MVFOL
5
4

The Essential Guide to

# Perfect Houseplants

**George Seddon and Andrew Bicknell with Elizabeth Dickson**

SUMMIT BOOKS
NEW YORK

*Drawings and paintings by Christine Hart-Davies*
*Copyright © 1984 by George Seddon,*
*Andrew Bicknell and Elizabeth Dickson*
*All rights reserved*
*including the right of reproduction*
*in whole or in part in any form*
*Published by SUMMIT BOOKS*
*A Division of Simon & Schuster, Inc.*
*Simon & Schuster Building*
*1230 Avenue of the Americas*
*New York, New York 10020*
*Originally published in Great Britain in 1984*
*by Elm Tree Books/Hamish Hamilton Ltd.*
*SUMMIT BOOKS and colophon are*
*trademarks of Simon & Schuster, Inc.*
*Manufactured in the United States of America*

*10  9  8  7  6  5  4  3  2  1*
*First American Edition*


*Library of Congress Cataloging in Publication Data*

*Seddon, George.*
    *The essential guide to perfect houseplants.*

    *Includes index.*
    *1. House plants. I. Bicknell, Andrew. II. Dickson,*
*Elizabeth. III. Title. IV. Title: Perfect houseplants.*
*SB419.S3825  1985      635.9'65      85-4758*
*ISBN 0-671-55726-2*
*ISBN 0-671-55641-X (pbk.)*

# Contents

# Introduction

This is a book about how to make plants look at home and feel at home.

Making plants look at home involves common sense in choosing plants which are suitable for the kind of home in which you live and imagination in finding the perfect place for them. Elizabeth Dickson closes the book with ideas to stir the imagination. With photographs of a wide range of rooms she shows how plants can be used to enhance the effect their owners set out to achieve. She makes it clear that plants should be an integral part of the overall theme of decoration and furnishing, and not intrude on or detract from it. The examples, of course, are not meant to be slavishly followed, for every person's rooms are different rooms from everyone else's rooms and each should be an expression of the individual's personality.

Most of the book, by George Seddon and Andrew Bicknell, is taken up with the practical aspects of making a plant feel at home – which means choosing the right plant in the first place and then looking after it with well-informed loving care. In the illustrated A-Z catalogue (pages 62–165), which takes up the major part of the book, the authors describe some plants to choose from; these are the most popular or the most readily available plants which are not excessively demanding.

The catalogue divides them into four groups according to the temperatures in which they should be grown. Two groups are of plants which are most likely to succeed in homes which are not centrally heated or only partially centrally heated. Such homes are likely to have some rooms which are considerably cooler than others, satisfying the needs of plants which require to be cool either all the year round or in winter. The other two groups in the A-Z are of plants more suitable for houses with full central heating, providing greater warmth in winter for those plants which need it. Entries in the A-Z catalogue include a photograph of the whole plant, supplemented with details of leaf size and character, estimates of how big the plant is likely to grow indoors, and other relevant facts.

A distinctive feature of the A-Z is 'The Year's Care' section devoted to each plant. In an easy-to-follow way it outlines the routine care of the plant during the four seasons of the year, during both growing and resting periods: temperature, light and watering needs; when to feed, when not to feed, when to prune, when to propagate and so on.

However, there are many aspects of plant care which are common to different groups of plants and these are fully explained in the section called Basics (pages 8–61). Besides temperature, it covers such important subjects as watering, feeding, light, humidity, composts, the techniques of potting-on, pruning, propagating, and ways of dealing with pests and diseases. The numerous detailed drawings by Christine Hart-Davies in this section clearly illustrate how the various operations of plant care are carried out.

Indoor gardening need not be totally confined with the walls of a house, so the next section of the book – 'Out-doors, but almost indoors' – includes plants suitable for window boxes, balconies and patios and such areas as can be seen close up from indoors. Extending indoor gardening in this way gives people in flats or gardenless houses a chance of at least a little 'outdoor' gardening. It provides a better environment for non-tropical plants than they would have indoors, without losing the intimacy which people have with houseplants. Also by extending the choice to some outdoor plants, especially annuals, a whole new range of colour is made available. There is nothing like opening the curtains on a brilliant window box to lift the spirits on a grumpy morning.

# Basic facts that decide the choice of a plant

Plants grow in the most extraordinary places and in the most extraordinary ways. In the jungle regions of Brazil bromeliads perch on trees and even telegraph wires, collect water, decaying leaves and insects in a vase of leaves and flourish. By contrast, in the deserts of South West Africa there is a succulent (endearingly called 'Baby Toes') which grows buried in the sand except for a window peeping above ground to let in the sun. In all parts of the world, except those permanently covered by ice, there are multitudinous plants which have no difficulty in growing in what we look on as the most adverse conditions, yet no plant of its own accord grows in a house, at least not until the roof falls in and sun and rain and decay can enter. Then they invade.

When Noah built his ark to preserve the world's animals for posterity he seems to have made no provision for plant life; wisely, for even if the animals and the three children had left them alone the odds are that they would not have made the voyage. Outdoors they stood a far better chance. Consider the olive, not a moisture-loving tree, but even after ten months under water it was still able to produce a branch for the celebrated dove to take back to the ark. In fact, there is no such thing as an indoor plant; it is only an outdoor plant which has been abducted to live indoors.

Not all of them settle down, perhaps because we have chosen the wrong plant in the first place or because we have treated the potentially right plant in the wrong way. The 'right' plant to choose is one which will find indoors at least some of the conditions which were an essential part of its original habitat. The obvious starting point is temperature.

Different plants start into growth at different temperatures. Above that there is a range of temperatures in which they will grow best, and way beyond that there is an extreme high at which they will die. Below the starting point for growth there is a fairly narrow range of temperatures in which they rest. Below that there is a bottom low at which many will die. To a certain extent plants will get by in less than their optimum conditions, but they cannot be pushed too far.

A glance back over the past 150 years or so shows how these basic facts determined the kind of houseplants grown at various times. At the start of the last century the craze for cacti started, followed by one for ferns and such hardy foliage plants as aspidistras and Norfolk Island Pines. All these plants had one thing in common, whatever their other needs – they had to be kept cool, either all the year or when they were resting. This was something that Victorian houses were well able to provide. Of course there were other limits to their choice of plants, for they had to stick to those which could withstand the darkness of foggy Dickensian winters and asphyxiation from gas fumes indoors.

Our houses have changed since then; they are warmer, lighter and less polluted. As a result favourite houseplants have become exotics from the tropics, which need warmth. The problem is now reversed; with more effective heating our houses can be too warm in winter for a host of plants which must, or should, have a resting period. The importance of a rest period can hardly be exaggerated, but is too often ignored. Everyone who has kept a tortoise or watched a dormouse sleeping all through a TV wildlife documentary knows how important hibernation is for some animals. Winter is approaching, food is going to be scarce, so to conserve energy they put themselves, as it were, into cold store.

Plants which grow outdoors in temperate regions behave in a similar way. The temperature falls to a point at which the plant stops growing. It then needs less energy and therefore less food, which is just as well, because the plant has to manufacture the major part of its own food from light and there is not enough light in winter for it to produce enough food to sustain growth. Bring such plants indoors and the warmth induces them, against their habit, to go on growing, but unhealthily because they will be suffering from light starvation.

Tropical plants have a different life style in their native haunts from that of temperate plants. Temperatures are usually high enough to keep them growing all the year, but since levels of light show little change as well the plants can manufacture enough food to give them the energy to grow healthily. But bring them indoors and they will keep on growing if the rooms are warm enough in winter, but they will suffer from light starvation. For their future health, they must be forced to take at least some rest, even though this is against their nature. It can be done by moving them to a cooler room – if in a fully centrally heated house there is one – and then watering less and feeding not at all.

Temperature levels, therefore, are not the only considerations in choosing a plant, since they are inextricably connected with the levels of light, but they remain the essential starting point. The conventional approach is to divide plants into three groups within narrow limits; those which thrive best in the ranges 45–55 deg F (7–13 deg C); 55–65 deg F (13–18 deg C) and 65–75 deg F (18–24 deg C). However, American indoor plant books, especially those written before oil prices went through the roof in the 70s, generally advocate temperatures considerably higher. This suggests that it was the owners rather than the plants they had in mind. This is a more practical approach, because nobody is going to court hypothermia just to keep a cactus contented in winter.

In the summer months how cool or warm a house is depends basically on the temperature outdoors, and we have no say over that. Even so some rooms are warmer or cooler than others. For most of the year, when we light fires or turn on the boiler, we have more control over how warm we want to keep the home, or at least part of it. Since readers either have central heating in some form or have not, the plants included in the book have been divided according to the kind of warmth they are likely to encounter and be able to cope with. Those plants which must have cool resting periods in winter may be most suitable for houses with no central heating, or with central heating in only part of the house since they are likely to have at least some rooms cool enough for such plants. Those plants which need considerable warmth day and night in winter as well as in summer are most suitable for houses with full central heating. Even so, plants in warm rooms will stay healthier if a place can be found for them to rest for a time at rather lower temperatures.

The plants in the A–Z catalogue, which starts on page 129, have been divided into four groups.

**1** Plants which need cool conditions, either in winter or all year, and given that are reasonably easy to look after.
**2** Plants which need to be cool, but will require rather more attention in other ways.
**3** Plants which need greater warmth in winter than those in the first two groups, but are otherwise reasonably tolerant.
**4** Plants which need warmth, but are more demanding of attention.

Before buying a plant which catches your eye and your fancy, consult the A–Z to see whether you can provide the temperatures in which it can grow and rest.

Of course, plants have other needs besides adequate levels of temperature and light and suitable periods of rest. These – such as watering, fertilising, pruning, repotting – are part of the routine of looking after the chosen plant. Each entry in the A–Z traces in detail the care of the plant throughout the year, both when it is growing and when it is resting. Some basic knowledge of how a plant works helps in understanding why you are urged to do this and not to do that.

## The year's care

The seasons occur at different times of the year in the Northern and Southern hemispheres. Therefore references in 'The year's care' section of the A–Z catalogue relate to seasons and not to calendar months. The conversion table from seasons to months is:

| Northern hemisphere | | Southern hemisphere |
|---|---|---|
| January | Winter | June |
| February | Late winter | July |
| March | Early spring | August |
| April | Spring | September |
| May | Late spring | October |
| June | Early summer | November |
| July | Summer | December |
| August | Late summer | January |
| September | Early autumn | February |
| October | Autumn | March |
| November | Late autumn | April |
| December | Early winter | May |

## Plant names

In each of the four sections into which the A–Z catalogue is divided the plants are arranged alphabetically by their botanical names. This is done to avoid confusion, for a plant may have several popular names, and some of them it may share with other plants. The botanical name belongs only to that plant and to no other. The botanical name is in horticultural Latin, which is based on a curious mixture of Latin and Greek. The first word in the name is the plant's genus, a group of plants with the same botanical characteristics, though they may not look alike. The second word describes the species to which the plant belongs within the genus. All plants in the species will be recognisably alike, though there may be some differences which are indicated by a third name – the variety to which the plant belongs. By custom botanical names are printed in italics. However, if the variety is not one that occurs in nature but has been cultivated ('cultivar') it is printed in roman characters and is enclosed in single quotation marks.

If a plant in the A–Z has a common name it is given after the botanical name. If it has more than one the most widely used name is chosen.

# Basic facts that affect the care of plants

## The leaves

Leaves are remarkable feats of engineering. They breathe in air and absorb the carbon dioxide in it and with light and water convert it into food. They breathe in air and with the oxygen convert the food back into energy for the plant's growth. They breathe out the waste gases from these processes, as well as excess water. They can even take over some of the normal functions of the root and absorb water and mineral salts directly. Some can miraculously propagate themselves. However, their main role is to manufacture food.

## Photosynthesis

The major raw materials of a plant's food are air, water and light. The process by which these are converted into food is called photosynthesis. On a leaf, largely on the underside, are numerous pores, or stomata, which can open to admit air. The small amount of carbon dioxide present in the air is extracted. Water is drawn up from the roots to provide hydrogen and this is combined with the carbon dioxide to make a simple sugar. The energy necessary for this conversion is provided by light absorbed by leaf cells containing chlorophyll (the pigment that makes leaves green). The oxygen released in this process is given off as waste through the stomata, and the sugar can be stored in the leaves or other parts of the plant. Photosynthesis can take place only in light, but the levels of light needed for efficient food conversion vary from plant to plant, primarily depending on their original habitat.

## Respiration

The stored sugar is used to create energy to make the plant grow, and this is done by respiration. Oxygen is needed. The stomata admit air and the oxygen in it combines with the sugar to produce energy, leaving carbon dioxide and water as waste. These are given off through the stomata. Unlike photosynthesis respiration does not need light, and most of it may take place at night.

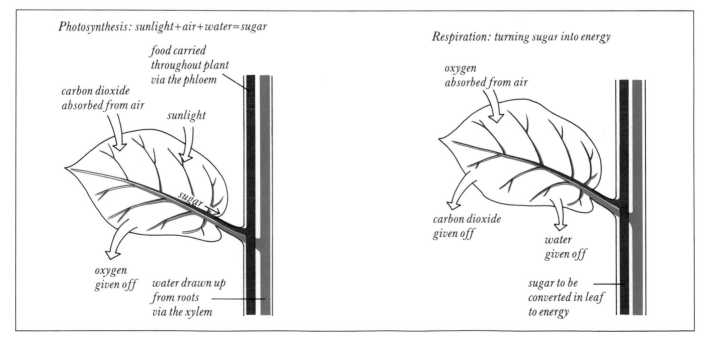

Photosynthesis: sunlight+air+water=sugar

carbon dioxide absorbed from air

food carried throughout plant via the phloem

sunlight

sugar

oxygen given off

water drawn up from roots via the xylem

Respiration: turning sugar into energy

oxygen absorbed from air

carbon dioxide given off

water given off

sugar to be converted in leaf to energy

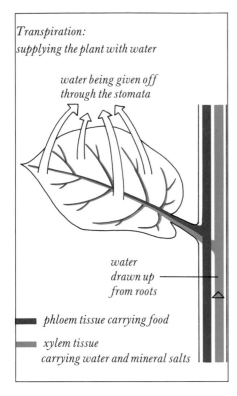

*Transpiration:*
*supplying the plant with water*

*water being given off*
*through the stomata*

*water*
*drawn up*
*from roots*

phloem tissue carrying food

*xylem tissue*
*carrying water and mineral salts*

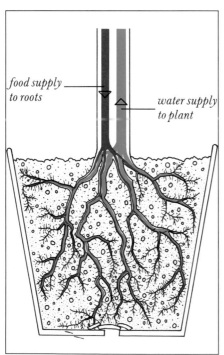

*food supply*
*to roots*

*water supply*
*to plant*

## Transpiration

Giving off water – transpiration – is another important role for the leaf. (Much of the water vapour escapes through the stomata, but there is also evaporation through the surface of the leaves and stems.) When water escapes a kind of pull is exerted throughout the plant and water is pumped up from the roots to replace that which has been lost. In this way water taken up by the roots is circulated to all parts of the plant.

There is potential danger in this. In hot dry rooms the plant may lose water faster than it can be replaced and that is when the plant wilts, often dramatically. The collapse is caused more by the dryness of the air than the warmth; in a humid jungle there would be no such problem. Wilting can happen not only at the height of summer, but also in winter in centrally heated rooms, where the air is desert dry. This danger explains the emphasis in the A–Z catalogue on the need for providing extra humidity in such conditions.

# The roots and stems

The roots are the suppliers of water and the elements which the plant cannot extract from the air. By the process of osmosis, the water and the mineral salts from the compost which have dissolved in it are drawn into the plant through the fine hairs of the roots. Water can move through the semi-permeable wall of the root hair if the concentration of minerals in the water is weaker than the concentration of minerals in the sap inside the root hair. However, if we apply strong doses of fertiliser to the compost, the process of osmosis, which ensures a continuous supply of water to the plant, may be reversed; the mineral solution in the compost becomes more concentrated than in the sap, water flows from the roots into the compost, the plant becomes dehydrated and wilts. Since plants in pots need only minute amounts of minerals they must be fed sparingly. Never apply a stronger dose of fertiliser than that recommended by the makers — indeed, a weaker and less frequent dose is better.

Disaster also follows over-watering. Less than half of a good porous compost is solid matter and the rest is water and air. The air there is as vital to the plant as the water because roots need oxygen. If the compost is kept sodden all the time the air is excluded, the roots cannot function, so the plant goes short of water even though the roots are drowning in it, and it wilts and dies. That is the simple reason for the constant warnings about the danger of over-watering.

The stems form the vital link between roots and leaves – multi-lane highways servicing the plant. They are complicated structures, but two plant tissues in them are especially important. The tissue called xylem holds the leaves up to catch the light and also conducts water and mineral salts from the roots. The other tissue, called phloem, is the supply line for the synthesised food. Both operate throughout the plant; in the leaves their routes follow the easily recognisable mid rib and network of veins.

Stems may need supporting, but they do not demand as much constant looking after as leaves and roots. Only when we are pruning or propagating them do they take over the star role.

For detailed information on plant care see:

Light and cleaning, pp.84–87.
Watering, pp.88–91.
Humidity pp.92–93.
Feeding, pp.94–95.
Pruning pp.96–100.

Repotting, pp.101–103.
Composts, pp.104–105.
Propagation, pp.109–119.
Pests and diseases pp.120–127.

# Plant habits and habitats

The childhood image of what a plant should look like stays with us all our lives. As in a child's drawing, it is a stem sticking out of the ground with leaves on it and a flower at the top. Many plants roughly conform to that image, though experience has taught us that below the ground there are roots. However, because of their natural environment, some types of plant have managed to change this basic structure, usually to make sure that they get enough light and water, so that the species can go on surviving.

The most remarkable change is among those plants which have almost dispensed with roots. These are the epiphytes, or air plants, which grow not in the ground (terrestrial plants) but clinging to a rock or another plant, but only for support and not as a parasite feeding off it.

## Bromeliads
Reaching upwards for light and water

Bromeliad

*Aechmea fasciata*, a very popular bromeliad, is an epiphyte from the forests of southern Brazil, where it grows high among the trees to be sure of good light. Water and decaying vegetation and insects are collected in a 'vase' formed at the base of the leaves and the plant absorbs both food and water through the scales on the leaves; what few roots exist are used as anchorage. Other bromeliads which need less light grow lower down the tree and they are likely to have softer, thinner leaves. When grown indoors they should have more shade than the tree-toppers. Oddly enough, bromeliads take readily to life in a pot. There are terrestrial bromeliads, but the only one widely grown as a houseplant is the pineapple, *Ananas comosus*.

## Succulents and cacti

Putting something by for a dry day

*Echeveria derenbergii,* with its fleshy leaves, is an obvious example of a succulent plant. The characteristic common to most succulents is that they are able to store water in their leaves and stems, which are also constructed to cut down evaporation. This enables them to live through long periods of low rainfall in their native habitat. *E. derenbergii* comes from high unforested areas of Mexico, and like many succulents, needs bright light. Most are easy to grow indoors, but they do better with a cool winter rest, and readily adapt to taking one.

Cacti are also succulents, but they have one botanical feature which distinguishes them from other succulents – they have areoles, small protuberances which are modified side shoots, from which spines and flowers grow. A more obvious difference is that while other succulents usually store more water in their leaves than in their stems, cacti store it in their stems,

Echeveria

Rebutia

Orchid

which have taken over the role of leaves and replaced them. The stem of *Rebutia miniscula* is globular, a shape giving the maximum amount of water storage space and the minimum surface loss of moisture. Rebutias come from regions of Argentina and Bolivia with hot summers and occasional heavy rain but cold dry winters. So, like many desert cacti, they can stand a lot of heat and sun in summer but must have a cool winter rest. If that can be provided they will do well. Most jungle cacti are epiphytes from the tropical forests of South America, and with that background do not want a summer baking and a chilly winter.

## Orchids
Storing food and water
*Dendrobium nobile* is a fine example of an epiphytic orchid; most orchids grown as houseplants are epiphytes. Generally they have several stems and these grow from a rhizome attached to the tree or rock on which the orchid has established itself. Their thick stems are known as pseudobulbs, though some resemble bulbs more than others and some look like flattened stems. All serve the same purpose – to store food and water to call upon in times of drought. In their native surroundings in India and Burma dendrobiums enjoy heavy rain at certain times of the year, followed by long periods without rain, when they rest. They need to follow this same pattern of rest when brought indoors.

# Light

'What a nice light room you've got,' is the kind of remark that is enough to make a plant laugh. For some plants it is not light enough and for others it is too light to be nice. When we go into a room we have an instant overall impression of lightness or gloom. However, no room, small or large, is uniformly light, and our eyes are largely unaware of these varying intensities of light unless they are trying to read or do petit point. Our flesh is far better in responding to differences of temperature. While we have thermometers to confirm how hot or cold we feel, few people use light meters. If they did they would have their eyes opened to the enormous variations of light and shade in a room – variations in different parts of the room, at different times of the day, and from day to day throughout the year. Life is too short to trail round the house with a light meter plotting the changes from hour to hour all the year round, but if you get into the habit of looking at a room from time to time from the point of view of the plants you will realise where some plants may safely be placed and where others cannot go if you want them to thrive, or even live.

The level of light in a room depends in the first place on which way the window faces, and even if there are two windows they are frequently on the same wall. The levels vary depending on whether the sun is rising, high in the sky, or sinking. They are obviously lower in all rooms in winter. The level also drops, more dramatically than we realise, only a few feet from a window.

## South, south-east and south-west facing

Windows in a south-facing wall let in most direct sunlight and those on south-east and south-west walls only a little less. In winter what sunlight there is moves round the walls of the room, but in midsummer when the sun is high in the sky it falls on a comparatively small area of the floor near the window. The rest of the room has bright light without direct sunlight.

## West facing

Second in the league, both for light and warmth. A window looking west may get little winter sun, but in summer it floods into the room as it sets and is still strong and can be quite hot.

## East facing

A room with an east facing window gets its bright sunshine in the morning, little in winter, but many hours in summer before you are likely to be up. When first the sun comes over the horizon the light may be bright or hazy, but it is not fierce until well into the morning, as it moves south, falling on different parts of the room as it does so.

## North facing

A steadier light than in other rooms and there is no direct sun except perhaps at the height of midsummer and any which enters the room then would not harm any plant.

Of course, whichever way a window faces the levels of light will be lowered, often drastically, by nearby buildings or trees.

## Shades of light in a room

Inside the room, beyond the sun's direct rays the level of light falls rapidly to between a fifth and a twentieth of what it was at the window. That is, for a plant, shade in varying degrees. The falling off is noticeable within 6ft (1.8m) of the window, if out of sun. There are also dark triangles of shade at each side of the window. Light walls help to maintain levels of light further into a room and dark walls lower them. A plant in front of a mirror benefits from reflected light, but reflected direct sunlight can harm it.

Plants range from sun lovers, such as cacti, to shade lovers, such as ferns, but the general run of plants falls between these extremes. When they are growing they need good or bright light, whether in warm or cool rooms. Some of them will benefit from a little direct sunlight, especially weak winter sun, and some will not. (For advice about individual plants see the A–Z entries). As a rule plants are more tolerant of levels of light below their optimum level than of light which is much brighter. Certainly the reaction to sunlight is more rapid – scorching and wilting – than it is to too much shade.

A variety of a plant which has variegated leaves needs better light than a variety with plain green leaves. The reason is that the pale or coloured part of the leaves are short of chlorophyll and to compensate for that the rest of the leaf needs brighter light for more efficient photosynthesis.

A plant may be regularly pinched out and skilfully pruned and still grow misshapen. Light is usually to blame for this. In poor light, especially in winter in a warm room, a plant becomes etiolated – the stems grow lanky and thin, the leaves are small and of poor colour, and there are fewer of them. Start by cutting back, if this is a plant to which it can be done, then move it to a better light and leave it there to grow sturdily again.

Unless a plant has reasonably equal light from all sides and from above, as it has out of doors, its natural response is to turn towards the source of light – indoors it will be the nearest window. If allowed to indulge the habit (phototropism) the plant will grow permanently disfigured. To avoid this turn the plant a little but regularly; a mark can be put on the side as a guide and a reminder.

But never move a plant when in bud or in flower; buds and flowers are likely to drop. Some plants are very touchy about a change of position.

When a plant is resting in winter it is in a period of no growth and it needs not only less warmth, less water and no food but by and large it needs less light. However, since winter levels of daylight are so much poorer than in summer a plant may have to be moved nearer to the window so that it still gets adequate light; seasonally adjusted light, as it were.

Not only the intensity of light but its duration is important for some

---

**Warning signs**

*Too much light*
Browning leaves and curling tips, especially on thin-leaved plants
Yellow or brown spots or patches on leaves
Leaves turn pale and dull
Leaves wilt in direct sun and young leaves suffer sun scald.

*Too little light*
Weak, lanky, straggly growth, with longer gaps between leaves on the stems
Variegated leaves lose variegations and revert to green
New leaves are smaller
Plant produces no flowers or flower buds drop before they open
Cacti grow exceedingly slowly

Some of these symptoms may have other causes. If in doubt look up 'Warning signs' in the sections on watering, humidity and feeding. See also pests and diseases, pages 54–61. Check in the A–Z entries that the plant is being grown in the temperature it needs.

---

flowering plants – the so-called short day and long day plants. Short day plants produce flower buds only when they have spent 2–3 months in more hours of darkness (roughly 14 hours a day) than in daylight (10 hours). Long day plants will flower only when they have had more than 12 hours of daylight each day for two months or more.

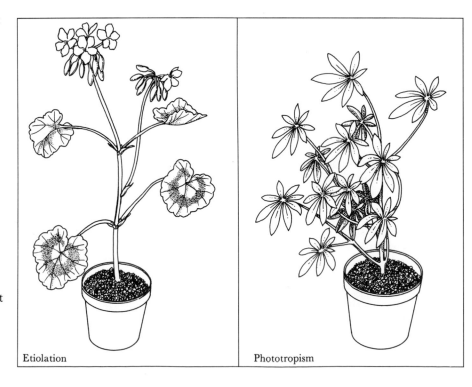

Etiolation                                  Phototropism

The plant's need for the kind of light in which it will thrive reasonably well often conflicts with our wish to put it somewhere in the room where we think it looks best. If we ignore the plant's needs totally it will soon have its revenge by ceasing to look its best, so a little give and take is needed. Put the plant where you want it to be for four weeks, say, with intervals of at least two weeks where it will flourish best. However, there are problems. No plant should be moved suddenly from a poor to a bright light; do it in a few stages. There is rather less risk in moving a foliage plant from a brighter to a poorer light. A flowering plant is more likely to be affected and it should never be moved when in bud or in flower. (Particular care should also be taken in moving plants outdoors for summer – put them in shade to begin with – and back indoors for winter – put them as near to a window as possible until they have grown accustomed to the change.)

The alternative to shuttling plants around indoors is to take artificial light to them. Artificial light, which is basically recycled sunlight, provides the energy which the plant may be going short of. This is using light not just to make a plant look pretty, but to keep it healthy.

Ordinary incandescent filament bulbs are virtually useless. They give out three times as much heat as light and if they are placed near enough to the plant to give it enough light to promote growth they are liable to fry the leaves. Fluorescent tubes give out far more light than heat so they can be placed nearer the plant. They also provide a more suitable type of light: pairing a 'natural light' ('cool white') tube with a 'daylight' tube combines an appropriate mix of the blue end of the spectrum – affecting the growth of the plant – and the red end – affecting the production of flowers.

A lighting unit is basically two or four fluorescent tubes and a reflector to deflect their light down on the plants, increasing the amount of light they get by three quarters. Flowering plants need good light so the tubes are hung between 9 and 12in (22.5–30cm) above the top of them, whereas they can hang higher (12–18in, 30–45cm) above foliage plants. If the leaves should scorch the tubes are too low; if the plants become etiolated the tubes are too far away. Lower or raise them only a few inches at a time until you get the distance right.

It is comparatively easy to install a lighting unit above a shelf or shelves, hiding the light behind a wooden valance 5–6in (12.5–15cm) deep. An excellent place would be the space in a chimney breast after a fireplace is removed. Mirrors behind the plants both reflect the light and give a feeling of depth. Because of risks from watering all cables should be waterproofed and properly earthed and fused. Stand the plants on waterproof trays; they can be put to use to increase humidity by filling them with pebbles in water.

A unit can also be installed in a large terrarium.

If a lighting unit is the main or only source of light, as in a passage or basement, foliage plants should be lit up for 12–14 hours a day and flowering plants for up to 16 hours. A time switch is a good investment. The plants should not be lit for 24 hours, for they need some rest.

Photosynthesis comes to a stop in the dark, but the plant continues to convert into energy the sugar compounds created by photosynthesis under lights.

Houseplants which have been introduced from sub-tropical parts of the world are accustomed to days and nights of roughly equal length the whole year and they stay in active growth. Normal practice is to force them to rest during the short days and poor light of winter, but with adequate artificial light they can be allowed to go on growing. If they are, the A–Z routine of care for spring and summer must be followed for most of autumn and winter as well. A partial rest of a month or two is a good thing. To induce it, cut the artifical lighting by up to four hours a day, reduce watering and stop feeding.

Plants which in nature rest must be removed from the light unit during autumn and winter to a cooler place and be given no fertiliser and little water.

Among the plants suitable for growing under lights, as long as their temperature requirements are also met, are above all saintpaulias, for they can be kept in flower almost all the year, *Fittonia verschaffeltii*, *Guzmania lingulata*, peperomia, and orchids. Desert cacti do extremely well under lights when they are in growth, but they must be allowed to rest at low temperatures in winter.

Lighting unit

# Cleaning

Dirty leaves reduce the amount of light the plant needs for photosynthesis and hence cut down its food. The way to keep them clean depends on the kind of leaves they are.

**Large glossy leaves**
Support the underside of the leaf with one hand and wipe off the dust. Sponge lightly with a damp cloth, wrung out in tepid water. The underside of the leaf, although it seldom gets very dirty except in a household of heavy smokers, can be cleaned by similar gentle sponging. This is important, because most of the stomata are on the underside of the leaf and if they become clogged the plant cannot breathe efficiently. Do not use beer, oil, milk or any fancy preparation for leaf cleaning since they clog up the stomata.

**Hairy, scaly leaves
(also cacti and succulents)**
Do not wash. Brush off dust with a very soft brush. An artist's brush is good for small leaves.

**Very small glossy leaves**
Mist-spray to squirt off the dust, but not to make the leaves sopping wet.

How frequently leaf cleaning has to be done depends on whether you live in a heavily polluted town or in a remote part of the country. Leaves get dirtier in winter, but they often look dirtier in summer; there is nothing like a shaft of sunlight for showing up dust – and not just on plants – and shaming you.

Dirty windows block out a surprising amount of light. The moral is clear.

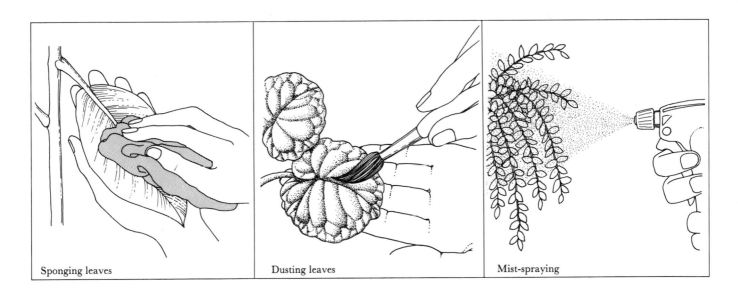

Sponging leaves

Dusting leaves

Mist-spraying

# Watering

One of the inescapable clichés of indoor gardening books is that more plants are killed by overwatering than by any other cause. Since plants can also be killed by underwatering – often more rapidly and dramatically – it would be more accurate to say that more plants die from *incorrect* watering than from any other cause. If that provokes the question 'What is correct watering?' the only honest answer is 'You will have to find out for yourself.'

If you want to know how acid or alkaline the compost is you can use a soil testing kit. With a thermometer you can tell precisely whether the temperature of a room is within the range suitable for plants there. With a light meter you can measure accurately the intensity of light in any part of the room. A hygrometer will show exact levels of humidity and so inform you whether the air is too dry for your plants. But while a moisture meter can indicate the level of moisture in the compost you still have to decide for yourself whether it is enough, too much, or too little for any particular plant. In any case one of the many things that life is too short for is to trail round a whole lot of plant pots day after day sticking a moisture probe into the compost. Until houseplant care is fully automated we have to acquire skills in watering with the help of eyes and fingers, plus a few basic facts, allied to experience.

The amount of water a plant needs depends on:

**1** Where the plant had its home in the wild – rain forest or desert, for example.
**2** How small or large the plant is, and how big the leaves are.
**3** Whether it is in active growth or resting.
**4** How cool or warm the room is.

Eyes can tell you instantly a lot about a plant's needs – and not just for water – if you get into the habit of really looking at it. This is one of the great advantages of growing only plants that you really like. A loved plant is a looked at plant and a looked at plant has a far greater chance of being a cared for plant.

Just looking at the surface of the compost cannot tell you what is happening below, but a finger can give some idea. Stick one into the compost – even if you do get some behind your finger nails – for about 1in (2.5cm) or more, to *feel* how wet, moist or dry it is there.

The trouble is that words cannot precisely convey degrees of moisture: how dry is dry, how moist is moist, how wet is wet? It is thus patently impossible to say how much water is needed to make a dry compost (how dry?) moist (how moist?). Should you water sparingly, moderately, plentifully, generously? And what do those words mean? (There is a similar dilemma in cookery books; how stiffly do you beat cream or whites of egg; how soft should dough be, how runny batter?)

The approach adopted in the A–Z entries is to concentrate on frequency of watering. The sequence is to water thoroughly – by three possible methods – until the compost can hold

Watering from above

no more; then let it drain and water again thoroughly when you finger, with some help from your eyes, tells you to do so. First, the three methods of thorough watering:

*1 From above, the easiest way.* Use a can with a long spout which can reach through the foliage to the whole surface of the compost. Pour tepid water on to the compost until it starts coming out of the drainage hole of the pot. After ten minutes or so empty all the water that has drained into the saucer. Only four plants mentioned in

the book can be safely left standing in water, for many it is fatal. (The four are the three carnivorous plants, *Dionaea muscipula, Drosera rotundifolia* and *Sarracenia flavia*, but during active growth only, and *Cyperus alternifolius*, the Umbrella Plant, all the year round.) When watering from above avoid wetting the leaves, which may mark them and encourages fungus diseases.

*2 From below, a safe way.* Place the pot in shallow tepid water, which by capillary action will be drawn up through the compost. Leave it until drops of moisture appear on the surface and the compost feels damp. Remove from the water and let any excess drain away before putting the pot back on the saucer. This is a good way of watering plants with leaves which are easily damaged by water – saintpaulias especially.

*3 By immersion, the most effective way.* Though effective it is admittedly tedious, and is possible only with plants of a reasonable size. Totally immerse the pot – not the whole plant – in tepid water in the kitchen sink or in a bucket. Air bubbles will be seen rising from the surface of the compost. When they stop (the spaces between the particles in the compost having then been filled with water), take the pot out of the water and let it drain for at least half an hour before putting it back on its saucer. As the water drains out the air rushes in to the

Watering from below

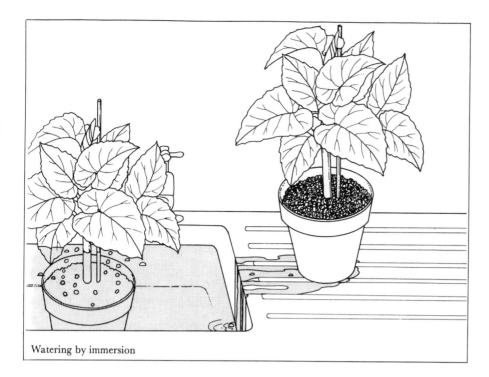

Watering by immersion

spaces left, providing a fresh supply of vital oxygen for the roots. Even if this method is not adopted for every watering it is advisable to do it occasionally as the best way of renewing the oxygen. Of course it works efficiently only if the compost is porous, as it should be, and not compacted.

**Note:** however you water always use tepid water. Water which is even a few degrees colder than the compost is liable to cause shock to the roots.

If you try to regulate the *amount* of water you give each time, as many people do, there is no way of knowing whether the compost is wet only on the surface while below it is dry. Little-and-often watering generally means not enough, and too often. Thorough watering, followed by thorough draining, ensures that the compost is moist throughout. It does not remain so long. The roots take up water, and it evaporates from the surface of the compost and the sides of a clay pot. The surface of the compost dries out most rapidly, but just glancing at it gives little idea of what is going on underneath. To find out

that stick your finger an inch or so into the compost.

For some plants the advice in the A–Z entries is to let the compost dry out almost completely between watering. That stage can be reckoned to have arrived when your finger reveals that the compost is dry 1in (2.5cm) or more below the surface. Then you water and drain thoroughly. Such drying out advice applies particularly to the resting period of plants which are kept in the cool.

For other plants the recommendation is to let the compost dry out a little, or slightly, between watering. If your finger, pushed into the compost, finds that around a depth of 1in (2.5cm) is only just damp, water again, thoroughly.

For plants that should always be moist the surface of the compost should never feel dry, but just moist – not sodden. For this it may be possible to rely on the evidence of eyes alone.

From this it is clear that the watering demands of plants differ and each has to be watered when it needs it. It is thoroughly bad practice to adopt a routine of watering everything regardless, when you happen to find time – say, weekly on Saturdays or Sundays. Watering, especially in summer, is the inescapable burden of growing houseplants. If the chore becomes intolerable the only sensible thing to do is to get rid of some of them; the slap-happy routine of watering may do just that for you.

**Holiday watering**

Watering the plants when the house is empty during holidays can be a major headache; deaths are then more likely to be from underwatering than overwatering. Not all friends who offer their services as plant sitters are to be trusted, too often they turn out to be dedicated overwaters.

The plants should get along quite well on their own if you are away for only a few days. After watering them thoroughly put them all together in a cool room where they will not get direct sun. If they are on pebble trays move those with them.

For the long holidays the simple method is to use capillary felt mats alongside the kitchen sink. One end of the mat is in water in the kitchen sink;

fill the sink and make sure the plug is watertight. The rest of the mat is spread over the draining board and the water is drawn up to it by capillary action. With flat-bottomed plastic pots the system works admirably if the pots are simply placed on the mat, but not so with clay pots. They need capillary wicks as well so that the water is drawn up into the compost. Push about 3in (7.5cm) of the wick through the drainage hole into the compost. There is no danger of overwatering by this method. It might be a wise precaution to ask a neighbour to refill the sink occasionally.

Alternatively, plants of a reasonable size can be enclosed in plastic bags, in the same way as they are used for propagation. Water the plants thoroughly, let them drain, put the bags over them, making sure that the leaves are not touching the plastic. Put them in a good light out of the sun and the water will be recycled, as in a bottle garden. This could work for several weeks. However, make sure that the plants are absolutely pest free before they are bagged – in those humid conditions the pests will prosper even more than the plants.

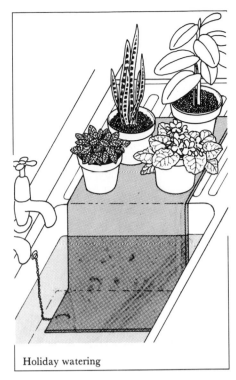

Holiday watering

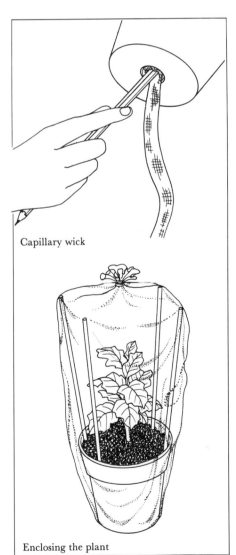

Capillary wick

Enclosing the plant

**Warning signs**
*Too much water*
Tips and edges of leaves turn brown
Lower leaves turn yellow and fall
Leaves of succulents and stems of cacti become bloated
Soft brown or black areas on leaves
Brown papery patches on leaves
Rotting leaves, stems and rosettes
In resting period leaves turn brown and fall
New leaves are soft and pale
Green slime appears on sides of clay pots

*Not enough water*
Leaves and stems wilt
Lower leaves dry up and fall
Brown crisp spots on leaves
Buds drop off
Flowers die quickly
Leaves of succulents and stems of cacti shrivel
In growing period leaves turn brown
All leaves drop off (if compost dries out completely)
Peat compost shrinks away from the sides of the pot

Some of these symptoms may have other causes. If in doubt look up 'Warning signs' in the sections on light, humidity and feeding. See also pests and diseases, pages 54–61. Check in the A–Z entries that the plant is being grown in the temperature it needs.

# Humidity

A plant takes up water through its roots and loses it through its leaves (transpiration). The hotter and drier the air the more likely it is that the leaves will lose water faster than the roots can replace it. The plant will then wilt. But if the air is moist, even though hot, the plant loses far less moisture and does not wilt.

Temperature and humidity are directly related – humidity is always measured as relative humidity (RH), relative to the temperature. As the temperature of the air rises the amount of water it can hold increases, so that far more moisture is needed to maintain the *level* of humidity. Human beings are satisfied with a fairly low level, but even they can suffer in the dry air of centrally heated and air-conditioned rooms in winter. Some plants, such as desert cacti, have evolved to cope with even lower levels of humidity; others, especially from rain forests, should ideally have high levels which bring humans out in a hot sweat.

A hygrometer measures relative humidity from RH 0 per cent (total dryness) to RH 100 per cent (total saturation). In fully centrally heated houses in winter relative humidity can drop to 10 per cent or lower – in terms of dryness suitable only for cacti, except that the temperature would be far too warm for them in what should be their

resting period. Most succulents are satisfied with a level around 30 to 35 per cent, but in general foliage plants need a level of RH 60 per cent. Plants with thin papery leaves, such as calatheas, suffer from the loss of moisture more quickly then fleshy leaved plants, and should have a level of RH 70 per cent or over.

How are the conflicts between human comfort and the needs of the plants to be resolved? In the first place the plant, as usual, has to compromise. While in a dry warm room it will not thrive as well as it would in a humid greenhouse, with a little help it may do tolerably well. This applies especially to many of the warmth-loving plants in the A–Z section which need more attention because of their needs for extra humidity.

One way of greatly increasing humidity for all plants (and humans) in a room or house is by using an electric humidifier. Non-electric humidifiers which hang on radiators are far less effective, but even a little extra moisture is welcome. The alternative is to concentrate on the plants by creating a humid micro-climate around them, either individually or in groups. This can be done in three ways:

**1** Mist-spray around the plant, aiming to add moisture to the air rather than to wet the leaves of the

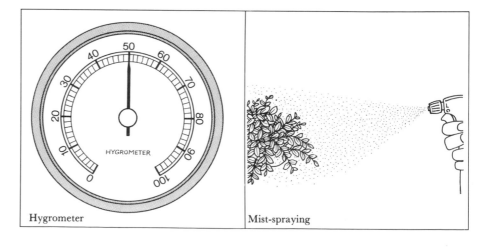

Hygrometer

Mist-spraying

plants. In particular, do not spray the foliage of hairy leaved plants. Over-enthusiastic spraying which gets a lot of water lodged among the leaves and stems has its dangers, especially in badly ventilated rooms. In a wet stagnant enviroment fungal diseases flourish.

**2** Put the pot within a larger container and fill the gap between the two with peat, which is always kept moist. The plant should be in a plastic non-porous pot so that the moisture in the peat is not drawn into the compost as it would be through a clay pot. A number of small plants can be grouped in one large container. This has the advantage that moisture given off by each plant makes the air around it more humid and all benefit from their closeness to each other.

Stand the pot on a tray of wet pebbles. The 'tray' can be any kind of dish which will hold water, but plastic pebble trays in many sizes are available at garden centres. These are usually about 2in (5cm) deep. Spread a layer of pebbles or gravel over the bottom of the tray and pour warm water over them, not quite covering them, because the pot itself must not be standing in water. The water evaporates, the vapour rising around the leaves. The warmer and drier the air the more rapid the evaporation. Keep the water topped up, but never above the height of the pebbles. Adding hot water when topping up gives a little added boost to the humidity. Here again plants in a group can be self-supportive by benefiting from each other's transpiration. Obviously the greater the area of wet pebbles under a plant the greater the evaporation and the higher the humidity. A pebble tray which is only slightly larger than the base of the plant pot is useless. As far as is reasonably possible match the size of the tray to the spread of foliage of the plant, or group of plants.

A pot within a pot

Tray of wet pebbles

**Warning signs**
*Air too dry and hot*
Leaves shrivel or wilt
Tips of leaves turn brown
Leaves drop
Buds drop

*Air too moist with bad ventilation*
Grey mould on leaves
Rotting stems and leaves of cacti and succulents

Some of these symptoms may have other causes. If in doubt look up 'Warning signs' in the sections on light, watering and feeding. See also pests and diseases, pages 54–61. Check in the A–Z entries that the plant is being grown in the temperature it needs.

# Feeding

Overfeeding is almost as deadly a sin as overwatering – deadly, that is, for the plant. It is usually the result either of carelessness in applying too much fertiliser or of misguided kindness. Nonetheless a plant does need some feeding. In the garden it can spread its roots in search of food, but when it has used up the food in the compost in a pot it depends on you to replenish it.

There is no need to start feeding immediately you buy a plant. Loam-based composts have both minerals in the loam and added fertiliser and in the growing season these should last the plant for up to three months. Peat-based composts have negligible natural fertility, but the fertilisers which have been added will be enough for the plant for around two months. Similar no-fertiliser periods apply after repotting into fresh compost and potting-on.

Feed only when the plants are actually growing, thus the last feed of the year will be in early autumn. If plants are given fertiliser later than that they will be seduced into growing, but in the poor light the growth will be weedy. There is also likely to be a build-up in the compost of minerals to a level which can burn the roots. However, plants from the Tropics which are kept growing with adequate artificial light must be fed the year round.

Never feed an ailing plant. It needs rest to recover, not to be prodded into growth.

When feeding is in order do not overdo it. This means:

1 Not giving a stronger dose than is recommended by the makers; weaker is far better.
2 Not giving fertiliser too often. When frequency of application is recommended in the A–Z entries this is the maximum frequency during the time from early spring when the plant is growing vigorously. If you want to restrain its exuberance, less frequent fertilising is one of the best ways of doing it, without going to the length of starving the plant. A plant which may be fed fortnightly for sturdy growth will come to no harm if the feeds are cut down to six, spread out over spring and summer.

The main elements a plant needs are:
Nitrogen (N) to encourage growth of leaves and stems. Too much produces soft growth, susceptible to disease.
Phosphorus (P) for healthy root growth.
Potassium (K), usually called potash, for flower production, sturdiness, resistance to disease.

In addition the plant requires certain trace elements, in minute amounts. These assist the functioning of the plant, rather than its growth.

All these elements should be included in any fertiliser you buy. The label on it gives the percentage of the three main elements, always in the same order N,P,K. A so-called balanced fertiliser might have the elements in equal proportions – say 777 – each a percentage. One of the popular balanced fertilisers on sale is a 14 14 14 mix, twice the strength, so that you need only half as much fertiliser to give the same strength of solution. If the first number in the code is the largest that fertiliser is rich in nitrogen; if the second it is rich in phosphorus, and if the third it is potassium rich. You can use a balanced fertiliser all through the growing season, or you can start in spring with a nitrogen rich mix to encourage growth, then follow with a regular balanced fertiliser, and finish towards the autumn with a potassium rich feed, to build up the plant for the winter.

Fertilisers are usually sold as concentrated liquids or powder which have to be heavily diluted in water, the most common and the easiest way of applying them. Never make the solution stronger than recommended, and do not apply it when the compost is very dry, since it is then most likely to harm the roots. Another way of applying a fertiliser is as slow release tablets or spikes, which are pushed into the compost. A large pot may need several spikes, inserted around the plant. The makers usually recommend how many will be needed for different sizes of pot. Push sticks in near to the sides of the pot, not close to the roots, which can suffer from fertiliser burn. The spike fertilisers act over a longer period than the liquid fertiliser – from three to six months. They are more expensive, but obviously save time. It is as well to keep some record of when you insert the spikes.

---

**Warning signs**

*Overfeeding*
Excessive leaf growth and few flowers or none
Soft pappy growth (excess of nitrogen)
Crisp brown spots on leaves and edges turning brown
White crusty deposits on clay pots

*Underfeeding*
Pale leaves (lack of nitrogen)
Weak stems, stunted leaves with purple blotches (lack of potassium)
Few flowers, edges of leaves brittle and brown (lack of potassium)
Yellowing of leaves, but not of veins (lack of iron)

Some of these symptoms may have other causes. If in doubt look up 'Warning signs' in the sections on light, watering and humidity. See also pests and diseases, pages 54–61. Check in the A–Z entries that the plant is being grown in the temperature it needs.

# Pruning

As we have to help our plants to adjust as far as possible to the unnatural environment of our homes, so we have to train them to grow in ways which look attractive to us. We certainly do not want them to behave as they may have done in their natural habitat – growing 60ft high or trailing all over the carpet as though it was the forest floor. This house training is achieved by pruning.

There are various methods of helping to keep a plant presentable:

**Trimming:** cutting back the brown tips of leaves; removing dead leaves and stems.

**Pinching out:** regular removal of the growing tip of stems to force the plant to grow bushy. (Also called 'stopping' or 'nipping'.)

**Minor pruning:** occasional cutting back of stems which have grown too long.

**Hard pruning:** drastic surgery to rejuvenate the plant.

Some plants cannot be pinched out or pruned because the stems if cut would not resprout. These include all the bromeliads, ferns and palms. Other common unprunable plants are: anthurium, araucaria, asparagus, aspidistra, caladium, calathea, chlorophytum, cycas, saintpaulia, sansevieria and spathiphyllum. All that can be done to such plants is trimming.

## Trimming

All plants will at some time have leaves which go brown, however careful you are.

To get rid of brown tips cut them away almost to the edge of the brown and not into the green part of the leaf. If you do, the brown will spread along the leaf.

If all the leaf is brown cut it away cleanly right at the bottom.

A dead branch or frond should be cut back close to the main stem.

This is merely tidying up; real pruning involves some cutting away of the living part of the plant to alter its habit of growth. It starts with pinching out, which involves removing the tips of young stems which the plant produces when it is actively growing.

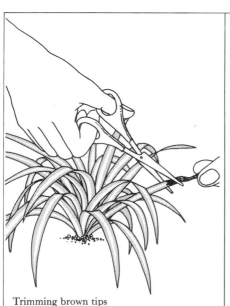

Trimming brown tips

Trimming brown leaves

Trimming dead branches

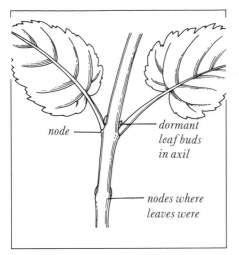

*node*

*dormant leaf buds in axil*

*nodes where leaves were*

## Pinching out

If regularly carried out this is the most effective way of making a prunable plant bushy and keeping it that way. With your fingers or sharp scissors remove about 1in (2.5cm) of the growing tip of stem just above the first or second node. (A node is the point where there is a leaf or a pair of leaves, or where leaves are about to appear, or where they were until they fell off). The effect of cutting of the tip is to stir into growth the dormant leaf axil buds lower down the stem. (The axil is the angle between leaf and stem.)

Side shoots appear from the axil and when they are long enough these also can be pinched out.

The pinching out routine should begin when the plant is still young and small; do not wait until it has grown too large and lanky.

## Cutting back

Even with regular pinching out, more vigorously growing plants may get a little out of hand and these need some growth cutting back. There may be a few overlong stems spoiling the overall shape of the plant; they may need cutting back only a few inches or they might be better cut back to only a few inches above the surface of the compost. There is no blue print for all plants, each one grows in its particular way. The vital point to remember is that the effect of all pruning is to promote more growth, not less. Cutting off one part of the stem stirs dormant buds lower down the stem into growth to produce two or more side shoots. As with pinching out the effect is to produce a bushier plant.

For this operation finger nails are not enough. Use either a very sharp knife or scissor type secateurs; these have cutting edges curved like the beak of a bird. Avoid the anvil type secateurs with straight edges which crush the stems and may make the mangled ends rot. Cut just above a node and cut at an upwards angle or straight across the stem, never downwards.

Pruning of this kind is best done at the start of the season of active growth, rather than towards the end of it.

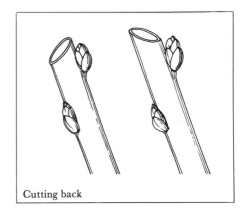

Cutting back

Pinching out side shoots

Drastic surgery

A plant which has been cut back very hard because it had been neglected is not a ravishing sight, but during the summer it should begin to look more respectable again. However, severe pruning can be avoided by regular pinching out, plus, perhaps, a yearly routine of cutting back of rampant growers.

Variegated trailing plants have a habit of producing shoots which are wholly green. All these stems should be pruned to compost level or the whole plant may revert to plain green.

Some flowering plants flower on newly grown wood while others flower on wood that grew the previous year. This means that care must be taken when pruning in the spring not to cut shoots which will provide flowers later in the year.

The habit of each plant is best learned and remembered by observing it carefully when it is in flower. If the flowers are on fresh green stems, that plant flowers on new wood grown that season. If the flowers are on darker brownish wood that is the previous season's wood. When observed, as Dickens' Captain Cuttle would have said, make a note of.

## Drastic surgery

Sometimes hard pruning may not be enough and a major operation is needed to give the plant a total face lift. Some plants which have withered because the compost has been allowed to dry out can be revived by cutting down the top foliage to the level of the compost, watering well and waiting for new growth to appear. This can be done, for example, with many ferns and with asparagus, none of them prunable in the ordinary sense. In the main, however, the plants which demand drastic surgery are single stemmed plants which lose their lower leaves, so that the stems are bare and leggy – such as dieffenbachia – or grow too tall, and perhaps are bare stemmed as well – such as *Ficus elastica*. Rejuvenating a dieffenbachia is simple. In spring cut the stem to within 5in (12.5cm) of the compost just above an old leaf joint. Keep it at around 60 deg F (16 deg C) and new leaves will grow from the stump.

A more complicated method can be used to bring a ficus down to size – by air layering. This retains the original shape of the plant and means that it is capable of growing tall again. About 2in (5cm) below the

Air layering

lowest surviving leaf make a clean, upward-slanting cut into the stem with a sharp knife, about a third of the way into the stem.

Dust the cut with hormone rooting powder and wedge the cut open with a matchstick to prevent it from healing. This is the point from which new roots will grow. Tie a poultice of wet sphagnum moss round the area of the cut. Cover the moss with clear plastic and seal it with adhesive tape, top and bottom, so that the moss does not dry out. Go on feeding and watering the plant as usual. In eight weeks or so roots should be seen through the plastic, growing in the moss. Carefully remove the plastic, cut the stem a little below the moss and pot the rejuvenated ficus, along with the moss containing the roots in the same type of potting compost as its parent. Subsequent care is as usual.

The bare lower stem of the original plant should put out new side growth; it will at least look different.

**Training into shape**

Keeping a plant in good shape may also involve giving it some support. Push a stout cane or stake into the compost, almost to the bottom of the pot, but not too close to the stem of the plant. Tie the plant loosely to it. Some plants will need more than one cane.

As the plant grows replace the cane for a longer, and possibly stronger one.

Training into shape

Plants with aerial roots (eg monstera and philodendron) are best supported with a moss stick into which the roots can be inserted. The stick can be put in the pot when the plant is being repotted. Use a wooden pole, at least 3ft (90cm) long. Wrap sphagnum moss around it from the top to about 4in (10cm) from the bottom – that bare part will be in the compost – as you go, binding the moss tightly to the pole with fine wire. Put the stick in the pot with a little compost to anchor it.

Place the plant alongside the stick and fill the pot with compost. Loosely tie the plant to the stick and insert the aerial roots into the moss.

There is little point in a moss stick unless the moss is always kept moist; spray regularly, daily in summer.

As well as providing water for the aerial roots the moist stick will increase humidity around the plant.

Some plants are traditionally trained round a hoop – bougainvillea, hoya, jasmine, passiflora and stephanotis among them. To make a hoop about 15in (37.5 cm) high use a piece of stout plastic-covered wire about 3ft 6in (1.05m) long. Stick one end of it most of the way into the compost at the side of the pot and bend it over in the shape of a hoop, pushing the other end into the compost at the opposite side of the pot.

With the greatest gentleness twine the stem of the plant in and out round the wire. To keep the stem secure loop thin string round hoop and stem. When the stem has reached the other end of the hoop it can be trained to go round again in circles or to turn back on itself and go round the other way.

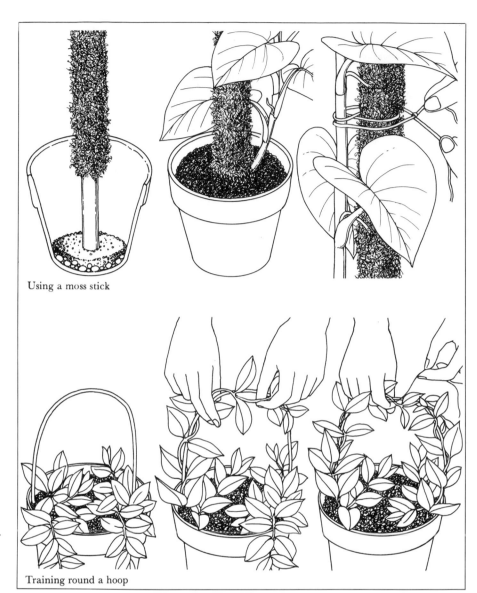

Using a moss stick

Training round a hoop

# Repotting and potting-on

In the garden as a plant grows its roots spread further and further to satisfy its increasing need of food and water. The sensible gardener avoids disturbing those roots until, perhaps, the plant has grown so big that it needs dividing. It may then seem odd that the indoor gardener is urged to put his plants through the yearly trauma of being taken out of their pots, and put back into the same pots, or possibly larger ones. The advice is not as mad as it seems.

The reason for putting a plant into a larger pot, even if it seems to be doing quite well where it is, is simple. A plant in a pot cannot spread its roots as it could in the soil outdoors. As it grows and the roots are almost filling the pot it must be given more room to expand; there are only a very limited number of plants which do not apparently object to having their roots tightly packed in a pot – that is, potbound. The extra fresh compost in the larger pot gives an additional supply of food for the plant to root about in.

Even if a plant is a slow grower and has not filled the pot with roots it is still advisable to repot it every year merely to give it some fresh compost. The old compost has probably been regularly fertilised and there is a risk that an excess of mineral salts or, in hard water areas, of lime has built up in the compost. Signs that this is happening show in nasty brown (mineral) or white (lime) deposits on the sides of clay pots or on the surface of the compost in non-porous plastic pots. Also constant watering over a year alters the texture of the compost. It becomes compacted and liable to be waterlogged and the resulting lack of air in the compost means that the roots are starved of oxygen. So the plant is taken out of the pot, some of the old compost is gently teased out of the roots and the plant is put back in some fresh compost in a clean pot of the same size. The correct name for this operation is repotting.

If the plant is moved into a larger pot this is known as potting-on. Depending on how vigorously the plant is growing it may have to be potted-on every year, or every two or three years. Many young plants are sold in $3\frac{1}{2}$in (8.75cm) pots and when potting-on becomes necessary the next size to choose could be 5in (12.5cm). It would then move up 1in (2.5cm) or more at a time to 10in (25cm). If it was then still alive and worth keeping, that might well be its last potting-on because the next sizes – 12in and 15in (30 and 37.5cm) are inconveniently large.

Do not be tempted by the bright idea of saving yourself a lot of trouble every year by putting a small plant into a big pot right at the start. It does not work. It will be a long time before the roots reach far into the surrounding compost and when they do the compost there will be sodden and sour because there have been no roots to take up water and fertiliser. Here again the situation of a plant in a pot in entirely different from a plant in the garden. The soil round a plant does not go sour just because there are no roots in it. The water disperses elsewhere into the soil and the soil itself is kept aerated by all the living things in it, which are not, or should not be in potting compost. Nor is garden soil so unremittingly dosed with fertiliser. One simply has to become reconciled to the chore of regular repotting and potting-on.

There comes a time when both repotting and potting-on have to stop – probably when a 10in (25cm) size of pot has been reached.

Top dressing then takes the place of potting-on and repotting. Carefully remove the top 2in (5cm) of compost and replace it with fresh compost without taking the plant out of the pot. The nutrients in the new compost will gradually seep down with normal watering.

## How to repot and pot-on

The usual time for changing pots or compost is in spring when active root growth has begun. It is better to wait until flowering plants have flowered.

Water the plant a few days before repotting to make it easier to get it out of the pot. Have everything ready – thoroughly clean pots, crocks and moist compost; the shorter the period the plant is out of its pot the less it will suffer.

## 1 To remove the plant

Place one hand over the surface of the compost, holding the stem between fingers. Turn the pot upside down and gently knock the rim against the edge of a table. If that is not enough to shift the root ball run a knife round the inside of the pot.

If the plant is so potbound that a mass of roots has grown through the drainage hole, break the pot with a blow of a hammer – it is better to lose

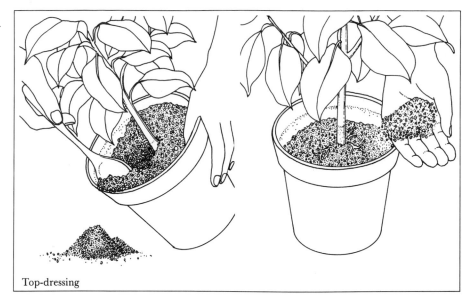

Top-dressing

the pot than lose the plant by damaging the roots when pulling them through the drainage hole.

## 2 Repotting

Carefully remove some of the compost from the roots. Cut away any rotten roots but treat the root hairs with great respect. Put the plant back in a clean pot of the same size and carefully firm fresh compost round the roots. Do not overdo the firming, especially with peat-based compost, in order not to restrict free drainage.

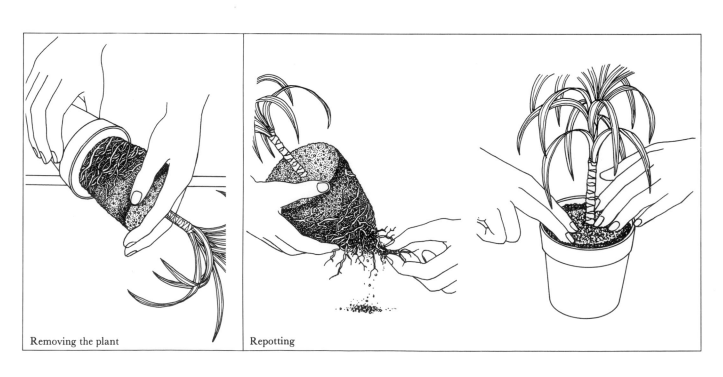

Removing the plant                    Repotting

### 3 Potting-on
Have a slightly larger pot ready, and put crocks in the bottom if it is a clay pot. Put a layer of fresh compost deep enough to keep the plant at the right level in the new pot. In a small pot the compost should come up to within $\frac{1}{2}$-$\frac{3}{4}$in (1.25-2cm) of the rim of the pot when you have finished replanting. This space allows room for watering. In large pots it can be between $1\frac{1}{2}$-2in (3.75-5cm). There is a simple way of getting everything right – the plant in the centre of the pot and at the right level. Put the old pot on to the layer of new compost at the bottom of the larger pot and pack compost around it up to the correct level, fairly firmly but not overtight. When the old pot is removed a mould is left which the root ball largely fills. Firm the compost against the root ball, adding more if necessary.

### 4 After replanting
Whether it has been repotted or potted-on, water the plant and let it settle down for a week or so in a shady place; it helps to mist-spray the leaves a little. Until the roots have spread into the new compost the plant will need less watering than before and there will be enough nutrients in the new compost to make fertilising unnecessary for two months (peat compost) or three (loam-based compost).

### Special cases
#### Cacti
Remove every cactus from its pot in early spring, and pot on if the roots crowd the pot. Otherwise repot in fresh compost. Beware of spines; hold the cactus with either a few layers of folded paper or with tongs. When replanting do not press the compost down hard.

#### Succulents
Repot or pot-on every year, according to the state of the roots. Spines are not the problem, but some succulents are very brittle and must be handled with extreme care. Hold the stems near the base to avoid rubbing off the bloom covering the leaves.

#### Bromeliads
Bromeliads do not have vigorous root systems and do not have to be potted-on frequently; most of them will never need more than a 7in (17.5cm) pot. Because they do not rely totally on roots for their food it is less vital to renew the compost every year as it is with other plants.

### For more information
Choice of composts and pots, pages 104–106.

For individual plants, A-Z sections pages 129–230.

Potting-on

Repotting a cactus

# Composts

When buying a plant you can inspect it carefully for signs of pest, disease and ill health, but you have to take on trust one of the most important things – the compost in which it is growing. Only later does the most common defect emerge – it is not free draining. This is because the texture is not coarse enough; it may indeed be almost fine dust. The result is that the compost holds too much water and not enough air. The fault can be remedied when repotting by replacing the old compost with a better one.

Do not use garden soil, for it may be chock full of invisible pests and diseases, be too acid or alkaline, and not even fertile. Instead buy a specially prepared compost, sterilised and fertilised. Garden centres usually have a wide range of them and cheapness is not the first consideration in deciding which to buy. The first choice is between a loam-based compost, in which the main ingredient is *sterilised* soil, plus peat and sand, and a peat-based compost made of peat and sand.

For most plants there is nothing to beat a good loam compost because the soil in it has its own natural fertility as well as the added fertilisers. But how good it is depends on the quality of the soil, and like many other things, loam is not what it used to be. The best is made of rotted-down turves and these are in short supply. Much of the soil now used is not fibrous enough because it contains too much clay and the compost becomes compacted and waterlogged. The standard loam-based composts are from formulas devised by the John Innes research station in the 1930s. The basic John Innes compost is 7 parts of sterilised loam (to provide food), 3 parts peat (to hold water) and 2 parts coarse sand (to ensure free draining). This compost is the one to use for sowing seed and raising cuttings, for the natural nutrients in the loam are adequate for the young roots. When the seedlings and cuttings

are well established they are moved into a potting compost, which is the basic formula with added fertiliser in powder form – providing nitrogen, phosphorus and potassium. The fertiliser is added in varying strengths to give three grades of compost. John Innes No 1 is for young plants in small pots, J.I. No 2, with twice as much fertiliser as No 1, is for mature plants, and J.I. No 3, with three times as much fertiliser, is for large plants in large pots.

There is no such standard formula for composts based on peat (called peat moss in the United States). Peats are formed when bog plants decay without oxygen. Sphagnum peat is composed of dead sphagnum moss and sedge peat is derived from grasslike sedges. Both are acid and sphagnum peat, especially, is above the level of acidity preferred by most houseplants (pH 5.5 to pH 6.5) so some form of calcium carbonate is added to peat-based composts to bring down the acidity to these levels.

To make the peat more free draining one part of coarse (sharp) sand may be added and one part of perlite, which both holds water and makes the compost more porous. (The white specks in some composts are perlite – volcanic rock which has been heat treated and ground.) The best peat composts are made of coarsely milled peat, providing spaces for air in between the particles; they are generally light brown. Composts made of dusty peat – sedge peat often is – are worse than useless, because they pack down with constant watering, never drain properly and exclude oxygen from the roots. They are usually very dark brown, almost black when wet.

Some plants do better in a loam-based compost and some in a peat-based compost, and such preferences are pointed out in the A-Z sections. By and large plants can thrive equally well in either. If you change from one type of compost to another when repotting the plant will adjust, perhaps more readily than you will to the inevitable changed pattern of fertilising – more frequently if you change from loam to peat, less frequently if from peat to loam – and to a lesser extent, watering, depending on whether the pot is plastic or clay.

Some plants require either slightly different or entirely different composts from the standard mixes. The reason is always to make the compost more free draining. Generally this is done by adding coarse sand, grit, or perlite to the ordinary loam-based or peat-based composts.

**Cacti:** Add one part of coarse (sharp) sand or perlite to every two parts of loam-based or peat-based compost. If peat-based compost is used avoid the dark finely milled peat which is not free draining. When repotting do not firm down peat compost much.

**Succulents:** Like cacti, other succulents need porous composts. As a general rule add one part of coarse sand to two parts of loam-based compost. Some do better with even more sand – lithops, for example. If using peat instead of loam, avoid finely milled peat.

**Bromeliads:** Composts for bromeliads should be free of lime and

porous. Leaf mould – leaves which have decayed for several years and are crumbly – is often added.

**Palms:** For most of the palms in the A-Z, peat-based composts are recommended, with the addition of coarse sand.

**Ferns:** Peat-based composts are satisfactory, but with the addition of sand unless the peat is very porous. A mixture of loam-based compost, leaf mould and sand can be used for larger ferns which might be top heavy in a peat compost.

**Orchids:** All the orchids (except *Paphiopedilum callosum*) included in the A-Z are epiphytic and usually grown in a mix of equal parts of peat, sphagnum moss and osmunda fibre. Sphagnum moss is the living moss from which sphagnum peat is derived and osmunda fibre is the chopped up fibrous roots of the osmunda fern, or Royal Fern. This fibre is in short supply and expensive and chopped up tree bark is now often substituted. This orchid mix is the most porous of all composts. The paphiopedilum can be grown in a porous peat-based compost but also thrives in the peat, sphagnum moss and osmunda fibre compost.

**Carnivorous plants:** These need the same type of compost as the epiphytic orchids, above.

# Pots

Most houseplants are now sold in plastic pots, whereas a generation ago they were in clay pots. Each has its advantages and disadvantages. Clay pots, being porous, allow water to evaporate through the sides. This diminishes the risk of sodden compost, but in hot weather the compost may dry out quickly. Lime from hard water and fertilisers also seep through the sides, leaving ugly white or brown deposits. Clay pots are heavy, a drawback when handling them, but a great plus in that their weight provides ballast to prevent a large plant from overbalancing, especially if the pot is full of loam-based compost. To water a plant in a clay pot with capillary matting a wick has to be inserted in the drainage hole. Clay pots cost more.

Plastic pots are lighter and fall over easily. Water cannot escape through the sides so there is a risk of overwatering. They do not need a wick for use with capillary matting. If black they look fairly innocuous, but the usual shades of green are very unnatural against the green of the leaves. This does not matter if they are out of sight within another container. If the space between the pot and the outer container is to be filled with moist peat as a way of increasing humidity, a plastic pot should certainly be the choice. A porous clay pot would draw moisture from the peat as the compost dried out, defeating the object of the operation which is to provide a humid microclimate around the plant, not an alternative to watering.

When repotting a plant it can be moved from a plastic to a clay pot, or the other way round. But roots grow in different ways in a porous and a non-porous pot. Some of the water in a clay pot moves through the compost to the sides and the roots spread out to follow this moist path. No water can escape through a plastic pot and the roots spread downwards before spreading outwards. However, when changed from one type of pot to another the plant will adjust before long to the changed conditions.

All pots, clay or plastic, should be thoroughly cleaned when repotting. Never put a plant in a dirty pot.

# Hydroculture

Looking after a large number of houseplants is an exacting occupation – seemingly endless watering, feeding, pruning, potting, pest spotting. Some of the tedium can be avoided by growing plants in water instead of in compost – so-called hydroculture, or hydroponics. On the other hand, for the dedicated indoor gardener it may also take away the pleasure, just as a keen cook gets no satisfaction out of convenience food.

If it is true that overwatering is the main cause of death among houseplants how does it come about that they thrive with their roots always in water? The reason why plants die in perpetually sodden compost is that all air is excluded, depriving the roots of the oxygen they need. But when grown in water plants develop different, fleshier roots which can extract oxygen from the water and store it.

In hydroculture the risk of overwatering is replaced by the danger of overfeeding. The plant gets its food from fertiliser dissolved in the water and the regular topping up of water and fertiliser can easily lead to a harmful build-up of mineral salts. So the main chore of hydroculture can become the regular removal of the plant from its container to give the roots a good wash to rid them of these salts.

Pots for hydroculture may be a single container or a double container. Single containers can be improvised, but avoid any made of metal, which may be corroded by fertiliser. Glass is safe from corrosion, but looks unsightly when algae start growing on the inside. Most pots sold specifically for hydroculture are made of plastic.

Plants which have been raised in water, and therefore have the fleshier roots, are not as widely available as plants raised in compost. A plant can be transferred from compost to water, but it has a major setback while it is developing a new set of roots and a

mature plant is likely to die. The first important step in making the transfer is to wash all the compost from the root ball. The washing must be gentle but thorough; any scrap of compost that goes into the water solution will make it foul.

## Single container method

In a single container the plant grows in aggregate, which may be pebbles, gravel, or expanded clay granules. The plant is planted in the aggregate as in compost and the roots grow down into the water/fertiliser solution at the bottom of the container.

When planting fill the container with the aggregate, anchoring the plant in it as you go. Using a special hydroculture fertiliser – which is weaker than standard compost fertiliser – make up a solution no stronger than that recommended by the makers. Pour in enough to fill between a quarter and a third of the container. There are available simple gauges which can be pushed into the aggregate to show how deep the solution is. As it evaporates it is topped up at intervals to restore the level. Because the topping up can lead to a build up of salts, every month or

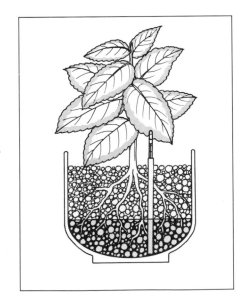

two the solution has to be poured off – not the easiest operation – and replaced by fresh solution. Also every year both aggregate and roots have to be washed.

## Double container method

A double container is easier to deal with, and it is better to buy one than to try to improvise.

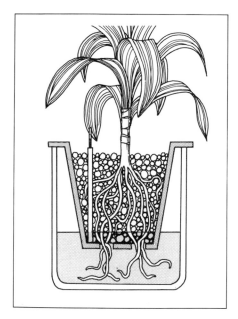

The outer container holds the fertiliser solution and there is usually a built-in gauge indicating both the maximum level of the solution and the minimum, to show when it has to be topped up. The inner container holds the aggregate and the plant, which may have been inserted straight into the aggregate or may be in a small pot of its own; through the holes in the pot the roots can grow into the aggregate and the solution. The inner container is suspended from the outer container so that the bottom is a little way into the fertiliser solution, which needs topping up as the gauge indicates. The washing out of excess salts still has to be done every month or two, but more simply by lifting the inner container and washing the aggregate under the tap.

Because root systems in hydroculture spread less than in compost, 'potting-on' is needed far less frequently. It merely involves removing the plant from its old container, washing out the roots and aggregate and moving it to a larger container, single or double, with additional aggregate – as in potting-on in compost.

Hydroculture has come far in the last decade and many refinements, such as the slow controlled release of fertilisers to avoid mineral build-up, have been introduced. The most labour saving development in hydroculture, favoured by merchant banks and multinational companies, is to hire contractors to look after and replace the plants. A more frugal, labour-saving approach is to buy plastic plants; no watering, feeding, repotting, pruning, pests or diseases, just an occasional dusting, but hardly indoor gardening.

# Propagation

Even the healthiest houseplant does not live for ever and there is much to be said for building up a new generation of plants to follow on as the others age or die. This is what propagation is about.

It is very easy to induce many plants to reproduce themselves – indeed some go more than half way to doing it for you even indoors, just as they do in the wild. What for us may be the simplest methods of propagation – by division and taking cuttings – the plants cannot do for themselves. On the other hand, the commonest natural form of reproduction, by seed, can be one of the trickiest to attempt indoors, especially with plants from very warm climates. However, it is the only way of growing annuals, and the kind we need for window boxes and other containers are fairly easy to raise.

The A-Z catalogue of plants gives the appropriate method, or methods, of propagation for each plant. The techniques are explained in the following pages. Listed roughly in order of difficulty, with the easiest first, they are:

### Vegetative propagation
By division – clumps of roots, rhizomes, tubers.

Planting offsets – including bromeliads, succulents, cacti, clivia and palm suckers.

Layering plantlets and stems of trailing plants.

Taking cuttings – stem tip cuttings, heel cuttings, stem cuttings of cacti and succulents, stem sections, leaf and stalk cuttings, leaf cuttings.

### Sexual propagation
Raising plants from seed.
Raising ferns from spores.

## Vegetative propagation

### Division
When dividing a plant growing in a clump it is best to take the word literally and split the plant into two parts and not into a large number of bereaved looking objects. Water the plant a day or two before you intend to divide so that it is easier to take out of the pot. Have ready two thoroughly cleaned pots big enough to take the sections of the divided plant, crocks and the appropriate compost, already moistened. Put some crocks and a layer of compost at the bottom of each pot. Remove the plant from the pot, as when repotting. Prising the roots gently apart by hand is by far the best method because this is likely to do the least damage to the roots, especially the fine root hairs.

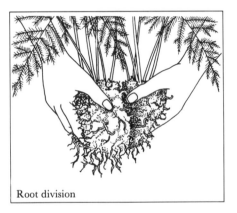
Root division

If the root ball is made up of tough roots it may have to be cut through. Always use a very sharp knife. Repot the divided parts in fresh compost as quickly as possible so that the root hairs do not dry out. Plant to the same depth as before. Keep the plants out of sun for a week or two after the operation and do not water again until the compost begins to dry out; divided plants need less frequent watering than before because until the root hairs are re-established they will be taking up less moisture.

Plants growing from rhizomes or stem tubers are easily reproduced from sections of the rhizome or tuber. A rhizome is the thick fleshy stem from which both roots and stems can grow. It either grows underground or, as is usual indoors, on the surface of the compost. The comparatively few tuberous houseplants have stem tubers, growing underground or on the surface. All the orchids in the A-Z section, except vanda, grow from rhizomes and can be propagated by division. Other plants which have rhizomes or tubers include achimenes, *Begonia tuberhybrida*, cyrtomium, pellaea, smithiantha and spathiphyllum.

Take the tuber or rhizome from the pot and remove old compost from around the roots. New plants will grow from pieces which have only one growth bud, but it is far better to cut off sections with several buds to produced a decent sized new plant. The sections should be placed on a layer of sharp sand on top of a layer of compost in a shallow pot or tray.

Put them in a propagator to provide warmth and humidity and move them into small pots when the shoots have grown well, planting them in the same way as was the old tuber or rhizome.

## Offsets
Many plants produce offsets, small editions of themselves, either at the base of the plant, where they may or may not have roots, or from below ground where they will have roots.

One rule common to the propagation of all offsets is not to be in too great a hurry to remove them – let them become well-established before severing them from the parent plant.

## Bromeliad offsets
The rosette of most bromeliads dies after flowering, but puts out offsets as it does. Do not remove the offsets until the parent plant is dead and the offsets have developed their rosette formation and are several inches high. All the bromeliads in the A-Z section can be propagated in this way, but some are more lavish in producing offsets than others.

Remove the whole plant from the pot, and cut away the offsets with a sharp knife, carefully in order not to damage the young roots.

Reject any offsets which do not have roots. Plant the others in a free draining compost suitable for bromeliads, and keep them in the warmth, about 75 deg F (24 deg C).

**Succulent offsets:** Non-branching succulents may produce offsets round their base. Those which come away easily from the plant can be potted up immediately, but if you have had to use a knife let the cut heal for two or three days before planting, or the offset will rot. Press the offset into the

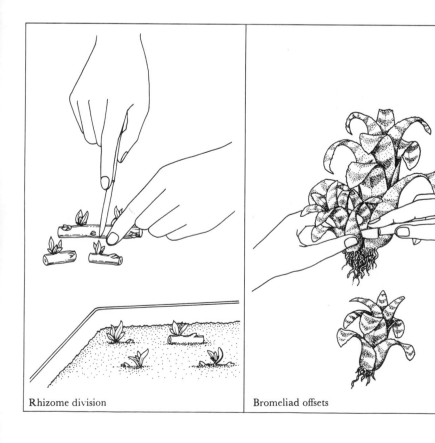

Rhizome division

Bromeliad offsets

potting mixture and in a few days it will root, if kept in a temperature of about 70 deg F (21 deg C).

**Cacti offsets:** Some cacti produce offsets at the base of the plant – among them are gymnocalycium, lobivia, mammillaria and rebutia. Gently pull them away and plant them. If they have to be cut away let the cut surface dry and heal for a few days before planting in a suitable cacti compost. They do not need to be kept in a propagator and normal late spring and early summer temperatures are suitable. Keep out of the sun until well established.

**Clivia offsets:** A clivia is one of the plants which grows offsets from below the surface of the compost. Let the offset grow at least three leaves about 9in (22.5cm) long, before removing it in spring or summer, after the plant has flowered. Propagation is done at the same time as repotting. Cut the offset away from the parent with a very sharp knife.

Try to sort out which roots belong to the offset and disentangle them as carefully as you can – they are very brittle. An offset without roots will not grow. Plant it in a potting mixture and keep it in ordinary room temperatures, but out of sun.

**Palm suckers:** While palms have usually to be grown from seed – a long process – two of them in the A-Z, *Chrysalidocarpus lutescens* and *Chamaerops humilis*, produce suckers which can be removed along with the roots and potted up. Plant the chamaerops in a loam-based potting compost and keep it in normal room temperatures. Chrysalidocarpus will need far more nursing. Remove the sucker in spring, plant in a mixture of two parts loam-based compost and one part coarse sand, and keep it in a warm room. For the first month enclose it in a plastic bag, as described on page 112. After moving it out of the bag the palm should be watered infrequently until it is growing well.

### Layering

**Plantlets:** A very few plants produce offsets on their stems or leaves; these are known as plantlets. The most reliable way of propagating them is by layering, which allows the young plant to grow its own roots while still being nourished by the parent. The three most notable examples are *Chlorophytum comosum, Saxifraga stolonifera* and *Tolmiae menziesii.*

The chlorophytum is the easiest. It puts out long stems carrying flowers, which are followed by plantlets. Pin

Clivia offsets

Plantlets

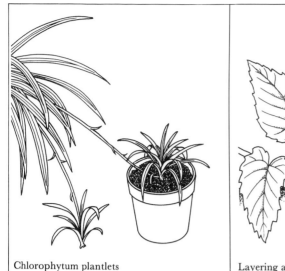

Chlorophytum plantlets

Layering a trailer

Bulbils

down a plantlet at the end of the stem into a pot of moist rooting compost placed alongside the parent plant. Let it become well established and obviously growing before severing it.

Saxifraga and tolmiae are dealt with in a similar way.

**Other layering:** Many trailing and creeping plants which do not produce plantlets can be induced to root by layering and later severed from the parent plant. Examples are cissus, *Duchesnea indica*, fittonia, hedera and pellionia.

**Bulbils:** Bulbous plants produce small bulbs alongside them. Remove and plant them when repotting.

It will be several years before they flower.

### Cuttings

In the wild plants do not reproduce themselves by cuttings – except by accident when a bit gets broken off and with luck, manages to take root. But once domesticated most plants are liable to find themselves cut into pieces to make more; short lengths of young shoots, bits of ancient stem, leaves with stalks, leaves without stalks, chopped up leaves – all are expected to turn into magnificent plants, and often they do. Some plants cannot be grown from cuttings, and none is versatile enough to grow from every type of cutting, so you should never expect a hundred per cent success. The best time to take cuttings is after plants have begun active growth; late spring and early summer

are good because there may be enough natural warmth (around 65 deg F, 18 deg C) for the cutting to root. However, normal room temperatures are not enough for many indoor plants and they must be raised in a heated propagator where the compost itself is kept at temperatures of 70–75 deg F (21–24 deg C) or more; hence the phrase 'bottom heat'.

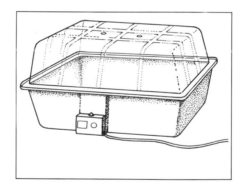

Even if bottom heat is not necessary cuttings need a humid atmosphere so that the leaves do not dry out and shrivel before the roots have begun to grow. There are many simple unheated propagators available, and far cheaper than the heated.

A propagator to be used for cuttings needs to be taller than one for growing from seed. Use shallow containers rather than the normal pots, which cut down head room.

Alternatively a plastic tent can be improvised for each pot containing a cutting or cuttings. This is made from four canes, a plastic bag and a piece of string or elastic band. Make a few small holes in the bag to admit air

Plastic 'tent'

Stem tip cuttings

and to prevent excessive condensation.

The essential part of this construction is that the bag must be large enough not to touch the leaves of the cutting, which would go mouldy and rot.

Have everything ready before taking the cuttings. Plastic pots are better than clay pots for cuttings for they do not allow moisture to escape through the sides of the pot. If you use a clay pot the whole of the pot must be enclosed in the bag. Have them already filled with moist rooting compost, peat or loam-based, as recommended in the A-Z entries. Have a small dish of hormone rooting powder in which to dip the cuttings before planting; this encourages and hastens rooting.

**Stem tip cuttings** (also referred to as softwood cuttings): These are the growing shoots of soft-stemmed plants, and the prunings of some plants may provide a supply of them. They should not be too young or soft or they may rot before they root. As a rough guide cuttings are about 3–4in (7.5-10cm) long, but may be less on small growing plants. The better rule is that the cutting should have at least three nodes – the points where leaves join the stem. Cut the stem just below

a node, using a very sharp knife; crushed and jagged edges rot. To make sure of a clean cut it may be better to make a cut lower down the stem and trim it to size when you have removed it from the plant and can handle it better. Remove the lower pair of leaves, or two pairs if need be; none must touch the compost when planted.

Moisten the end of the cutting and dip it in hormone rooting powder. Make a hole in the compost with a pencil so that you do not have to force the cutting in – that way the stem might lose its rooting powder and be damaged. Gently press the compost round the stem, just firmly enough to keep the cutting upright. Try to get the planting done as quickly as possible before the end of the stem begins to dry out. Put the pot in its plastic tent or in the propagator with the lid on.

If after a day or two there is excessive condensation on the sides of the bag, take it off, turn it inside out and replace it. If in a propagator open the ventilator. Stick your finger into the compost occasionally to see whether it needs watering. If it does, immerse the pot or tray in shallow water and let it drain afterwards; do not water from above. Keep the cuttings out of

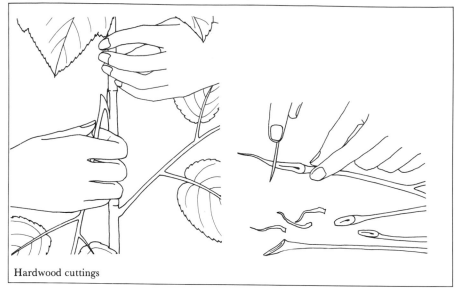

Hardwood cuttings

the sun, but not in deep shade. The cuttings of some plants root quickly, of others very slowly, and a proportion of cuttings of all plants never root at all, but as long as the cutting does not collapse there is always hope. Remove any which start to go mouldy. When the cuttings have taken and are obviously growing, gradually acclimatise them to the drier atmosphere of the house, removing the tent or lifting the lid of the propagator for an increasing number of hours each day.

**Hardwood cuttings** (also called heel cuttings): These cuttings are side shoots from plants with hard stems and they are taken with a 'heel' from that stem.

Holding the stem in one hand give the side shoot a downwards tug. Trim the heel with a sharp knife, dip it in hormone rooting powder and treat it in the same way as a stem-tip, or soft cutting. Heel cuttings take longer to root.

**Stem cuttings of cacti and other succulents:** The stems of branching desert cacti, such as opuntia, are easy to propagate and root readily. Holding a branch with tongs or thick layers of paper to protect you from the spines cut it off with a sharp knife.

Let it dry out for two or three days and plant in a porous potting mixture suitable for cacti. It will need warmth (around 70 deg F, 21 deg C), but not humidity, so there is no need to put it in a plastic tent.

To propagate jungle cacti: for epiphyllum take a cutting of a 5in

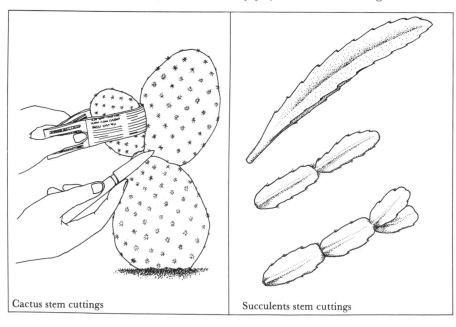

Cactus stem cuttings

Succulents stem cuttings

(12.5cm) branch; for rhipsalidopsis, two joined segments and for schlumbergera, two or three joined segments.

Let them dry out for a day and plant them in a porous potting mixture. All should begin to grow after a few weeks.

Branching succulents can be propagated by removing a branch, letting it dry out for three days, and planting it in a free draining compost. The cutting may need supporting with a small stick.

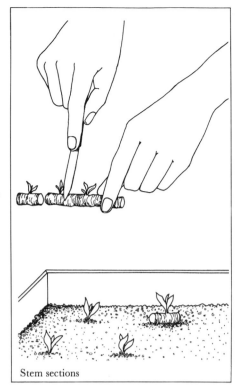

Stem sections

**Stem sections:** Making plants grow from small pieces of old stems can be done with only a few plants and since the operation involves the mutilation of the old plant it is done only after it has become leggy. Aglaonema, dieffenbachia and dracaena are suitable for this treatment. Cut about 6in (15cm) off the top of the plant and treat it as an ordinary stem cutting. Cut the rest of the stem a few inches from the compost and in time it will put out new growth.

You are now left with a length of bare stem. Cut it up into pieces about 2in (5cm) long; each piece must have at least one node, better if more. Lay them flat horizontally on the surface of a pot of moist peat moss.

Cover them with a plastic tent. Keep the peat moss moist. In time the sections root and sprout and after a couple of shoots have appeared harden them off gradually over a fortnight by removing the tent for longer periods each day. When thoroughly established they can be transplanted into potting compost.

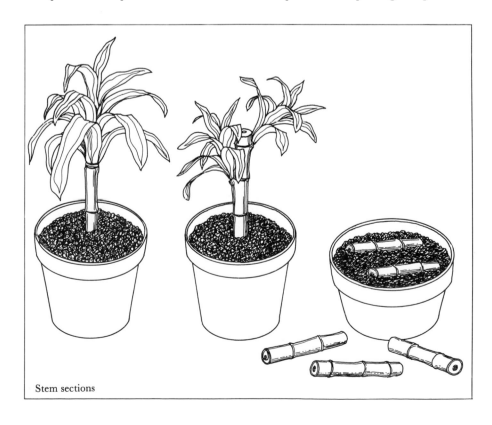

Stem sections

## Leaf cuttings

Leaves without stalks can produce new plants. The limited number of plants which can achieve this wonder include *Begonia rex*, the succulents crassula and echeveria, and peperomia and saintpaulia.

## Saintpaulia leaves with stalks:

Put a layer of peat compost in a shallow pot with a layer of damp sand on top. Break off a few healthy leaves with their stalks right from the base; if you leave a bit rot sets in. Cut the stalks to 1in (2.5cm) and dip the ends in hormone rooting powder. Make holes with a pencil in the sand and push in the cuttings to a depth of about $\frac{1}{2}$in (1.25cm); they get a better hold if inserted at an angle of 45 deg. The leaves must not be touching each other.

Gently firm the compost round each cutting. Place the pot in a plastic tent. At length – it may be a couple of months or more – plantlets will appear round the base of the leaf.

Remove them from the leaf when they are about $\frac{1}{2}$in (1.25cm) tall, and pot them.

Saintpaulias are often propagated by suspending the leaf stalk in water. Fill a shallow glass jar almost two-thirds full of water, adding a few bits of charcoal to keep the water sweet. Cover the top with aluminium foil held in place with a rubber band. Make a few small holes in the foil for the cuttings. Break off some leaves with stalks and trim the stalks to about 2in (5cm) before pushing the cuttings through the holes into the

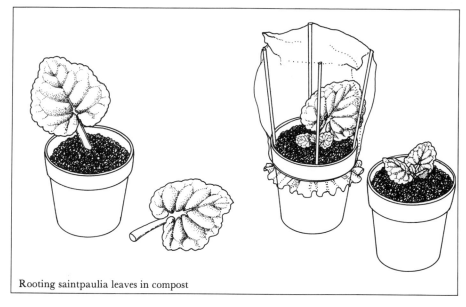
Rooting saintpaulia leaves in compost

water. Roots will take about a month to form and plantlets will follow. Remove them from the leaf stalk and pot them.

It may be interesting to watch the process of roots developing in water but propagation by this method is not a particularly good idea. Roots need oxygen. Plants grown in water develop thick white roots which can absorb oxygen from water. Plants in compost develop different types of roots which get oxygen from the air between the particles of the compost. So when you move a plant from water to compost it has to start growing a new lot of roots and often gets a severe setback at this stage. The shock can be reduced by moving the plant to the compost when the roots are still small – no more than $\frac{1}{4}$in (.6cm) long. The adjustment is then easier.

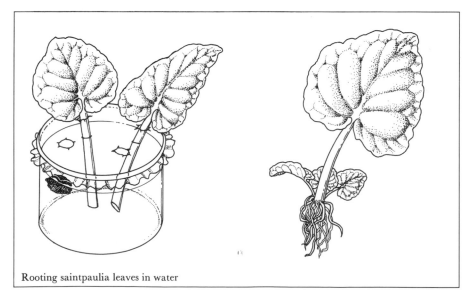
Rooting saintpaulia leaves in water

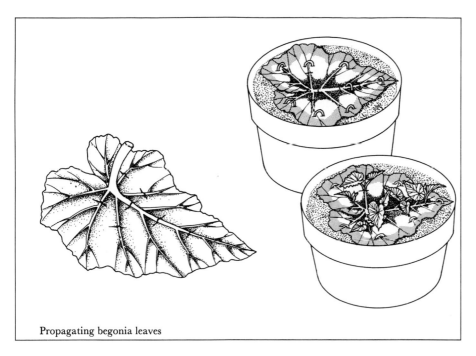

Propagating begonia leaves

**Begonia rex leaves:** They can be rooted with a stalk in the same way as saintpaulias, but there is another way, using just the leaf. A heated propagator will be needed.

Prepare a shallow pot of damp sand. Take a whole leaf of *Begonia rex* and lay it on a flat surface underside up. With a sharp knife or razor blade make two or three cuts across the centre vein and one or two cuts across the larger of the veins that join the central vein. Turn the leaf over carefully and lay it face up on the surface of the damp sand. To hold it in close contact with the sand pin the leaf down at a number of points with loops of wire.

Propagating sansevieria leaves

Keep the plant in the propagator at a steady 70 deg F (21 deg C) with the sand always moist. When after several weeks plantlets begin to grow from the cut veins gradually reduce the temperature, but only a little. When the plantlets have two recognisable leaves 1in (2.5cm) or so long sever them from the leaf and plant them in potting compost in individual pots.

**Sansevieria leaves:** If the leaves of sansevieria are cut across the leaf into pieces of about 1in (2.5cm) each one can produce a new plant. It is important to plant the bits with the bottom end down, and to remember which is which nick a little piece out of the lower edge of each piece as you cut it. Let them dry out a little and then push them into a layer of damp sand which has been put on top of a layer of compost.

Put them in a propagator and keep them at a temperature of 70 deg F (21 deg C). When there are three young leaves ease them away from the old leaf and plant in loam-based compost. It is hardly worth the trouble, because however vividly variegated the parent plant was, the offspring will have only green mottled leaves. The operation could fill an idle hour on a wet afternoon.

## Sexual propagation

### Raising plants from seed

The most natural thing in the world is for a plant in the wild to grow from a seed. In a house raising plants from seed may be either ridiculously easy – mustard and cress on a piece of wet blotting paper – or virtually impossible. They must have warmth to germinate (at least 65 deg F, 18 deg C) and seeds from sub-tropical plants are likely to need 70–80 deg F (21–27 deg C) and that means raising them in a heated propagator. They also need humidity (which a propagator would provide) and a good light after they have germinated. You need patience and a capacity to accept inevitable failures – failure to germinate, collapse from damping off, losses when transplanting. You also need room; not just for the propagator but for all the pots for the seedlings after they have been transplanted. Books may furnish a room, but small pots merely clutter it up. If you have a greenhouse many of the problems are solved, but raising plants from seed inside a house is not a practice to embark on without much thought, especially as it can easily become an obsession and get out of hand. Nevertheless, there is an excitement in it which other forms of propagation do not have, and success brings a very satisfying smugness, as though you were the plant's creator.

Use seed trays or shallow pots and fill them 2in (5cm) deep with a sowing compost (page 104). Seeds which are large enough to handle easily can be spaced in rows on the compost and then covered lightly with sifted compost. Small seeds should be scattered very sparingly, a pinch at a time between thumb and finger, and covered with a sprinkling of sand, or if very small merely mist-sprayed. After sowing put the tray in very shallow tepid water and let the water soak up right through the compost until the surface glistens with moisture. Let the compost drain thoroughly before putting the tray in the propagator.

Germination is often rapid, in a week or so if conditions are favourable, but some seeds are laggards. When seedlings begin to break through the compost give them a little more ventilation in the propagator and a brighter light. Keep the compost moist by standing the tray in shallow tepid water and then letting the compost drain. Moisture is vital; seedlings have shallow roots and can die in a few hours if they get dry. The first leaves to unfold are so-called seed leaves, which do not look at all like the plant's normal leaves. Thin out crowded seedlings as soon as they are large enough to handle. The next pair are true leaves, and when these have appeared and the seedlings are about 1in (2.5cm) high transplant them. Do not let them grow too big, the later they are moved the greater the setback. Loosen the seedling from the compost with a stick and lift it out by a leaf, preferably by a seed leaf, which in any case will soon die. Never take hold of a seedling by the stem, which is very fragile.

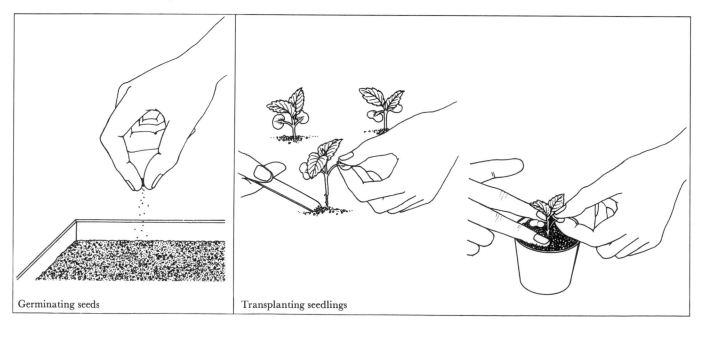

Germinating seeds                    Transplanting seedlings

The seedlings are replanted in small pots using a potting compost. (See page 104). Discard all weak seedlings, but transplant more than you think you need because there will be some casualties.

The length of time it takes a perennial plant to grow from a seed into an attractive mature plant varies enormously – it may be years. Vegetative propagation by division and cuttings give far faster results. An annual plant goes through its whole life cycle in a year or less, while a biennial lives through two seasons, flowering in the second. Many of these are suitable for window boxes and containers and can be grown from seed without the need of a heated propagator because they germinate at lower temperatures. Raising such plants from seed is far cheaper than buying small plants from a nursery and with seeds there is usually a greater choice of varieties.

### Raising ferns from spores

The greatest challenge in propagation is growing ferns from spores. Many ferns produce them in great quantities in spore cases (or sori) growing on the underside of fronds, visible as brown spots. Detach a frond when the spots darken and put it in a paper bag for a week or two to let the sori dry out and burst to release the spores, which look

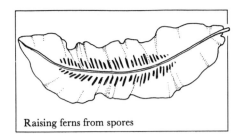
Raising ferns from spores

like small specks of dust. Fill a tray with moist peat moss and scatter the spores from the bag on to it. Enclose the tray in a plastic bag and keep it in the warmth in a bright light and sit back and wait.

After a month or two a green film appears on the surface of the compost. These are prothalli, the first stage in the life cycle of a fern. With minute heart-shaped leaves they do not look at all like a fern, but in the fullness of time these minute plants develop sexual organs, which the fern itself totally lacks. A moist compost and a humid atmosphere is vitally important at this stage, for the male cell literally has to swim to the underside of the prothallus to make contact with the female egg cell. The result of their congress is to create a young sexless fern. It is hard to imagine anything more complicated than that.

# Pests

There are two main kind of pests which an indoor plant suffers; those which suck its sap and those which chew its leaves. If they are not destroyed the plant probably will be. Happily, there are far fewer pests indoors than there are outdoors and you will be unlucky if you see all of them.

The immediate step to take if you have any suspicion that something is wrong is to remove the affected plant away from all the others. Pests and diseases spread at breakneck speed.

## Suckers

Among the more likely of the really unpleasant pests are eight sap suckers.

### Scale insects

**What they are:** Scale insects are so small that it is usually only when they are there in large numbers that you notice them. They haunt the underside of the leaves, especially around the mid rib, and before long the damage they do shows through to the surface of the leaves. The minute insects cover their bodies with a tough protective shield – the scale. Under it the mother lays her eggs (in many species without the need of a male) and then dies. When the young insects emerge they move to another part of the plant, and establish themselves there, having built scales for protection. If female they stay there sucking sap for the rest of their lives. The males are mobile, moving around

to mate, without feeding, and eventually turn into winged insects, so small as not to be noticed.

**What they do:** Scale insects pierce the leaves and stems and suck the sap, weakening the plant and disfiguring the foliage. There are many species, each with its favourite plants to suck. Among indoor plants most liable to be affected are ferns, palm, begonia, dracaena, azalea, ivies, pelargoniums, ficus, bromeliads and cacti.

**What to do to them:** If there are only a few young scales they can be prised off the leaves with a finger nail. If many, spray with malathion. To destroy tough mature scales apply a systemic insecticide to the compost, and this will kill the young as they emerge. Also give the systemic treatment to infected ferns, cacti and other succulents since they are damaged by malathion sprays.

### Aphids

**What they are:** Aphids – greenfly and blackfly – are omnipresent houseplant pests. Some are winged, some wingless; some start as eggs as a result of mating, some are born alive without mating (parthenogenesis). Whichever way they arrive they do so in vast numbers. In summer a female can produce seven young a day, and just over a week later these young have joined the production line, and so on.

**What they do:** In their hundreds they suck the sap of leaves and, especially, young shoots, causing

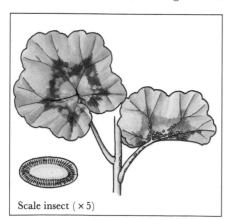

Scale insect (× 5)

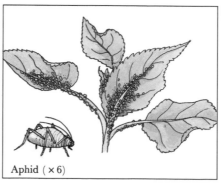

Aphid (× 6)

stunted and distorted growth; spread virus disease; and leave behind large quantities of excrement (honeydew) which encourage the growth of sooty mould. Some species attack roots, and they can make the plant wilt.

**What to do to them:** Spray the leaves with soapy water, or a solution of derris, pyrethrum or malathion. Do not spray ferns, cacti and other succulents with malathion. Derris kills fish, so remove a fish bowl or aquarium to another room before spraying. The alternative is to apply a systemic insecticide to the compost. This is also the way to get rid of root aphids.

### Red spider mites

**What they are:** These mites, little more than red or greenish dots, have no wings but four pairs of walking legs, so they can get around. One of the main problems is that it is almost impossible to see them and they betray their presence only by the damage they have done. They are particularly liable to strike and breed quickly in hot dry weather, and many plants are then at risk.

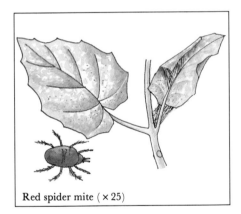

Red spider mite ( × 25)

**What they do:** They pierce the undersides of the leaves and suck sap. The damage shows as yellow spots on the upper surface of the leaves. In a heavy infestation the yellowness spreads all over the leaves, which begin to fall. The plants may eventually die. Aspidistra, cissus, dracaena and schefflera are among the plants frequently attacked.

**What to do to them:** Spray with a solution of derris or malathion, but do not use malathion on cacti, succulents in general, or ferns. To try to ward off the mites spray the plants frequently in hot dry weather.

### Leaf hoppers

**What they are:** The adults are pale yellow jumping insects about 1/8th in (3mm) long, which leap about when disturbed and flee, often to land on another plant. The whitish nymphs are sluggish; when they moult they leave their skins behind, which show up as white specks on the leaves.

Leaf hopper ( × 5)

**What they do:** Both adults and nymphs suck sap from the undersides of the leaves, inhibiting the growth of the plant. The holes they make produce white or yellow mottling on the top surface of the leaves.

**What to do to them:** Spray with malathion (not, to repeat the important warning, on ferns, cacti and succulents) or use a systemic insecticide, which will also deal with the emerging nymphs.

### Cyclamen mites

**What they are:** Invisible to the naked eye. Under a microscope they reveal themselves as oval see-through bodies on eight short legs. Whereas red spider mites flourish in hot dry weather, cyclamen mites like it cool and humid. Given these conditions new generations emerge in less than a month. The mites feed on flower buds as well as on the juicy young leaves.

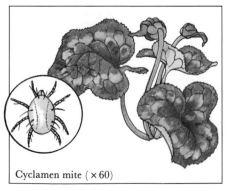

Cyclamen mite ( × 60)

**What they do:** Suck sap, and in doing so scar leaves, distort or destroy flower buds and cause leaves to drop. They also spread fungal diseases. Plants, besides cyclamen, susceptible to attack are African violets, azalea, begonia, fuchsia, impatiens and pelargonium.

**What to do to them:** Throw the plant away if the attack is bad, for the sake of your other plants. A minor attack can be dealt with by using a systemic insecticide.

## Mealy bugs

**What they are:** These are pale yellow or pink wingless insects, about 1/6th in (4mm) long, related to scale insects, but they cover themselves with a white waxy substance instead of scales. This, at least, makes them easier to detect. On the other hand, they are mobile and given to hiding in the more inaccessible parts of a plant.

**What they do:** Mealy bugs suck sap from stems and leaves, stunting growth, causing leaves to turn yellow and fall, and promoting sooty moulds by their excrement (honeydew). Some attack roots, especially of cacti, and are not discovered until the plant begins to wilt for no apparent reason. Plants often liable to attack are

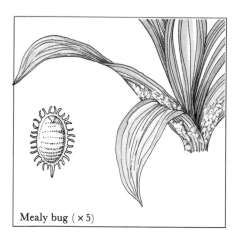

Mealy bug ( × 5)

African violets, begonia, cacti, dieffenbachia, dracaena, ferns and palms.

**What to do to them:** Remove obviously infested leaves. Spray the plant with malathion (not ferns, cacti, succulents), paying particular attention to the undersides of the leaves, and the crevices and curled leaves in which the bugs may be hiding. Or use a systemic insecticide; especially for cacti, and this is the

only way of dealing with mealy bugs round the roots.

## Thrips

**What they are:** Thrips are small flying insects, brown or black, and less than $\frac{1}{16}$ in (2.5mm) long. They live and breed on the undersides of leaves. Evidence of their presence are scratches along the leaves where they have scraped the surface to suck or to lay eggs (in many species the young are produced from unfertilised eggs). They are most active, and reproductive, in warm dry weather.

Thrip ( × 7)

**What they do:** Their sap-sucking stunts and distorts growth of both shoots and flowers and their piercing of the leaves disfigures the plant. This is made worse by their reddish excreta, on which fungus readily grows. As active fliers they are efficient carriers of virus diseases from plant to plant. Among plants at greatest risk are begonia, croton, cyclamen, ferns, orchids and palms.

**What to do to them:** Spray with malathion (not cacti, succulents, ferns) for immediate results and apply the slower-acting systemic insecticide to guard against a repeat attack.

## Whiteflies

**What they are:** Small (1/20th in – 1.25mm) insects, covered in a white

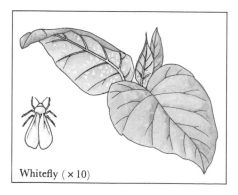

Whitefly ( × 10)

waxy coating, which live on the undersides of leaves, but if disturbed rise up in a cloud and flap about like dwarf moths. Reproduction is largely parthenogenetic and prolific, and given good summer weather generation follows generation every month.

**What they do:** Both adults and young suck the sap; the plants develop yellow mottling and if the flies are not destroyed the plants may die. The flies' excrement (honeydew) attracts sooty mould.

**What to do to them:** Spray with derris or malathion to kill the flies, but many will fly away as you begin. To kill them if they return, as well as the nymphs which emerge from the eggs left behind, use a systemic insecticide in the compost.

**Another reminder:** do not spray ferns, cacti and other succulents with malathion – they will be permanently damaged.

## Chewers

The chewers are rather less of a menace indoors than the suckers. They are more at home outdoors in window boxes and containers, but some of them do stray at times into the house. Two of the nastiest to be found there are fungus gnats and leaf miners.

### Fungus gnats

**What they are:** It is not the gnats – small black flies – which do the damage but the small white maggots which emerge from the eggs, which are laid on the surface of the compost, especially after it has been watered.

**What they do:** The maggots operate underground, consuming not only organic matter in the compost but chewing at the roots as well, leaving wounds open to bacterial diseases.

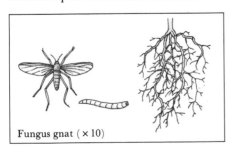

Fungus gnat ( × 10)

**What to do to them:** Kill both eggs and maggots by soaking the compost

with malathion. Always use sterilised compost.

### Leaf miners

**What they are:** Pernicious larvae which are the offspring of certain species of moths, beetles and flies which lay their eggs in the leaves of plants.

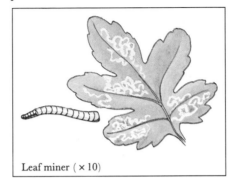

Leaf miner ( × 10)

**What they do:** The larvae suck sap, but the main damage is caused by their tunnelling inside the leaf, making white drunken patterns on the surface.

**What to do to them:** Sprays do not reach the larvae inside the leaves so remove and destroy all seriously mined foliage. Apply a systemic pesticide to the compost.

Outdoors the champion chewers are caterpillars, slugs and snails.

### Caterpillars

**What they are:** It is unfortunate, from a gardener's point of view, that such beautiful insects as butterflies and moths have to go through a destructive caterpillar adolescence. Their parents seldom lay eggs on indoor plants, but outdoors they can still be a fearsome pest though the use of pesticides on commercial crops is reducing the caterpillar (and sadly, the butterfly) population.

**What they do:** Some, such as cutworms, live in the soil and feed on underground stems, but the most

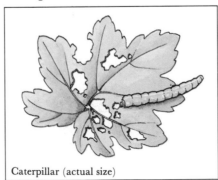

Caterpillar (actual size)

common caterpillars are those which voraciously devour leaves, often during the night. As though the chewed leaves were not insult enough they leave behind much excremetal evidence of their presence.

**What to do to them:** Pick them off and destroy them if there are only a few. If many, spray with derris.

## Slugs and snails

**What they are:** Two havoc creating hermaphrodites (snails with shells and slugs without) which are not easy to get rid of. Most feed above ground, usually in the dark, especially on warm humid nights. Slugs are far more destructive than snails, in particular the brown field slug and the black garden slug.

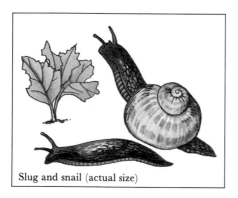

Slug and snail (actual size)

**What they do:** The foliage feeders tear leaves and flowers to pieces and injure stems with the help of a 'tongue' which has thousands of extremely small teeth.

**What to do to them:** Lay bait of methiocarb, but to protect it from rain (and to protect children and pets from eating the pellets) place it under an upturned plant pot slightly raised from the ground. Some gardeners tempt them with a saucer of beer in which the slugs drown, others hunt for them in the dark and drown them in salt water; both macabre operations.

## Earwigs

**What they are:** These insects have chestnut brown bodies about 1in (2.5cm) long, with a fearsome looking pair of pincers at the tail. They forage at night and hide during the day, often in among flower petals.

**What they do:** They chew leaves, but their main offence is to eat petals and gouge out young flower buds, which are ruined.

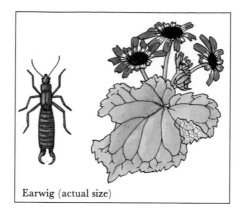

Earwig (actual size)

**What to do to them:** Shake them out of their hiding places in the flowers and then spray malathion over the lower part of the plant and on the ground around where the earwigs have fallen.

## Ants

**What they are:** The common black ant, about 1/5in (5mm) long, is the one most likely to visit our window boxes. Ants are not much of a pest themselves but a sign that there are aphids and other excreters of honeydew around; that is what the ants are after.

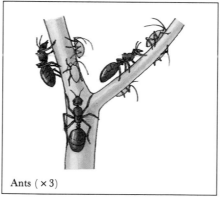

Ants ( × 3)

**What they do:** They are liable to carry aphids and mealy bugs from plant to plant. They also make nests in containers, disturbing the roots.

**What to do to them:** They can be killed with ant sprays, or malathion, but if you get rid of the honeydew pests the ants will go.

Worms are in no way pests, but in pots can be a nuisance by disturbing the roots. They will be present indoors only if you used garden soil in potting, or if they found a squat in a pot while it was out of doors in summer. This trespassing can be prevented by standing the pot on a hard surface and not on the soil.

## Pesticides

All pesticides are deadly because their purpose is to kill. They kill in different ways and some are more indiscriminately deadly than others. Sprays or dusts can bring instant death to insects which come into contact with them, or they may kill when insects eat parts of the plants which have been sprayed or dusted. Other poisons are absorbed by the plant into the sap and over quite long periods will go on killing pests, whether suckers or chewers. These are systemic pesticides. Contact pesticides act at once, but usually have to be repeated. With systemics there is an initial delay before they are taken in by the plant, but then they are long acting.

The pesticides likely to inflict the fewer casualties on harmless or beneficial insects (such as bees) are the least persistent – derris (rotenone) for aphids and mites and pyrethrum (or the similar resmethrin) for a large number of pests. However, derris will kill fish, so cover their bowl or spray elsewhere. Malathion is more deadly (and evil smelling). It kills most pests, but it will also kill ferns, cacti and succulents and should never be used on or sprayed near them. These pesticides, either singly or in combination with others, are produced in enormous profusion by the chemical industry under a great variety of names. They may be sold as a powder to dust the plant, as a liquid to spray on the plant, either with a manual sprayer or from an aerosol, or as a liquid to dilute and soak the compost.

Among the systemics dimethoate is most frequently chosen for spraying. Systemics can also be used as granules, preferably scratched into the compost rather than scattered on the surface because they may give off a stench when wet. The pesticide reaches the roots after watering to be taken up into the sap. Alternatively there are 'plant pins' impregnated with butoxicarboxim, which are pushed into the compost and act in a similar way.

**Warning:** All pesticides are dangerous to some degree and should be handled with great care. Follow exactly the instructions on the packets on how to apply the poison. Never make solutions stronger than recommended.

To avoid risks spray outside. If you cannot and the plant is not too big put it in the bottom of a plastic bag, spray, quickly pull the bag right over the plant and seal the top. Leave it in the bag for a quarter of an hour.

If you have to spray indoors and the plant is too big to go into a bag open the windows wide to clear the air as quickly as possible. Take care to spray the undersides of the leaves where pests love to hide and not just the top surface.

Cover up furnishings near the plant–they can be badly marked. Never spray near food. If using an aerosol hold it at least 12in (30cm) away from the leaves or they may be damaged. Never use an aerosol anywhere near a fern. In short, do not get spray-happy with pesticides.

# Diseases

Many of the ailments of plants are caused not by pests but by diseases, though pests often spark them off. Diseases caused by fungi or by bacteria may be curable; those caused by viruses are not.

## Sooty mould

This black mould is a fungus growing on the excrement ('honeydew') of aphids, and it interferes with photosynthesis and clogs the stomata of leaves. Wipe off the mould with warm soapy water and then spray the leaves to get rid of the aphids.

Sooty mould

## Botrytis (or grey mould)

A fluffy and grey mould on stems, leaves, flowers and even the compost. It is encouraged by overwatering and excessive mist-spraying. Saintpaulias and other plants with similarly soft stems are most at risk. Cut away the diseased part of the plant. If there is any left worth saving spray it with fungicide. Thereafter cut down watering and mist spraying and increase ventilation.

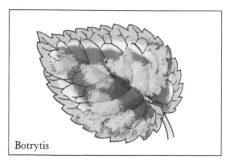

Botrytis

## Blackleg (another form of grey mould)

This mould mainly attacks cuttings of fleshy plants, causing them to turn black and rot at the base. Overwatering is responsible, in combination with a compost which is not porous enough. Cuttings which are dipped in a hormone rooting powder that includes a fungicide are more likely to ward off attacks.

## Damping off

A number of fungi attack seedlings which topple over and die within hours. Remove the stricken seedlings immediately and apply a fungicide to those which remain. The usual cause is the use of unsterilised soil harbouring the fungi; always use sterilised compost and soak it with a fungicide before sowing. Thin seedlings before there is any danger of overcrowding.

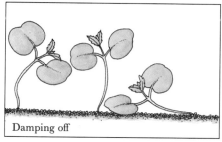

Damping off

## Mildew

White powdery mould on leaves and stems caused by overwatering and under ventilation. Remove the mildewed leaves or stems and spray the plants with fungicide.

Mildew

## Crown and stem rot

The fungus responsible makes the stems slimy and mushy. It spreads rapidly and can be deadly. The main cause is overwatering. A badly affected plant is best thrown away. If caught at a very early stage remove the rotten stems and dust the compost with a fungicide powder; then let it dry out for a time. Afterwards water from below, especially saintpaulias, the most likely victim of the disease. Other plants often affected are begonias, pelargoniums, cacti and other succulents.

Crown and stem rot

## Root rot

This fungal disease causes the plant to wilt and the leaves to yellow and curl. When the plant is taken out of the pot the root or tuber will be found to be rotten and slimy and the compost sodden, since overwatering is often to blame. Probably best thrown away, but if not too badly affected it might be possible to save the plant. Remove dead leaves, gently wash compost from the roots, cut away mushy roots. Repot in fresh, free-draining compost, watered with a fungicide solution. Water very seldom until the plant is growing well again – if it does. Once again it is saintpaulias, begonias, cacti, other succulents as well as palms which are threatened by this fungus.

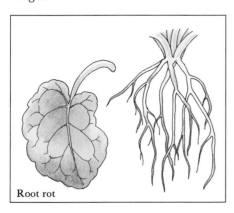
Root rot

## Leaf spot

Brown and yellow damp-looking spots can be caused by bacteria and fungi encouraged by overwatering, under ventilation and poor light. Remove spotty leaves, spray with fungicide and thereafter cut down on watering.

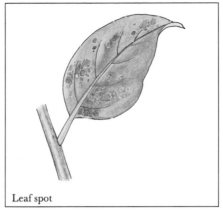
Leaf spot

## Viral diseases

They are usually introduced by sap suckers, but can be carried from plant to plant on our hands. The signs are stunted, distorted growth and yellow mottling of the leaves. There is no cure, and to try to prevent the infection from spreading throw away the plant, throw away the compost, and either throw away the pot or clean and sterilise it. Then thoroughly wash your hands before touching another plant.

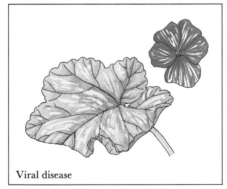
Viral disease

## Fungicides

Two systemic fungicides – benomyl and thiophanate-methyl – deal with many fungal diseases. They are available for use as a spray or for soaking the compost. Like pesticides they should not be breathed in, but they are said to be slightly less dangerous to animals and humans than most pesticides.

# The right plant A-Z

# Easy plants for cool rooms

The plants in this section of the A–Z – the largest of the four sections – need to be kept in cool conditions either all the year round or in their resting period. In all 139 plants are listed under 65 entries, and they include many of the most popular houseplants. The individual entries will help in deciding which plants are most likely to thrive in your home. How their demands can vary, even within the cool, easy category, can be judged by a few examples.

Among the year-round cool plants are *Araucaria excelsa* (Norfolk Island Pine), *Chamaerops humilis* (European Fan Palm) and *Euonymus japonicus* and these grow best around 55 deg F (13 deg C), but in any kind of house they will have to put up with higher temperatures than that in summer. They rest best at about 45 deg F (7 deg C), and no centrally heated houses are going to get anywhere near as low as that. *Monstera deliciosa* and philodendrons thrive in summer temperatures of 65–75 deg F (18–24 deg C), and in winter should go no lower than 55 deg F (13 deg C), which should be possible in a partially centrally heated house.

There are many desirable flowering plants to choose from in this section. Some need to be fairly cool even in the growing season, especially when flowering, because in warm rooms the flowers drop rapidly. Flowering plants also need a cool resting period if they are to produce flowers in the following year. This is particularly so with flowering succulents.

While desert cacti flourish in great heat in summer, a really cool winter rest is vital. For example, *Cereus peruvianus* (Tree Cactus) thrives even in a temperature of 80 deg F (27 deg C) – when humans tend to wilt – but in winter rests around 45 deg F (7 deg C) – at which humans shiver.

Not all plants go to these extremes and many adjust to higher or lower temperatures. However, there are limits beyond which a plant cannot be pushed and still live, and temperature limits are among them.

---

**Warning signs**
*Temperature too high*

Leaves and buds wilt and drop
Leaves droop
Leaves shrivel and turn brown
Flowers fall prematurely
Cacti, succulents and other plants fail to flower if kept too warm in winter

---

The entries in this section are listed here according to the type of plants they are.

**Flowering**
Abutilon pictum 'Thompsonii'
Browallia speciosa 'Major'
Campanula isophylla
Clivia miniata
Fuchsia magellanica
Impatiens wallerana
Jasminum polyanthum
Myrtus communis 'Microphylla'
Passiflora caerulea
Pelargonium
Plumbago capensis
Solanum capicastrum
Sparmannia africana

**Fruiting**
Nertera granadensis

**Foliage**
Araucaria excelsa
Asparagus densiflorus
Aspidistra elatior
Aucuba japonica 'Variegata'
Chlorophytum comosum 'Vittatum'
Cissus antarctica
Coleus blumei
Cyanotis kewensis
Euonymus japonicus
× Fatshedera lizei
Hedera helix
Monstera deliciosa
Pellionia pulchra
Philodendron
Pilea cadierei
Rhoeo spathacea
Rhoicissus capensis
Saxifraga stolonifera
Tolmiea menziesii
Tradescantia fluminensis
Yucca aloifolia
Zebrina pendula

**Cacti**
Astrophytum myriostigma
Cereus peruvianus
Echinocereus pectinatus
Ferocactus latispinus
Gymnocalycium baldianum
Lobivia hertrichiana
Mammillaria bocasana
Parodia chrysacanthion

**Succulents**
Aeonium tabulaeforme
Aloe variegata
Beaucarnea recurvata
Crassula aborescens
Echeveria derenbergii
Faucaria tigrina
Gasteria verrucosa
Haworthia margaritifera
Lithops lesliei
Sansevieria trifasciata 'Laurentii'
Sedum morganianum
Senecio rowleyanus

**Bromeliad**
Neoregelia carolinae 'Tricolor'

**Palms**
Chamaedora elegans
Chamaerops humilis
Cycas revoluta
Raphis excelsa

**Fern**
Cyrtomium falcatum

**Orchid**
Vanda cristata

**Bulbs**
Lilium longiflorum
Zephyranthes grandiflora

period, temperatures in the range 45–55 deg F (8–13 deg C) are best. A good light is still necessary, especially for the variegated plants in order to maintain the brilliant colouring. Water occasionally, but only enough to prevent the compost from drying out completely. No feeding is necessary during this time.

## Aeonium tabulaeforme

Succulent   Canary Islands

On a short, barely visible stem, *Aeonium tabulaeforme* produces a rosette of closely packed green leaves, forming an inverted saucer shape up to 12in (30cm) in diameter. In summer, a mature plant of about three or four years will send up a stem some 2ft (60cm) long, bearing yellow flowers on a cluster of branches. *A. haworthii*, also a native of the Canary Islands, is a complete contrast – a bushy, branching plant up to 2ft (60cm) in height. The woody branches carry rosettes of fleshy blue-green leaves edged with red. Yellow flowers, tinged with pink, appear in late spring. Once a rosette has flowered it dies.

*Abutilon pictum*
'Thompsonii'

### The year's care

**Spring and summer:** Temperatures between 55–65 deg F (13–18 deg C). Abutilons need plenty of air and bright light but they should be protected from direct scorching sun. Water frequently, but do not leave the pot standing in water; the roots do not take kindly to that. Apply a liquid fertiliser once a week, for the lower leaves tend to fall if the plant is not fed sufficiently. To promote bushy growth prune back hard in spring to a height of about 18–24in (45–60cm).

**Potting-on:** In spring each year in a loam-based compost. Abutilons grow rapidly and they may need to be potted-on again later in the year. They certainly will if roots start growing through the drainage hole of the pot.

**Propagation:** The plain leaved species can be raised from seed sown in spring, but the variegated forms can be produced only by taking stem cuttings. This can be done in summer, using a loam-based compost.

**Autumn and winter:** From autumn until early spring, the dormant

## Abutilon pictum
### 'Thompsonii'

Flowering Maple
Flowering shrub   Brazil

The elongated, deeply lobed leaves, similar to those of the maple, are dark green, attractively mottled with yellow. Lantern-shaped orange and red-veined flowers appear, often continuously, from spring to autumn, but the flowering season may extend beyond then. Abutilons – which are not maples, but members of the mallow family – grow rapidly, reaching a height of 4ft (1.20m). In Victorian times these plants were as popular as aspidistras and went out of vogue as quickly. They are now staging a comeback, not only as houseplants but outdoors in formal bedding. *A.p.* 'Thompsonii' is the most readily available as a houseplant but there are others worth growing. *A. hybridum*, with large dark green lobed leaves, and *A. megapotamicum*, (trailing abutilon) with heart-shaped leaves, either dark green or variegated, have equally striking red and yellow flowers.

### The year's care

**Spring and summer:** Both plants enjoy normal summer temperatures and should have a well lit sunny position to make sturdy growth. Water about once a week to keep the compost just moist and feed once every two weeks.

*Aeonium haworthii*

**Potting-on:** In spring every year in a free-draining loam-based compost. When replanting *A. tabulaeforme*, arrange the rosette at a slight angle in the pot to allow water to drain off.

**Propagation:** In spring take leaf cuttings of *A. tabulaeforme* and stem cuttings of *A. haworthii*. Both can also be raised from seed.

**Autumn and winter:** A temperature between 45–50 deg F (8–10 deg C) is necessary to allow the plants to rest. But during this period aeoniums need as much sun as they can get; a window-sill is ideal unless there is a danger of frost. Water plants about once a month. If the compost dries out too much the fleshy, moisture-retaining leaves will begin to shrivel. If, on the other hand, leaves become bloated-looking that is a sign of overwatering. Do not feed while the plants are resting.

## Aloe variegata

Partridge breasted aloe
Succulent   South Africa

*Aloe variegata* is the most popular of the smaller aloes, no more than 12in (30cm) in height. It forms a rosette of ranked triangular leaves, which are green banded with white. At first the rosette is at soil level, but as the lower leaves die and fall a stem will begin to form. The pink tubular flowers appear in spring and summer, carried on stems about 12in (30cm) long. *A. aborescens* is no dwarf: it can grow to 10ft (3m) or more. While it is still manageably young its attractiveness lies in its foliage, since growing as a houseplant it will seldom produce any of its red tubular flowers. It is commonly called the candelabra plant because of the way in which it grows. It sends up a woody stem around the top of which, in the form of a very loose rosette, hang tooth-edged narrow leaves up to 9in (22.5cm) long.

### The year's care

**Spring and summer:** Aloes are tolerant plants and will thrive in normal room temperature and a dry atmosphere. Bright direct sunlight is best for *A. aborescens*, and other spiny-leaved types, but while *A. variegata* needs good light to maintain its bright variegations, it should not be exposed to direct sunlight. Frequent watering will be necessary to quench the thirst of these plants; make sure that the compost is always moist, but not sodden. Avoid watering directly on to the rosette of *A. variegata* as any water collecting there may cause the plant to rot. Feed with a liquid fertiliser once a month.

**Potting-on:** *A. variegata* every two or three years in spring in a free-draining loam-based compost. *A. aborescens* will have to be potted-on every year until you despair of coping with its ever-increasing size. Be careful when handling the plants because if you damage the fleshy leaves they will be permanently scarred.

**Propagation:** By offsets which grow from the base of the plant. If removed when they are small and still rootless they do not easily produce roots of their own. If you wait until they are larger they will probably have produced small roots while attached to the mother plant. Plant those offsets which have roots in a loam-based potting compost. This should be kept just moist until the offsets are well established. Until then do not expose them to direct sunlight, but they will need a good light. If there are no offsets aloes can be raised from seed.

**Autumn and winter:** Temperatures between 45–50 deg F (8–10 deg C) are necessary to ensure that flowers appear. Keep the plants in a bright light. Water them only about once a month so that the compost does not dry out completely. Do not feed.

## Araucaria excelsa

Norfolk Island Pine
Conifer   Norfolk Island, north west
    of New Zealand

This plant will grow to a height of about 5ft (1.5m), but do it very slowly. The modest 18in (45cm) specimens usually on sale may take ten years to reach that height. Plants of 4ft (1.2m) or more can sometimes be brought but they are far more expensive; however, the cost may be worthwhile because the plant, with proper care, will live for many years. The overall pyramid shape is formed by horizontal layers of bright green branches in groups of four or more from an erect woody stem. The densely packed needles on the

*Aloe variegata*

*Araucaria excelsa*

*Asparagus densiflorus*

## Asparagus densiflorus
### (Syn: A. sprengeri)

Emerald Feather
Foliage    South-East Africa

Although referred to as a fern, *Asparagus densiflorus* is a member of the lily family. This species plant is no longer seen in cultivation, but its cultivars, among them *A.d.* 'Sprengeri', often simply called *A. sprengeri*, are very popular. *A. sprengeri* is a many-branching plant of trailing stems up to 15in (37.5cm) long. They are covered with what look like small green leaflets but are in fact phylloclades, that is, flattened stems which function as though they were leaves. They turn prickly as the plant matures. Flowering is very rare in asparagus grown as an indoor plant and if flowers do appear they are green and inconspicuous, and are followed by red berries. The more compact *A. setaceus* 'Nanus', known as the bride's bouquet fern or lace fern, is equally popular. The foliage of this plant is even more feathery and a richer green than that of *A. sprengeri*, but it is more erect growing. Both plants are most effective when used in hanging baskets.

### The year's care

**Spring and summer:** Temperatures in the range 55–65 deg F (13–18 deg C) are enough for these plants but they will tolerate anything up to 70 deg F (21 deg C). Put them where they will have plenty of light, but not

branches give the plant a beautiful feathery appearance. Its shape is similar to that of a Christmas tree, but do not be tempted to use it as one, because even fairy lights would singe the leaves.

### The year's care

**Spring and summer:** A temperature in the region of 55 deg F (13 deg C) will ensure steady growth. If the temperatures are too high the needles are likely to turn yellow and fall. Good light, but not direct sunlight, is essential. Site the plant where there is plenty of ventilation; it could go outdoors for a time, perhaps on a balcony, as long as there is shade from the sun. In hot weather, mist-spray it occasionally. Frequent watering will be required to keep the compost moist, but not sodden. Feed once every two weeks.

**Potting-on:** In spring every third year, using a loam-based compost.

**Propagation:** By sowing seed in spring, but it will be a long, long time before the plant reaches a decent size.

A cutting taken from the growing tip is an alternative, but by inducing the growth of extra shoots from the tip where the cutting was taken it will ruin the desirable pyramidal symmetry of the plant. All in all, it is better to buy a new plant.

**Autumn and winter:** The best temperature is around 50 deg F (10 deg C) and it must not fall below 40 deg F (4 deg C). On the other hand, too high a temperature in the resting season is as bad for the plant as it is in the growing season. High winter temperatures will cause the lower leaves to fall, and since fresh growth will not replace these fallen leaves you will be left with a bare stem; new growth is always at the top of the plant. In winter give the plant as much light as possible, and turn the pot from time to time so that all sides of the plant get their share, so maintaining the symmetrical growth. Water just enough to keep the compost barely moist. Too much water in winter is another reason why lower leaves drop. No feeding is necessary.

direct sunlight. A spell out of doors –
but out of the sun – will do no harm.
Frequent watering is necessary. The
compost must never be allowed to dry
out completely or the foliage will fall
and the plant become a straggly and
unattractive mess. If this should
happen cut down all the stems to
compost level and thoroughly water
the compost. This is best done by
putting the pot in a bucket with water
not quite up to the rim of the pot.
Leave the water to be drawn up into
the compost until moisture begins to
glisten on the surface. Then remove
the pot and allow excess water to
drain away. New shoots will soon
appear. During the growing season
feed every two weeks.

**Potting-on:** In spring each year in a
loam-based compost.

**Propagation:** By dividing the plant
in spring. If the plant has become
spindly, cut down the stems to
compost level, remove the soil ball
from the pot and cut it up as you
would a cake into 4in (10cm)
portions. Plant each piece in fresh
compost and new growth will soon
appear. Plants may also be raised
from seed, but this is a slow business.

**Autumn and winter:** For *A. sprengeri*
the winter temperature should not fall
below 45 deg F (7 deg C) and it will
tolerate higher, normal room
temperatures. In warm rooms it will,
of course, need more frequent
watering than it would in a cool
place. *A. setaceus* does better in winter
at around 50 deg F (10 deg C); give it
a light position. The compost should
be kept just moist and not allowed to
dry out completely. Do not feed either
variety.

# Aspidistra elatior

Cast Iron Plant
Foliage   China, Japan, Eastern
   Himalayas

Aspidistras, beloved of the Victorians,
were often placed in cold, draughty,
dark and rarely used rooms, where
they still positively thrived – hence
the common name of Cast Iron Plant.
Nonetheless, neglect is not to be
encouraged; the normal care given to
other plants will be repaid in
healthier looking, larger leaves. The
dark green leathery lance-shaped
leaves, up to 2ft (60cm) long, are

*Aspidistra elatior*

borne on single short stems. Small
purple flowers, though rare in
cultivated specimens, grow at soil
level and are easily missed. There is a
variegated form, *A.e.* 'Variegata',
which has white to cream stripes
along the length of the leaves, but this
is not often seen on sale.

## The year's care

**Spring and summer:** A
temperature around 60 deg F (16
deg C) will be ample for strong
growth. Keep the plant in a shady
position out of direct sunlight, but in
deep gloom it will make poor growth.
Variegated plants need brighter light
to maintain their creamy markings,
but here again not direct sunlight.
Water fairly frequently, keeping the
compost always just moist. If the
plant becomes waterlogged or is
allowed to stand in water in its saucer
the roots are liable to rot. Wipe dust
off the leaves regularly, for both the
sake of appearance and the health of

the plant. Feeding once a month will
be sufficient.

**Potting-on:** In spring once every
three years in a loam-based compost.
These plants do better if potbound.

**Propagation:** By division when
repotting. Some roots may break off
during this operation but small pieces
which have tiny buds attached can be
propagated. Several sections can be
planted in one pot with the buds
pointing outwards and upwards.
Given time each piece should throw
up one or two leaves.

**Autumn and winter:** The ideal
temperature at this time of the year is
50 deg F (10 deg C), but
temperatures up to 60 deg F (16
deg C) will be tolerated. Keep the
plant in a shady position. Water
occasionally to make the compost
barely moist; once a week should be
enough, and less frequently at low
temperatures. Whatever the
temperature the plant should not be
fed during the resting period.

*Astrophytum myriostigma*

# Astrophytum myriostigma

Bishop's Cap
Desert cactus    North and Central
America

Astrophytums are globular cacti with pronounced divisions between the four or five ribs, which are covered with many irregular white scales. It has no spines; instead the areoles, the protuberances from which spines grow, sprout fine, fluffy grey hairs. Funnel-shaped yellow flowers with red throats appear in succession through the summer from the top of the plant, either singly or in groups of two or three. *A. myriostigma* does not begin to flower until it is three to four years old. When fully mature it will achieve about 8in (20cm) in both height and girth. As it ages it tends to lose its globular shape and becomes elongated. *A. ornatum* has lines of silvery scales and is even more segmented. The areoles on the edges of the eight dark green ribs sprout inch long (2.5cm) stout yellow-brown spines. Large yellow flowers appear only when the plant is mature; you may have to wait ten years or more.

### The year's care

**Spring and summer:** For both varieties a normal warm room temperature is suitable and a sunny window-sill would be a good position. However, *A. myriostigma* needs protection from harsh, fierce sun; *A. ornatum* is much more tolerant. Water when the compost has become almost dry. When the plant has grown large enough to cover most of the surface of the compost, the best method of watering is to immerse the pot in shallow water for a short time. Feed once every two months.

**Potting-on:** In spring each year, if the roots have filled the pot, using a loam-based compost to which equal parts of grit and sharp sand have been added. A free-draining compost is essential.

**Propagation:** From seed sown in spring. When seedlings appear after a few weeks, take care not to overwater them.

**Autumn and winter:** Astrophytums need a rest period at a temperature around 45 deg F (10 deg C). They will still require a good light with as much sun as is available. Water only occasionally to prevent the compost from drying out completely. If the ribs begin to look shrivelled watering is certainly necessary. No feeding.

# Aucuba japonica
'Variegata'

Spotted Laurel, Gold Dust Plant
Evergreen shrub    Japan

This aucuba has shiny serrated leaves with are heavily flecked with yellow. It can reach 6ft (1.8m) but most of the varieties cultivated as indoor plants grow to no more than 3ft (90cm). Regular pruning will keep them compact and bushy and prevent them from getting out of hand. In spring, bright red berries follow the insignificant maroon flowers, but only on female plants and only if they have been pollinated by flowers of male plants. Aucubas are tough, undemanding plants and their tolerance makes them suitable for halls and landings where many other plants will not grow.

### The year's care

**Spring and summer:** Coolish conditions between 55–60 deg F (13–16 deg C) best suit *A.j.* 'Variegata'. It tolerates partial shade, but good light will ensure that it maintains its colourful variegations. Frequent watering is necessary to keep the compost moist. Feed once every two weeks with liquid fertiliser. Pruning should be done in spring as active growth begins.

**Potting-on:** In spring when the plant has outgrown its pot, in a loam-based compost.

*Aucuba japonica 'Variegata'*

**Propagation:** Take stem cuttings in late summer, using a rooting compost of peat and coarse sand.

**Autumn and winter:** A temperature around 45 deg F (7 deg C) is the ideal, but slightly higher temperatures are tolerated. If the plant is kept in a centrally heated room at too high a temperature red spider mites will be encouraged. The gloomy light of winter does not affect aucubas adversely if they are in the cool. Do not feed, but regular cleaning of the leaves is a good idea.

# Beaucarnea recurvata

Pony Tail, Bottle Plant, Elephant's Foot
Succulent   Mexico

This oddity of a plant will give the inexperienced owner little trouble. The drooping leaves, 3ft (90cm) long and about 1in (2.5cm) wide, are thrown up from a bulbous root which protrudes above the surface of the compost. As the plant matures and the lower leaves fall a stout green-brown trunk forms and the bulb itself becomes larger and more distorted. Its use is to act as a reservoir of water in times of drought. Beaucarneas are slow growing to reach the still manageable height of 3ft (90cm).

### The year's care

**Spring and summer:** Beaucarneas are thoroughly at home in

*Browallia speciosa* 'Major'

temperatures of 75 deg F (24 deg C) or more. Bright sunlight is essential, but with shade when it is really scorching. Poor light results in pale leaves and weak growth. Water frequently to keep the compost moist at all times. Give a liquid feed once a month.

**Potting-on:** In spring once every two or three years will be often enough, for the plant seems to do best when potbound. Use a free-draining mixture of loam, peat and sharp sand.

**Propagation:** From seed sown in spring or with offsets, which can be removed from the base of the parent plant when repotting.

**Autumn and winter:** Resting conditions are a temperature around 45 deg F (7 deg C) and a strong light. If the plant is kept at this low temperature it will require only occasional watering; the bulb is itself a store of water to be called on. If that shows signs of shrivelling watering is necessary. Do not feed.

# Browallia speciosa
'Major'

Sapphire Flower
Flowering annual   Colombia, South America

Browallias are normally treated as annuals and after flowering the plant

*Beaucarnea recurvata*

is discarded. They can be bought as plants in or about to flower, but it is far cheaper and fairly easy to raise them from seed. Successive sowings will provide plants to flower in summer, autumn and winter. *B.s.* 'Major' is a bushy plant around 2ft (60cm) tall, with bright green slender pointed leaves on short stems. The tubular flowers are violet with white centres. *B.s.* 'Silver Bells' has white flowers. *B. viscosa* 'Sapphire' makes a more compact plant of about 12in (30cm) with flowers of a brighter violet than 'Major's'. They are somewhat smaller – 1–1½in (2.5–3.75cm) – but their profusion

*Browallia speciosa* 'Silver Bells'

makes up for their size. The oval green leaves feel sticky when touched. There is a white flowered form of this variety, *B.v.* 'Alba'. Half a dozen browallias in a hanging basket make a delightful summer show.

**The year's care**

**Spring and summer:** These tough flowering plants need temperatures in the range 50–60 deg F (10–16 deg C). They need plenty of light, but bright reflected light and not direct sunlight, which can burn the delicate flowers. Water frequently to keep the compost moist but it must not become waterlogged. As soon as flower buds form, feed every two weeks until flowering is over. Pinch out the growing tips of plants at intervals to encourage bushiness. Remove faded flowers to promote new bud growth.

**Potting-on:** These plants are not repotted.

**Propagation:** By successive sowing of seed. For winter flowering plants, sow in late summer or autumn. For summer flowering sow in late winter and early spring. Use a loam-based seed compost.

**Autumn and winter:** Plants should be kept at temperatures no higher than 65 deg F (18 deg C) and if it is somewhat cooler the flowers will last far longer. To ensure prolonged flowering a light position is vital. The plant will not need frequent watering if growing in a cool room. When buds have formed feed once a month until flowering is over.

# Campanula isophylla

Bell Flower, Star of Bethlehem
Flowering perennial   Northern Italy

This trailing campanula gives a startling display of flowers in summer, but dies down in winter. It can be used either in a hanging basket or trained up a trellis frame. The stems, some 12in (30cm) long, are covered with small pale grey-green, heart-shaped leaves. The star-shaped flowers, about 1in (2.5cm) across, appear from late summer to early autumn and can be so profuse that they hide the foliage. There are two forms which are usually grown: *C.i.* 'Alba', with white flowers, and *C.i.* 'Mayi', with blue; a combination of

*Campanula isophylla* 'Alba'

the two makes a most attractive display. Take care when handling the stems as they break easily and exude a white milky liquid.

**The year's care**

**Spring and summer:** Temperatures in the range 45–55 deg F (7–13 deg C) are best, but they will certainly rise higher at this time of the year, and as a result the flowers drop rapidly. In very warm weather plants growing in a pot and not in a hanging basket can be placed on a tray of wet pebbles. They can also be sprayed, but not when in flower; that is certain to damage the delicate blooms. A very light position is most important to ensure luxuriant flowering but the plants should not be exposed for long to the sun. Good ventilation is also necessary; a period outdoors will do the plants good, but they must be brought in before there is the least danger of frost. During the active growing period campanulas need frequent watering to keep the compost moist; in warm weather this may mean once a day. Feed once every two weeks. Pinch out the growing tips to encourage bushiness when the plant has put out new growth in the spring. When flowering is over at the

end of summer cut back all the stems to within 2in (5cm) of the surface of the compost.

**Potting-on:** In spring each year in a loam-based compost.

**Propagation:** From cuttings in spring when there has been new growth. Take great care when handling them because of the brittle stems. Choose cuttings about 3in (7.5cm) long with at least three pairs of leaves.

**Autumn and winter:** Plants need to be kept frost free at a temperature about 45 deg F (7 deg C). There is little to see of the plant after it has been cut back but give it plenty of light. Watering once every two weeks should be enough to keep the compost barely moist during the rest period. Feeding is not necessary.

# Cereus peruvianus

Tree Cactus
Desert cactus   South-east America

This columnar cactus, bluish green in colour, is hardy and fast growing. Even indoors it can reach 6ft (1.8m), but if confined to a 6in (15cm) pot it should stay a more acceptable 2–3ft

*Cereus peruvianus*

(60–90cm). The column has from five to eight ribs edged with regularly spaced areoles, from which short brown spines protrude. In the wild it sends out in summer white, scented tubular flowers up to 12in (30cm) long, but it rarely flowers indoors. Even if it does you might well miss them for they open only at night.

### The year's care

**Spring and summer:** *C. peruvianus* will flourish in temperatures even up to 80 deg F (27 deg C) and in full sun, though there must be good ventilation. Turn the pot regularly so that all sides of the plant receive equal shares of sun to maintain erect growth. A window-sill is ideal (until the column grows too tall). Plants will benefit from a period out of doors. Water fairly frequently to keep the compost moist. A liquid feed every two months will be adequate.

**Potting-on:** If the plant is being confined in a small pot to restrict growth pot-on in spring every two or three years. If you aim for a 6ft (1.8m) monster pot-on every year. Use a loam-based compost with added sharp sand to make it free-draining.

**Propagation:** From seed sown in spring, but this is slow. The alternative produces quicker results though it means virtually sacrificing the parent plant. Though plants cultivated indoors will stay columnar, they can be induced to branch if you cut off the top of the column. The cactus then produces branches from the base and these can be removed and planted. The chopped off top, after being allowed to dry out for a

few days, can also be potted. What remains of the original column is hardly worth keeping.

**Autumn and winter:** The plant needs a rest period in a temperature around 45 deg F (7 deg C) but still in a well-lit position. Remember to turn the pot regularly. Keep the compost almost dry during this period; any sign of shrivelling means that it is too dry. Do not feed.

## Chamaedorea elegans

Parlour Palm, Good Luck Palm
Palm    Mexico

This is a good palm for a beginner, easy to care for and staying a reasonable size. Plants are usually sold when they are about 12in (30cm) high and, growing only slowly, they will indoors reach about 4ft (1.2m). The long yellowish-green stems may grow to 2ft (60cm) and arch elegantly, bearing narrow 6in (15cm) leaflets in pairs, but rather out of line with each other on the stem. The flowers are not particularly striking, yellow mimosa-like sprays followed by berries, but they may not always be produced indoors.

### The year's care

**Spring and summer:** *C. elegans* will be happy in normal room temperatures of around 65–70 deg F (18–21 deg C). A partly shaded position is best and the plant should certainly be kept out of hot direct

*Chamaedorea elegans*

sunlight. This preference is not an invitation to plunge the palm into gloom, for the result would merely be spindly growth. It is reasonably tolerant of dry air, but if the atmosphere is too dry the leaf tips may turn brown and there could be attacks by red spider mites and scale insects. To avoid this stand the pot on a tray of wet pebbles or surround the pot with moist peat to create humidity. Water frequently, keeping the compost moist at all times. Liquid feed should be given once a month.

**Potting-on:** Small young plants should be potted-on every other year in spring in a peat-based compost in which one third part of sand has been mixed. When the plant matures it should be potted-on when the roots completely fill the pot, until it becomes too big to repot; then renew the top layer of compost. With less frequent potting the growth of the plant can be held in check.

**Propagation:** In spring from seed – a long process and hardly recommendable. A heated propagator will be needed to provide the considerable bottom heat of 75 deg F (24 deg C). The seedlings must be allowed to reach a good size before transplanting since they are very delicate and easily broken when handled. If you want another palm, better to buy a new young one.

**Autumn and winter:** The minimum temperature is 55 deg F (13 deg C) and the maximum not much higher, since the palm must have a resting period. Keep it in a partly shaded position. The compost should be barely moist. Do not feed.

## Chamaerops humilis

European Fan Palm
Palm    Europe, in particular Spain
        and Southern Italy

This hardy palm, the only one native to Europe, will, unlike the tropical species, tolerate cold rooms in winter. *C. humilis* has stems up to 4ft (1.2m) long, the first 12in (30cm) covered in sharp spines, then erupting into showy fan-shaped fronds. Each frond is dissected almost to the stalk, forming long, thin, beautifully coloured grey-green pointed segments. The overall width of the fronds is about 2ft (60cm). Flowers and fruit will never

*Chamaerops humilis*

be seen on these palms when cultivated indoors. *C.h.* 'Elegans', with silvery leaves, is a smaller form, making it the most suitable as a houseplant in small rooms.

**The year's care**

**Spring and summer:** An even temperature around 55 deg F (13 deg C) would be best, but higher temperatures are tolerated. Many palms prefer somewhat shady conditions but *C. humilis* requires excellent light, even two or three hours of sunlight a day will do no harm. If the plant is in shade at all times growth will slow down. Water frequently so that the compost is always moist. However, letting it stand in saucers of water is the surest way to waterlog the compost and cause the roots to rot. Feed once a fortnight. Do not be alarmed at the appearance of grey meal or hair on the newly emerging fronds; it is not a disease and soon falls off.

**Potting-on:** In early spring, but only every two or three years. Each time

pot-on to a pot 1in (2.5cm) larger until you reach the manageable maximum of 10–12in (25–30cm). Take care when repotting as the roots are fragile and easily damaged. Use a free-draining mixture of two thirds peat compost and one third sand.

**Propagation:** From seed sown in spring, or by the removal of suckers when repotting. Turn the plant out of

*Chlorophytum comosum* 'Vittatum'

the pot and carefully ease away some of the compost to see where the sucker joins the main plant. Pull the sucker away, along with the decent number of roots to support it.

**Autumn and winter:** Plants will be happy in unheated rooms at around 45 deg F (7 deg C), but below 40 deg F (4 deg C) permanent damage may be done. Keep the palm in a well-lit spot. The compost should be just moist when the plant is resting at low temperatures. Do not feed.

# Chlorophytum comosum 'Vittatum'

Spider Plant
Foliage   South Africa

Chlorophytums are cheap to buy when small and the easiest of plants to care for. *C.c.* 'Vittatum' produces clumps of long thin arching leaves up to 18in (45cm) long, with a creamy white streak down the middle. During the spring and summer months pale yellow, straw-like stems emerge from the centre of the rosette of leaves and they soon put out small, delicate, white flowers. These are followed by tiny plantlets, often several to a single stem, and they grow rapidly. It is from these plantlets that new generations of chlorophytums are created. As the plantlets increase in size they weigh down the stem, which may snap off from the parent plant. If this happens, the plantlets, which by now have the beginning of roots, can be potted up to make new plants. Chlorophytums are excellent in hanging baskets, which show off the gently arching leaves and the runners laden with small plants.

**The year's care**

**Spring and summer:** This plant is remarkably tolerant of both warm and cool conditions. It will grow in bright light or partial shade, but only bright light will maintain the colour of the variegated foliage. However, too much hot sunlight may scorch the leaves. *C.c.* 'Vittatum' needs frequent watering to keep the compost moist at all times. If it is too dry the leaf tips have a tendency to turn brown. Feed every two weeks.

**Potting-on:** In spring, using a loam-based compost. Potting-on may be necessary every year, and it certainly is if the fleshy roots begin to force the compost and plant up to the rim of the pot.

**Propagation:** There are two methods of propagating spider plants. Plantlets may be detached from the runner and either planted straight into a loam-based compost, or first rooted in water. When the roots are seen to be well-developed in the water, the plantlet is then transferred to compost. The better method of propagation is layering. Pin down the plantlet, still attached to the runner, into a pot of loam-based compost. When it has become established it can be severed from the parent plant. The chances of success are far greater this way since the plantlet has been supported by the parent while its own roots develop. Propagation is best attempted in spring and summer.

**Autumn and winter:** Do not allow winter temperatures to fall below 45 deg F (7 deg C). The plants should be kept in a well-lit place with some direct weak winter sun. The dry atmosphere of centrally heated rooms does not seem to bother *C. comosum*. Water often enough to keep the compost barely moist at all times. Do not feed.

# Cissus antarctica

Kangaroo vine
Foliage climber   Australia

Cissus can be grown as a trailing or climbing plant. As a trailer it is particularly effective in a hanging basket; as a climber its tendrils will curl around any support offered it. The cissus species are members of the vine family and are very similar in habit and appearance to the grape vine. Indoors *C. antarctica* can reach a height of 10ft (3m), forming a thick column of leathery shiny leaves, light green when young and turning dark green as they age. To contain its rampant growth upwards and convert it into bushiness, the growing shoots are pinched out regularly.

*C. striata*, from Brazil and Chile, is the smallest cissus available. Its delicate leaves, carried on red stems, are pink when they first appear and turn dark green on the upper surface while staying pink on the underside. The leaves are divided into five leaflets

*Cissus antarctica*

with finely serrated edges. This is probably the best cissus for a hanging basket. *C. rhombifolia* produces its leaves, slightly rhomboid in shape, in groups of three. New leaves have a metallic sheen caused by the fine hairs on their surface. As the leaves mature they turn dark green and the undersides are covered with fine brown hairs. *C. discolor*, from Java, may have the most magnificently marked foliage but its demands for warmth, high humidity and bright light make it a very difficult species to grow.

### The year's care

**Spring and summer:** Temperatures in the range 55–65 deg F (13–18 deg C) are ideal (leaving out *C. discolor*). All cissus require good light, but they should not be exposed to direct sunlight, which may cause the leaves to turn brown. Water frequently to keep the compost moist always, but if pots are left standing in water leaves will yellow and fall. Feed every two weeks. Growing tips should be pinched out regularly to promote bushiness. If stems become bare at the base cut them back to within 4in (10cm) of the compost level.

**Potting-on:** Pot-on each year in spring, using a mixture of loam, peat, leaf mould and sand, until the maximum manageable size of pot, 10–12in (25–30cm), has been reached. Thereafter remove the top 2in (5cm) of compost and replace it with fresh.

**Propagation:** From stem cuttings taken in spring and summer, or from seed in spring, but a bottom heat of 75 deg F (24 deg C) will be needed.

**Autumn and winter:** The minimum temperature is 50 deg F (10 deg C) and the ideal around 55 deg F (13 deg C). Keep all plants in a good light but not in direct sunlight. Water now and again to prevent the compost from drying out completely; it should be just moist. No feeding.

# Clivia miniata

Kaffir Lily
Flowering   South Africa

*C. miniata* has leathery dark green strap-shaped leaves, up to 2ft (60cm) long, which arch gracefully in pairs. Some plants have a very formal look, but others are far less shapely. Each plant produces one flower stem, or sometimes two, rising well above the leaves, and carrying in a mature plant a dramatic cluster of up to twenty orange trumpet-shaped flowers. While a clivia's overall height will be little more than 2ft (60cm) the spread of leaves may be more than 3ft (90cm). Given plenty of room it is a striking focal point plant.

### The year's care

**Spring and summer:** In early spring bring the plant out of its winter rest into a temperature of 65 deg F (18 deg C). Before long you should see the tip of the flower stem emerging from between the leaves. If the plant has not had an adequate cool resting period the flower stem may not appear until later, or even not at all. The flowers last about a fortnight, and when flowering is over the flower head should be cut off so that the plant does not waste its energy in producing seed. Remove the rest of the flower stalk only when it has withered completely. New leaves of a delicate pale green, gradually darkening, appear during the summer. They are long lasting, so the plant grows impressively larger and larger. Remove leaves only when they turn brown. Water fairly frequently and feed once a month.

**Potting-on:** Clivias appear to flourish when other plants would suffer from being potbound. However, when the thick fleshy roots push up through the

*Clivia miniata*

surface of the compost it is time to pot-on. Do this when flowering is over, using a loam-based compost.

**Propagation:** Offsets which the plant produces as it grows older, can be removed when repotting along with a good number of roots it shares with the parent plant. The offsets will fare better if they are allowed to grow four or five decent-sized leaves before being detached. Alternatively, offsets can be left to grow alongside the parent and in the fullness of time they also will flower. However the colony will eventually become so large as to need a tub rather than a pot. The more formally shaped clivias look better growing solo.

**Autumn and winter:** It is vital for the plant to have a cool resting period from autumn until late winter in a temperature of 50–55 deg F (10–13 deg C) to help to ensure flowering in spring. While the plant is resting allow the compost almost to dry out; watering once a month will be enough. No feeding is necessary.

## Coleus blumei

Flame Nettle
Foliage   Java

Although the coleus is a perennial it is most often treated as an annual.

Plants very quickly become large and woody and if they are cut back, new growth is weak and straggly. It is better to take cuttings and discard the old plant. These plants are grown for their richly coloured heart-shaped leaves, similar to those of the common nettle. The leaves may be green, brown, yellow, red or orange, or any conceivable combination of those colours. They look most striking when different coloured plants are grouped in a single container. *C. blumei* will grow more than 18in (45cm) tall, but can be kept bushy by pinching out growing tips.

**The year's care**

**Spring and summer:** The ideal temperature is about 60 deg F (16 deg C) and if it is much lower the leaves will begin to fall. To maintain the rich colouring bright light is essential. There can be a certain amount of direct sunlight, but fierce sun should be avoided. If they do not get enough light they will be etiolated. Frequent watering, probably daily, in hot weather is necessary to keep the compost always moist. A dry compost will cause the lower leaves to fall. The plants will also benefit from frequent mist-spraying. Feed every two weeks. Make it a regular practice to pinch out growing tips, and when doing this look out for mealy bugs and red spider mites, which can be a problem. Remove any flower buds that may form.

**Potting-on:** *C. blumei* grows so rapidly that it may need to be potted-on every two or three months during the growing period, for the roots need plenty of room. Use a lime-free loam or peat-based compost.

**Propagation:** By taking stem tip cuttings about 3in (7.5cm) long in

*Coleus blumei*

late summer. They can be rooted in water and then transplanted to compost or be planted direct into compost.

**Autumn and winter:** Overwintered plants will require a minimum temperature of 55 deg F (13 deg C). Give plants as much light as possible to help them to keep their colour. Inevitably there will be some paling in the gloomier winter days but the colours should sharpen up as the longer days arrive. The compost should be kept just moist while plants are resting. Do not feed.

## Crassula aborescens

Silver Dollar Plant
Succulent   South Africa

Very few of the three-hundred-odd species of crassula produce striking flowers and even they cannot be depended on to flower when grown indoors. Their popularity depends on the variety of shapes and colours of their fleshy leaves. *C. aborescens*, about 3ft (90cm) tall, has grey-green leaves, 1–2in (2.5–5cm) wide with red margins, carried on stout woody stems. It may produce white to pink flowers in spring, but it is unlikely. *C. argentea*, also about 3ft (90cm), has shiny, bright green oval leaves. In its natural habitat white to pink flowers in terminal clusters appear in summer, but here again flowers

cannot be relied on indoors. *C. falcata* takes its popular name of Sickle Plant from the shape of its leaves. They are grey-green, 4in (10cm) or more long, carried on stems of around 2ft (60cm). You are far more likely to see flowers on this species – large clusters of scarlet flowers which appear on long stems in summer; the stems may need staking to support the weight of the clusters. *C. lycopodioides*, Toy Cypress, grows to not more than 8in (20cm). The thin branching fingers are covered with tightly packed

*Crassula lycopodioides*

overlapping leaves. Insignificant green-yellow flowers grow from the leaf axils. *C. rupestris* (Buttons on a String) has small fleshy blue-grey leaves which appear to have been threaded on the stems. There are meagre clusters of small pink flowers in summer.

### The year's care

**Spring and summer:** All crassulas are quite at home in normal room temperatures at this period. A bright sunny position is essential, especially if you hope for flowers, but do not expose these succulents to fierce sun. Plants in poor light will develop spindly growth. Water fairly frequently to keep the compost reasonably moist; the fleshy leaves hold a certain reserve of water. Feed once a month. Look out for mealy bugs which may lodge themselves in the leaf axils.

**Potting-on:** Once every two years in a loam-based compost to which one part of sharp sand has been added.

**Propagation:** From leaf cuttings in spring and summer.

**Autumn and winter:** Crassulas need a rest, with temperatures between 45–50 deg F (7–10 deg C). Water occasionally to prevent the compost from drying out completely. If the leaves begin to shrivel, water at once. Do not feed.

*Crassula aborescens*

## Cyanotis kewensis

Teddy Bear Vine
Foliage creeper   India

*C. kewensis* is a trailing plant which is seen at its best in a hanging basket. It is similar in appearance to a tradescantia, to which it is related, but the main differences are that the cyanotis is covered with reddy brown hair and the leaves are smaller and fleshier. The top surface of the leaves is green and the underside purple. There may be small purple flowers in winter and spring, but they are rare indoors. *C. somaliensis*, from Somalia, is commonly called Pussy Ears because of the long white hairs which grow round the edges of the 2in (5cm) glossy green leaves. In spring purple-blue flowers may appear but, again, rarely on indoor plants.

*Cyanotis kewensis*

## The year's care

**Spring and summer:** Both species are satisfied with normal room temperatures. A well lit position is essential, to avoid spindly growth with gaps on the stems which ruin the plant's appearance; they look their best with tight, closely packed stems. Place pots on window-sills, or hang baskets near windows, so that the plants get direct sunlight. Water frequently to keep the compost moist, but avoid wetting the leaves, which are easily marked. Feed every two weeks. Pinch out growing tips to encourage bushy, branching growth.

**Potting-on:** In late spring, but as they are slow growing only every two or three years. Use a loam-based compost to which a third of sand has been added.

**Propagation:** In spring and summer, from stem tip cuttings with about four leaves.

**Autumn and winter:** Do not allow the temperature to fall below 50 deg F (10 deg C). Plants do not suffer in centrally heated rooms, but if the air there is too dry the leaf tips may turn brown. To increase humidity plants can be stood on trays of wet pebbles, but avoid spraying the leaves because of the risk of marking them. Good light is vital. Water only occasionally, but look out for shrivelling leaves, a sign that the plant is too dry. Do not feed.

## Cycas revoluta

Sago Palm
Palm   Japan, China

The stiffly arching fronds of this elegant palm give it the feathery

*Cycas revoluta*

appearance of a fern. Leaves up to 3ft (90cm) long are carried in rosette formation and are divided into narrow 6in (15cm) segments. It is slow growing, producing only one or two new leaves a year. Since it is usually young plants which are on sale they will stay a manageable size for many years, although eventually a plant might grow to 6ft (1.8m). As the plant matures it develops a knobbly ball-like base.

## The year's care

**Spring and summer:** A temperature around 65 deg F (18 deg C) is satisfactory. Good bright light, even sunlight, is needed to maintain even the slow growth of this palm. Water frequently in summer and feed every two weeks.

**Potting-on:** Every two or three years, in a loam-based compost with one third of sand added.

**Propagation:** From seed sown in spring, a slow process, demanding considerable bottom heat of 75 deg F (24 deg C) for germination.

**Autumn and winter:** The temperature should not fall below 55 deg F (13 deg C) and a little higher is better. However, they do seem to be able to stand some fluctuations in

temperature. Always keep them in a well lit spot; they need all the light they can get in winter. If the temperature is down to the minimum of 55 deg F (13 deg C) only occasional watering is needed to prevent the compost from drying out completely. The base from which the stems grow holds a certain amount of water which the plant can draw on if the compost should become too dry. Higher temperatures will involve rather more frequent watering. No feeding is necessary.

## Cyrtomium falcatum

Holly Fern, Fish Tail Fern
Fern   South-east Asia

*C. falcatum* is a remarkably long-suffering plant, putting up with cold, draughts and poor light, but that is no reason to make it suffer so. With more considerate care it will thrive better and look far more attractive. The stems, which grow from a rhizome, carry a silvery furry scale at their base. The dark green fronds, up to 18in (45cm) long, are covered with pairs of dark green glossy leaflets (pinnae), which resemble holly leaves. *C.f.* 'Rochfordianum' is a more compact variety with fronds about 12in (30cm) and larger pinnae. When

*Cyrtomium falcatum*

*Echeveria derenbergii*

bell-shaped flowers open in spring. In contrast *E. harmsii* forms a small branching shrub, and the loose rosettes of lance-shaped leaves covered with soft hair are carried on the end of the stems. The bell-shaped flowers, red and tipped with yellow, which are the most dramatic feature of the plant, appear in early summer on stems up to 8in (20cm) long. *E. gibbiflora*, which may reach a height of 18in (45cm), usually has a single stem bearing mauve pink leaves covered with warts. Red bell-shaped flowers are possible in winter, but rare on indoor plants.

**The year's care**

**Spring and summer:** Echeverias will thrive in normal room temperatures. They must have plenty of light, even direct sunlight, but not the hot midday summer sun. Water fairly frequently so that the compost is just moist. Too frequent watering will result in bloated soft leaves. Avoid watering into the centre of the rosette or the whole plant may rot. Low-growing rosettes are best watered by partly immersing the pots in water. Feed once a month. Be on the look out for mealy bugs.

**Potting-on:** Every year in spring in a loam-based compost, with a little sand added for good drainage. As plants mature they will probably need potting-on only every two or three years.

**Propagation:** By taking stem cuttings in summer, or by offsets in spring. Plants may also be raised from seed in spring but this gives slow results.

**Autumn and winter:** Echeverias will tolerate a minimum temperature of 45 deg F (7 deg C), but frost will

new fronds appear they are covered in white scale; this is not a symptom of disease – it will soon wear off.

**The year's care**

**Spring and summer:** Temperatures up to 65 deg F (18 deg C) ensure strong sturdy growth, but the warmer the room is the greater the humidity the plant will need. Either spray it regularly or stand on a tray of wet pebbles. Keep it in a bright spot, but out of the sun. Water frequently to make the compost throroughly moist and feed every two weeks.

**Potting-on:** Each year in spring, since it grows rapidly. Use a peat-based compost or a mixture of equal parts of loam, peat and sand.

**Propagation:** By division in spring when repotting. Make sure each piece of rhizome has some roots and at least four fronds. Sori containing spores develop on the underside of the leaves and they can be removed and propagated, but raising ferns from spores is an operation needing skill, warmth, high humidity and months and months and months of patience. It is better to stick to simple division.

**Autumn and winter:** Do not allow the temperature to fall below 50 deg F (10 deg C) and rather warmer temperatures are better. The plant should be placed where it can make the most of poor winter light. Water occasionally to keep the compost just moist. Feeding is not advisable during the resting period.

# Echeveria derenbergii

Painted Lady
Succulent   Mexico

Echeverias produce their leaves in the form of a rosette, some carried on stems, others stemless, resting on the surface of the compost. The leaves themselves vary in size, shape and *E. derenbergii* is a compact plant whose rosette of grey-green leaves, tipped with red, is carried on a short stem. More rosettes appear regularly from the leaf axils on the original rosette and from the rosettes stems of orange-red flowers are thrown up in early summer. The hybrid *E.* 'Doris Taylor' has rosettes of pale green leaves, covered with fine white hairs, on short reddish brown stems. Orange

bring certain death. Continue to give plants the best possible light, with direct sunlight. Water only occasionally to prevent the compost from drying out completely. Lower leaves tend to shrivel in winter and should be removed. This is not a sign of underwatering; all the leaves and not just the lower leaves, would be slightly shrivelled if that were so. Do not feed.

# Echinocereus pectinatus

Hedgehog Cactus
Desert cactus   Mexico

The columnar *E. pectinatus* grows about 8in (20cm) tall and 3in (7.5cm) wide. It is very slow growing and does not throw out additional stems from the base until the main stem has grown to about 4in (10cm). The erect column has many ribs, the edges covered with areoles, from which many spines protude. They are pinkish when the plant is young, but later they become white and so densely cover the green stem that the whole plant looks white. The short-lived bell-shaped pink flowers, which are about 3in (7.5cm) long, appear in summer.

**The year's care**

**Spring and summer:** *E. pectinatus* tolerates normal room temperatures and will stand temperatures up to 80 deg F (27 deg C). Full light with direct sunlight is essential if the plant is to flower. A well-ventilated position by an open window is desirable with a spell in the sun out of doors if possible.

*Echinocereus pectinatus*

The compost should be just moist throughout this period; if it is waterlogged the cactus will rot. Feed monthly.

**Potting-on:** In spring, when the roots have filled the pot, using a loam-based compost with either sand or fine grit added.

**Propagation:** By taking stem cuttings in summer or seed sown in spring. Cuttings should be allowed to dry out for a few days before being planted in compost.

**Autumn and winter:** The cactus should have a rest period at around 45 deg F (7 deg C), but must have as much direct sunlight as possible to ensure that it will flower during the following summer. No watering is necessary for plants overwintered at low temperatures, but those in warmer rooms will need occasional watering, say once a month. The compost should be made fairly moist. Do not feed.

# Euonymus japonicus

Japanese Spindle Tree
Evergreen shrub   Japan

Cool, light conditions are a must if a euonymus is to stay in good condition. *E. japonicus* 'Aureo-variegata' will grow to some 4ft (1.2m). Its dark green leaves, about 2in (5cm) long, similar to the laurel's in shape, are splashed with yellow. There is a dwarf version *E.j.* 'Microphyllus Variegatus' of around 18in (45cm). Its leaves are also smaller, about 1in (2.5cm) long, and green with a silvery white margin.

**The year's care**

**Spring and summer:** A temperature rising to no more than 55 deg F (13 deg C) would be ideal, but at this time of year even in the coolest room in the house it will be difficult to keep it down to that. It needs bright light, but should be shaded from direct sunlight. Water frequently to keep the compost moist and feed every two weeks. Growing tips should be pinched out in spring to encourage bushiness. If the plants get out of hand a little further pruning can be done. Make the cut just above the point where a leaf meets the stem. New growth will appear from there.

**Potting-on:** Every year in spring, using a loam-based compost.

**Propagation:** By stem tip cuttings in summer.

**Autumn and winter:** The plant must have a cool rest period at around 45 deg F (7 deg C). If it is

*Euonymus japonicus*

much warmer there may be problems from scale, red spider mites, and mildew, a white deposit on the leaves. The lower leaves will also tend to fall. However, a good light is needed to maintain the variegations, so in winter some direct sunlight will do no harm. If the plant is overwintered in a low temperature, only occasional watering will be required to keep the compost barely moist. Do not feed.

## × **Fatshedera lizei**

Ivy Tree
Hybrid evergreen shrub

*Fatsia japonica* from Japan and *Hedera helix hibernica*, the Irish Ivy, were crossed in a French nursery to produce this attractive ethnic hybrid. Both parents belong to the aralia family but are from different genera; fatshedera is thus a botanical rarity, between species of two different genera, and it has replaced in popularity its inferior fatsia parent. The fatshedera grows to little more than 4ft (1.2m), and the dark green and glossy leaves are both smaller and

more numerous than those of *F. japonica*. They tend to fall from the lower stems, but if there are several plants together in a pot the overall bushiness of the plants disguises the nakedness of some. Leggy plants can be cut back to induce new growth. There is a very striking variegated form, × *F.l.* 'Variegata', which has creamy white edges to the leaves.

### The year's care

**Spring and summer:** Fatshederas need a temperature of only 55 deg F

× *Fatshedera lizei*

× *Fatshedera lizei* 'Variegata'

(13 deg C) to sustain active growth. A light but slightly shaded position is best; × *F.l.* 'Variegata' will need better light to maintain the colour of the variegations. Water frequently to ensure that the compost is always moist, but not waterlogged, and feed every two weeks. The stems are thin and will need staking as the plant grows taller. Pinching out growing tips makes the plants bushier. The leggy ones should be cut back hard to within about 4in (10cm) of the compost. New growth soon appears.

**Potting-on:** Every year in spring, using a loam-based compost.

**Propagation:** By taking stem cuttings about 4in (10cm) long in early summer. Plant in a peat-based compost and keep in a temperature around 65 deg F (18 deg C). Transplant into a loam-based compost after roughly three months. Plants can also be raised from seed sown in spring.

**Autumn and winter:** Cool temperatures between 45–50 deg F (7–10 deg C) are the most suitable for fatshederas, but they will not object to higher temperatures, though red spider mites can be a problem if rooms are too warm. A well-lit position is necessary, especially for the variegated plants. Water occasionally so that the compost is barely moist. The frequency of the watering will depend on how warm the room is. Do not feed.

## **Faucaria tigrina**

Tiger's Jaws
Succulent    South Africa

These small, low-growing succulents are easy to care for and they flower readily. The pointed leaves, up to 2in (5cm) long, are arranged in pairs opposite each other and form a layered rosette. They are grey-green, covered with white dots, and edged with sharp teeth. Large yellow daisy-like flowers appear in autumn, opening in the afternoon and closing at night.

### The year's care

**Spring and summer:** Plants will be content in normal room temperatures. They must have direct sunlight if they are to flower. Water frequently to keep the compost moist all the time. Feed once a month.

*Faucaria tigrina*

**Potting-on:** How often to pot-on will depend on how quickly the rosettes cover the surface of the compost. It is usually necessary only once every three years. Do it in spring in a loam-based compost with added sand or grit. It is better to use a shallow pan than the normal deep pot.

**Propagation:** By division when repotting. Any rosettes which come away without roots should be left to dry out for a few days before potting up. Older plants develop short stems from which cuttings can be taken in early summer. Plants can also be raised from seed sown in spring.

**Autumn and winter:** Faucarias should have a rest period at around 45 deg F (7 deg C), but in a very bright position with direct sunlight. Water very occasionally to prevent the compost from drying out completely. Leaves will begin to shrivel if the plant does not have enough water. Do not feed.

# Ferocactus latispinus

Devil's Tongue
Desert cactus   Mexico

Of all the ferocacti, *F. latispinus* is the one most likely to flower indoors, given the right conditions. The shape is globular and it will take many years

*Ferocactus latispinus*

to reach its likely limit of 10in (25cm) in height and 8in (20cm) across. The many ribbed ball has groups of white and red spines along the rib edges, each group consisting of four short red spines, the lowest one hooked, surrounded by smaller white spines. Red flowers appear in summer but only on mature plants – that is when they are about 4in (10cm) across.

**The year's care**

**Spring and summer:** A warm position, with plenty of light and even direct sunlight, is best. Without excellent light thc plant will rarely flower and even if buds appear they will be reluctant to open. Good light will also maintain the colouring of the spines. A period out of doors in summer would do good. Water frequently to keep the compost moist. If it becomes sodden the roots rot, so a porous compost is a must. If the plant is kept dry too long red spider mites will be encouraged. Feed plants every two weeks.

**Potting-on:** Every year in early spring. Use a porous compost of one part sharp sand and three parts of peat compost.

**Propagation:** In spring by sowing seed, which will germinate easily.

**Autumn and winter:** A cool resting period at a temperature about 48 deg F (9 deg C) is necessary, but the plants must still have bright light and as much as sun as is available. A plant kept in these cool conditions will need very occasional watering; the compost should be barely moist. Do not feed.

# Fuchsia magellanica

Lady's Eardrops
Deciduous flowering shrub   Peru

Fuchsias are reasonably cheap to buy and they flower over a long period, but they need cool conditions indoors or the leaves and flowers drop. *F. magellanica* was the starting point of the many hybrids now available. It may be grown as a rather floppy shrub, as a standard, or as a trailer in a hanging basket, where the stems arch gently to show off the pendant blooms. The slender stems have oval mid-green leaves and the bell-shaped flowers grow in clusters, giving a show of colour from late spring through well into autumn. The flowers of the hybrids are often combinations of

*Fuchsia magellanica*

colours: white and red, purple and red, white and pink, but some are plain red or pink. Flowers may be more than 2in (5cm) long and some of the double-flowered hybrids reach a monstrously overblown size. If fuchsias are to be grown indoors it is better to buy them young in spring when they are no more than 6in (15cm) high, before flower buds have formed. *F. triphylla*, the honeysuckle fuchsia, from the West Indies, will tolerate warmer temperatures than most fuchsias. It has long lance-shaped leaves, which are green on top and purple underneath. Brilliant red tubular flowers are produced from summer through to autumn.

### The year's care

**Spring and summer:** When plants which you have overwintered start into new growth at the end of the resting period bring them into a temperature of between 55–65 deg F (13–18 deg C) – the lower end of the scale is better. Fuchsias require a great deal of light to ensure prolonged flowering, but they should be protected from direct sun. A well-ventilated spot near an often open window is fine, and a spell out of doors is even better. In very hot weather mist-spray frequently; dry air encourages aphids and red spider mites. When flowers have faded remove them and the attached seed pod, which is at first green, ripening to purple. If the pods are left on, the plant will concentrate its energy on producing seed instead of further flowers and the flowering period will end prematurely. Water frequently to keep the compost always moist. If the plant goes short of water the leaves will wilt dramatically, but they quickly recover if well watered immediately. Feed once a week.

**Potting-on:** In early spring in either a peat or loam-based compost. A 6in (15cm) pot is probably the largest a fuchsia will need.

**Propagation:** By taking stem tip cuttings, about 4in (10cm) long, in spring and summer.

**Autumn and winter:** When flowering is over cut back stems to within 6in (15cm) of the compost. Overwinter the plant at temperatures in the low 50s F (10–12 deg C). Hybrids of *F. magellanica* will tolerate lower temperatures, but not below 45

deg F (7 deg C). Frost is a certain killer. During this period, when the cut down stems will have lost their leaves, good light is not essential, until new growth starts. Water occasionally, about once a month, to keep the compost barely moist. No feeding is necessary.

# Gasteria verrucosa

Ox Tongue
Succulent   South Africa

*G. verrucosa* is easy to care for and in periods of active growth can stand both very warm and dry conditions. The thick, fleshy pointed leaves, up to 6in (15cm) long, are dark green and covered with white hairs. They are carried in opposite pairs, one set closely on top of another so that in all the plant grows to little more than 6in (15cm). Red tubular flowers, carried on long stems, appear from spring through to early autumn. *G. maculata*, another popular gasteria, is similar in form and colour to *G. verrucosa*, but the leaves themselves are strap-shaped and the whole plant is a little taller – about 8in (20cm).

### The year's care

**Spring and summer:** This plant will perfectly well survive warm, dry

normal room conditions during this period. Do not place it in full sun; a slightly shaded position is best, for direct sunlight tends to make the leaves turn brown. Water frequently to make the compost always moist and feed once a month.

**Potting-on:** Gasterias grow slowly, so potting-on should be necessary only every second or third year, in spring. To make a porous compost add one part of sand to a loam-based compost.

**Propagation:** By removing offsets when repotting. Any which have few or no roots should be allowed to dry out for a few days before being potted up.

*Gasteria verrucosa*

*Gasteria maculata*

**Autumn and winter:** Give the plant a rest period at a temperature not lower than 45 deg F (7 deg C) and keep it in a slightly shaded position. Water occasionally, say once a month, so that the compost is fairly moist. Do not feed.

# Gymnocalycium baldianum

Desert cactus   Argentina

*G. baldianum* has not only attractively coloured spines but flowers freely, even when young, during spring and summer. The stem is green and globular, growing to about 3in (7.5cm) and it has 10–12 ribs edged with groups of white or yellow spines growing from the areoles. Beneath each areole there is a small 'chin'. Red, daisy-like flowers, about 2in (5cm) across appear in spring and summer. *G. bruchii* is smaller, rapidly spreads its offsets to form a clump, and produces pink flowers in great profusion.

**The year's care**

**Spring and summer:** Both *G. baldianum* and *G. bruchii* will be happy in normal warm room conditions. They require full sun if they are to flower well; a bright window-sill with midday sun is ideal. Water frequently to ensure that the compost is always moist and feed once a month.

**Potting-on:** Until plants reach their maximum size of about 3in (7.5cm) pot-on each year in spring. Use a mixture of two parts of loam-based compost and one part of sand. Thereafter the plant can be repotted every two years to renew the compost.

**Propagation:** By removing offsets in spring. The *G. bruchii* cluster of offsets may become crowded and it is sensible to remove a few of them, leaving the rest undisturbed. Allow offsets to dry out for a few days before potting up.

**Autumn and winter:** Like cacti in general these plants need a resting period, with a temperature around 45 deg F (7 deg C). If they do not have this rest they will be reluctant to flower the following year. A bright position is necessary with as much full sun as possible. Poor light will not only make flowering unlikely, but will cause the globes to elongate. Water only occasionally, about once a month, to keep the compost barely moist. However, if the globes begin to shrivel it is an indication that watering is needed. Do not feed.

# Haworthia margaritifera

Pearl Plant
Succulent   South Africa

*H. margaritifera* is grown primarily for its remarkable fleshy foliage, for the

*Gymnocalycium baldianum*

*Haworthia margaritifera*

flowers are insignificant. The tough dark green leaves, soon forming a rosette, are covered in pearly looking warts. The leaves are about 3in (7.5cm) long and the rosette they form will grow to no more than 4in (10cm) high and 6in (15cm) across. Long slender stems from near the centre of the rosette carry the small white flowers which appear in summer and early autumn.

**The year's care**

**Spring and summer:** Warm normal room temperatures are suitable at this time of the year. Good light is needed, but the plant must be shaded from direct sunlight. If it gets sun the leaves are likely to turn reddish, but if it gets too much shade the dark green of the leaves turns pale. The correct balance of light is important, but at least the plant gives clear colour signals if it is wrong. Water frequently to keep the compost always moist, but the plant should be grown in a porous compost so that there is no danger that the roots will rot. Feed once a month.

**Potting-on:** In spring each year until the plant reaches its maximum size of around 4in (10cm) high and 6in (15cm) across. Use a mixture of two parts loam-based compost and one part sand. Plant in a shallow pot. When plants have reached full size they should be repotted every other year to renew the compost.

**Propagation:** By removing offsets when repotting. Any offsets without roots should be left to dry out for a few days before potting up. Haworthias can also be raised easily from seed sown in spring.

**Autumn and winter:** Give the plant a rest period at a temperature around 45 deg F (7 deg C) in a slightly shaded position. Water about once a month. If leaves begin to shrivel watering is required but do not get carried away and make the compost waterlogged. Do not feed.

# Hedera helix

Ivy
Evergreen climber   Europe

Ivies are tough, virtually indestructible plants and because of this they are often neglected by their owners. However, a little care and attention will be repaid with abundant strong growth. Ivies look particularly good in hanging baskets, although this is one of the areas in which they suffer the most neglect. Many cultivars have been developed

from *Hedera helix*, and most of them are self-branching so that they make fairly bushy growth if left to themselves. But even the self-branching ivies will benefit from pinching out the growing tips to encourage more dense foliage. *H.h.* 'Chicago', a vigorous grower, has small dark green leaves with purplish markings. *H.h.* 'Chicago Variegata' has creamy edges to the leaves. *H.h.* 'Glacier' has small midgreen leaves with white to pink edges, and is good for hanging baskets. Another good basket ivy is *H.h.* 'Sagittifolia' with small, slender arrowhead leaves of light green or green and cream in *H.h.* 'Sagittifolia Variegata'. The 'Sagittifolia' is a fast, dense grower. *H.h.* 'Lutzii' (not self-branching) has small three-lobed leaves with a yellow marbled effect. A most attractive variegated ivy with far larger leaves is *Hedera canariensis* 'Variegata' (Gloire de Marengo), the Canary Island Ivy.

The leathery leaves, up to 6in (15cm) long, are dark green at the centre with broad edges of creamy white. This ivy has no self-clinging roots and will need support if used as a climber. *Hedera colchica*, Persian Ivy, has the largest leaves of any ivy – heart-shaped and up to 10in (25cm) long and almost as wide. It is a vigorous grower.

### The year's care

**Spring and summer:** Ivies do not object to low temperatures and thrive best if they are below 65 deg F (18 deg C) in the growing period. Put them in a light but somewhat shaded part of the room where they will not be exposed to direct sunlight. Variegated ivies will need better light than the plain green to maintain their variegation. If the light is too poor they will revert to green, and this is especially likely to happen in weak winter light. Cut back any stems on which there are leaves which have reverted to green as far as the first still variegated leaf. Remove the plant into a good light and new growth

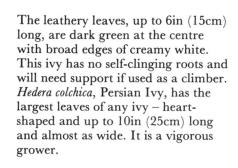
*Hedera helix*

*Hedera helix* 'Glacier'

*Hedera helix* 'Chicago'

should be variegated. Water fairly frequently to keep the compost moist. Feed every two weeks. Remember to pinch out growing tips in spring and once again in summer. If plants appear to be getting out of hand stems can be pruned back. Leaves should be sprayed and, if large enough, sponged to remove dirt; this will also discourage red spider mites which like dry, warm conditions.

**Potting-on:** Each spring in a mixture of loam, peat, sand and leaf mould, or, failing that, a loam-based compost with one third part of sand for good drainage.

**Propagation:** Take cuttings from the end of branches, about 4in (10cm) long, in summer. They can be rooted in water and potted up or planted straight into a rooting compost. Transplant into a potting mixture when the cuttings are established – in about a month or six weeks.

**Autumn and winter:** A resting period around 50 deg F (10 deg C) is required. Plants kept in warm rooms may become infested with red spider mites and a combination of warmth and poor light will certainly produce spindly straggly growth. On the other hand they should not be in the sun, even winter sun. Water occasionally to keep the compost just moist. Do not feed.

## Impatiens wallerana

Busy Lizzie
Flowering perennial   Tropical Africa

From *I. wallerana* many hybrids have been developed, compact and bushy, in place of the leggy stems and sparse foliage of the species. Whereas *I. wallerana* might grow to 2–3ft (30–90cm) the new compact hybrids will be no more than 15in (37.5cm). The elliptic bright green leaves, which feel rubbery, are carried on fleshy branching stems. Successions of flowers appear from spring until autumn, in shades of red, orange, pink and white, depending on which hybrid you buy. Some flowers are double and bi-coloured. These plants look particularly striking growing in a hanging basket, and very lively if colours are mixed. A recent introduction has been the 'New Guinea' hybrids, which are taller, about 2ft (60cm). Their leaves are

*Impatiens wallerana*

richly variegated, from creamy white to yellow, and the flowers are much bigger, though fewer. All impatiens should be pinched out to make them bushier.

### The year's care

**Spring and summer:** Temperatures in the range of 60–65 deg F (16–18 deg C) are best. Plants need excellent light for continuous flowering but they should be shaded from direct sunlight. If the atmosphere is too hot and dry red spider mites may be a nuisance and greenfly almost certainly will be. Water very frequently; they are thirsty plants and in hot weather daily watering may be necessary. If the compost does dry out the plants wilt with great suddenness, but a good watering will revive them. Feed once a month.

**Potting-on:** In spring, using a peat based compost. Prune all the straggly stems down to within 6in (15cm) of the compost.

**Propagation:** Either by sowing seed in spring or from cuttings taken in summer – by far the easiest method. Cuttings should be about 4in (10cm) long. They can be rooted in water, which they do very quickly and then planted in a peat compost, or planted directly into a peat rooting compost.

**Autumn and winter:** The ideal temperature is about 60 deg F (16

deg C) but plants will tolerate a somewhat lower temperature. Always keep them in a good light but out of direct sunlight. Only occasional watering is required to keep the compost just moist. With too much water during the resting season the plants can easily rot. Do not feed.

## Jasminum polyanthum

Jasmine
Flowering climber   China

Of the winter and spring flowering jasmines *J. officinale*, the Common Jasmine, is more suited to the outdoor

*Jasminum polyanthum*

life, while *J. polyanthum* has adapted to life indoors, but only if it is cool there. It is a vigorous climber, reaching a height of 10ft (3m), but it can be kept under control by hard pruning. The single young stem soon develops many branches and will need support. They carry dark green leaves divided into around six leaflets. Even young plants bear flowers and these appear in winter and spring as clusters of long-tubed white, very fragrant blooms. This is one of the few indoor plants which will flower in winter, and the young plants are quick to do so.

**The year's care**

**Spring and summer:** In spring temperatures should be no more than 60 deg F (16 deg C), even though they will obviously exceed that in summer. The jasmine requires plenty of light with a little direct sunshine but should not be in scorching sunlight. A position with plenty of fresh air will help to keep it in good condition. Water frequently to keep the compost always moist and feed every two weeks. In early spring when

the plant has finished flowering cut the stems back to within about 6in (15cm) of the compost.

**Potting-on:** In summer each year, leaving enough time for the plants to get thoroughly established after the hard pruning of spring. Use a loam-based compost.

**Propagation:** Take stem tip cuttings about 4in (10cm) long in summer and plant in a loam-based rooting compost. When they have rooted they can be transplanted into a potting compost, and several could be planted together in one pot. When they have reached about 12in (30cm) pinch out the growing tip of each to produce bushiness.

**Autumn and winter:** Cool temperatures around 55 deg F (13 deg C) are essential. If the room is much warmer the leaves will curl and fall and the flower buds will not open. Plants should always be in a well lit spot, where they can get as much winter sunshine as possible. Water about once a week to keep the compost just moist. Do not feed.

*Lilium longiflorum*

# Lilium longiflorum

Easter Lily
Bulb   Japan

Lilies are relatively short-stay indoor plants, because once the brief flowering season is over the slowly dying and yellowing stems are hardly attractive to look at. However, while the flowers last they are extraordinarily beautiful – trumpet-shaped, white with orange stamens, and measuring some 6in (15cm) across. They appear from late spring to midsummer depending on when you bring the bulbs out of their cool winter quarters; the time when they are in bud and flower is about three weeks. The stems, up to 3ft (90cm) tall, are covered with many narrow dark green pointed leaves, about 5in (12cm) long.

**The year's care**

**Spring and summer:** For flowers in late spring move the pot in which the bulb has spent a cool winter into a temperature of 60 deg F (16 deg C) in early spring. If you want later flowering leave the bulb longer in the cool. A well-lit spot, but out of direct sunshine, will encourage buds to develop. Water frequently to keep the compost moist but if you make it waterlogged the bulb is liable to rot. When flowering is over water only occasionally to keep the compost barely moist. Feed every two weeks from the time the first shoots appear in spring until flowering is over. The stem will yellow and gradually die down.

**Potting-on:** *L. longiflorum* can be potted-on when the stem has completely withered and comes away easily from the bulb, but it is a gamble whether it will flower a second year indoors. It is better to plant it outdoors and let it build up its strength to flower there in future years.

**Propagation:** Before planting the lily outdoors you can remove the offsets and raise them in a loam-based or peat-based compost. You will have to wait three or more years before these get to the stage of flowering.

**Autumn and winter:** Plant new bulbs in autumn in either a loam-based or peat-based compost. Choose a clay pot, less likely to topple over

when the lily grows tall. Cover the bottom of the pot with a 1in (2.5cm) layer of gravel or grit for free drainage and plant the bulb with its base half-way down the pot. Keep it in a frost-free place in a temperature about 40 deg F (5 deg C). Plenty of light is needed. Water the compost occasionally to make it just moist, never sodden. The plant should not be fed until the new shoots begin to appear.

# Lithops lesliei

Living Stones
Succulent   South Africa

*Lithops lesliei* is a novel plant, using camouflage to merge with the stones among which it grows in the wild. They are often sold in pots with the compost already covered in grit, making the small leaves difficult to detect. Most of the plant is buried below the compost, with about 1in (2.5cm) of the fleshy, flat-topped leaves protruding above the surface. The leaves, which are grey-green with reddish brown spots on the upper surface, grow in pairs, joined together with only a slit between them. Yellow flowers on short stems appear from the slit in late summer and autumn.

### The year's care

**Spring and summer:** This plant is happy with normal room temperatures and will even find great heat bearable. A very bright position is necessary, with plenty of direct sunlight, to produce flowers. Water occasionally to keep the compost just moist; too much water will make the leaves bloated and soft to touch. Avoid watering into the slit. Feed once a month.

**Potting-on:** Lithops stay small and grow slowly so need to be potted-on only every second or third year in spring. Use equal parts of sand and loam-based compost for a very free draining mixture. Plant in shallow pots.

**Propagation:** By division when repotting or by sowing seed in spring, but there will be a long wait before there are any flowers.

**Autumn and winter:** Give the plants a rest period at about 50 deg F (10 deg C) in a light place with plenty of direct sun. Water occasionally to make the compost just moist. Once flowering is over in the autumn stop watering. The leaves will begin to shrivel and eventually die but a new pair will appear in their place, though this may not happen until the spring. The plants should not be watered until the new leaves emerge and then only occasionally. Do not attempt to remove the old leaves until they have shrivelled completely or the new leaves may be damaged. The resting plants should not be fed.

*Lobivia hertrichiana*

# Lobivia hertrichiana

Desert cactus   Bolivia

A lobivia (anagram of Bolivia) requires little attention and has the added attraction of flowering freely when young. The globular *L. hertrichiana* grows to no more than 4in (10cm) in height and diameter, but it will produce many offsets as it matures. The globe has several ribs with areoles along the edges, from which brownish spines protrude. If the plants are kept in a good light some spines may pale to yellow. Large scarlet flowers, up to 2in (5cm) across, appear during the summer, opening during the day and closing at night. Flowers do not last long, but several are usually produced over a period of weeks.

### The year's care

**Spring and summer:** A lobivia will tolerate normal room temperatures. It requires bright light with full direct sun if it is to flower and keep the spines a good colour. Water frequently so that the compost is always moist and feed every two weeks.

**Potting-on:** The plant does not make many roots, so potting-on will be necessary only every two or three years, in spring. It is time to do so when offsets cover the whole surface of the compost. Use a loam-based compost with sand added for good drainage and choose a shallow pot.

**Propagation:** By removing offsets when repotting. Make sure that each offset has enough roots to support it. Plants can also be raised from seed sown in spring.

*Lithops lesliei*

**Autumn and winter:** The plant needs a cool resting period at around 45 deg F (7 deg C) if it is to flower well the following year. It must be placed in a good light with direct sunlight. A lobivia overwintered at low temperatures will require very little watering, say once a month, to keep the compost barely moist. Do not feed.

## Mammillaria bocasana

Powder Puff
Desert cactus   Mexico

Many of the mammillarias are good cacti for beginners because they are easy to grow and flower freely when young; others are impossible. *M. bocasana* forms a cluster of blue-green globes about 2in (5cm) across and the cluster may have to be divided when it becomes too big. Unlike many cacti it does not have ribs but small tubercles (mounds) instead, which are about ½in (1.25cm) high. Each tubercle has an areole from which silky white hairs grow, concealing hooked spines – so take care when handling this plant. Small, cream to yellow, bell-shaped flowers encircle the head of each globe in spring, and they are followed by purplish red seed pods. In contrast, *M. elegans* is cylindrical, at first as a single stem but as it matures clusters of new stems appear from the base. Each cylinder bears a mass of short white spines. There are red flowers in spring, but they appear only when the cactus is

about four years old. *M. zeilmanniana* starts off as a single globe but later branches from the base, spreading over the surface of the compost. As the globes grow they become elongated, up to 4in (10cm) tall. Each areole has more than a dozen white spines with a few brown, and viciously hooked, spines in the middle. In this species beautiful red flowers encircle the globe in summer and appear on very young plants.

### The year's care

**Spring and summer:** These mammillaria will be happy in normal room conditions at this time of the year, but they must have a bright spot

*Mammillaria elegans*

with plenty of direct sunlight to promote flowering and maintain the colour of the spines. Turn the pot regularly for even growth. Water frequently, but allow the compost to dry out between waterings. Take care not to water in between the clumps of stems which are liable to rot. Either water round the outside edge of the clump or immerse the pot in shallow water. Feed once a month.

**Potting-on:** Repot in spring each year in a mixture of two parts loam-based compost to one part of sand or grit, and pot-on if the roots have become crowded. A porous mixture is essential for good drainage, which helps to prevent root rot.

**Propagation:** By removing offsets when repotting. Any which have few roots should be allowed to dry out for a few days before potting up. Plants look better growing in shallow pots.

**Autumn and winter:** Mammillaria must have a resting period with temperatures about 45 deg F (7 deg C). If they are deprived of rest they will fail to flower. But keep them in a well-lit position with as much sunlight as possible. Water about once a month to prevent the compost from drying out completely. Do not feed.

## Monstera deliciosa

Swiss Cheese Plant
Evergreen foliage   Central America

Before buying that young 18in (45cm) high seemingly well-behaved monstera be warned that it will in a few years grow to 6ft (1.8m) and more, with a 6ft (1.8m) sprawl of leaves; if you have plenty of room well and good but monsteras which have grown too large for you are very hard to give away. The mature dark green leaves, 16in (40cm) wide and 18in (45cm) long are deeply slashed and perforated. Aerial roots grow from the central stem. In the wild the plant uses them to fasten round tree trunks and branches and to take up moisture and food, supplying the length of the plant. In the home these roots may be pushed either into a moss stick which is kept constantly moist or into the compost in the pot in which the plant is growing. However, they rapidly fill the pot, pushing out the compost and leaving little room for the main roots to develop. Young plants often have

*Mammillaria bocasana*

*Monstera delicosa*

of compost – carefully in order not to damage the roots – and replace with fresh.

**Propagation:** By taking stem tip cuttings in summer or from seed in spring. Overgrown plants can be reduced to a manageable size by being air-layered in summer.

**Autumn and winter:** A monstera will tolerate a minimum temperature of 55 deg F (13 deg C), but can be overwintered in much warmer, centrally-heated rooms. A slightly shaded position is best, but occasional exposure to direct sun would do no harm. Water occasionally to make the compost barely moist. Do not feed.

# Myrtus communis
## 'Microphylla'

Myrtle
Evergreen shrub    Mediterranean

The myrtle has not only distinctive smelling foliage, but also fragrant flowers and fruit. It grows to no more than 2ft (60cm) and its many branches are covered with leathery, narrow, pointed leaves about 1in (2.5cm) long. The white flowers, which appear in late summer and early autumn, have dense clusters of yellow stamens in their centres. Flowers may be followed by red berries.

### The year's care

**Spring and summer:** A myrtle will do best in temperatures not above 55 deg F (13 deg C), but it will not suffer unduly in higher temperatures as long as it is in a well-ventilated position. It should also be in a bright light with a limited amount of sunlight, but shaded from the hot midday sun. Poor light will affect flowering and fruiting. Turn the pot regularly so that the shrub grows evenly all round. Pinch out growing tips to increase bushiness and lightly prune any stray branches spoiling the overall shape. It is a thirsty plant and will need watering frequently. It is averse to lime, so in hard water districts it should be watered with rainwater, if possible, but distilled water can be used instead. Feed every two weeks.

**Potting-on:** In a peat-based compost every spring.

plain unslashed lower leaves and others with only a few incisions. As the plant matures the new leaves will be increasingly divided and perforated, as long as the plant is well looked after. Mature plants can produce cream coloured spathes followed by an edible fruit described as tasting like pineapple, but fruiting is rare in plants grown indoors. *M.d.* 'Variegata' is a most attractive form, the leaves marked with white or cream.

### The year's care

**Spring and summer:** Temperatures between 65–75 deg F (18–24 deg C) are essential; if they are lower the plant will be reluctant to throw out new leaves. It should have a well-lit position, but needs shade from direct sunlight. While it will grow in quite shady places the new leaves then tend to have fewer incisions. Variegated plants must have good light at all times to maintain their colouring. Dust and wipe the leaves regularly. Water the plant once a week but let the compost almost dry out between waterings. More frequent watering may be needed in hot weather. If the plant is allowed to become too dry the leaf tips may turn brown. A moss stick used to support a plant should be sprayed daily to keep the moss moist. Feed every two weeks.

**Potting-on:** In spring each year in a loam-based compost until a 10in–12in (25–30cm) size has been reached. After that remove the top 2in (5cm)

*Myrtus communis 'Microphylla'*

to form a rosette. As the plant matures the leaves develop a pinkish tinge. The overall height of the bromeliad will be no more than about 10in (25cm), but because the rosette of leaves is somewhat flattened the spread is about 18in (45cm). The insignificant white flowers, which may appear at any time, grow from the centre of the rosette. Its central leaves stay red for many months until the parent plant begins to die down. As it does so it produces offsets.

### The year's care

**Spring and summer:** *N.c.* 'Tricolor' needs temperatures in the range of 65–70 deg F (18–20 deg C) and to maintain the bright variegations it should be in a well-lit spot but shaded from direct sunlight. Spray plants in very hot weather. Water fairly frequently to keep the compost moist but not sodden. The centre of the rosette should also be filled with water. Feed once a month.

**Potting-on:** Every two years in spring, using a peat-based compost. A 6in (15cm) pot is likely to be the largest it will ever need.

**Propagation:** In summer by taking cuttings, which will root more successfully if they are taken with a heel – a small section of the old bark. It may be several weeks before they root.

**Autumn and winter:** The plant should have a resting period at between 40–45 deg F (5–7 deg C). Much higher temperatures may cause leaves to fall and affect flowering the following year. A well-lit position, with weak winter sun, is a must. Water occasionally so that the compost does not dry out altogether. If kept at a low temperature the plant will need watering about every two weeks. Do not feed.

## Neoregelia carolinae
'Tricolor'

Bromeliad   Brazil

*N.c.* 'Tricolor' has brightly variegated leaves and, as a bonus, the inner leaves of the rosette turn bright red before the flowers appear. The toothed, shiny green leaves, striped with yellow, grow to 12in (30cm) long

*Neoregelia carolinae*

*Nertera granadensis*

**Potting-on:** In spring in a peat-based compost with added sand. Nerteras do not have deep roots and for that reason, as well as for display, are best planted in shallow pots, and 5in (12.5cm) diameter will be the limit.

**Propagation:** In spring, by dividing the plant or sowing seed with bottom heat of 70 deg F (21 deg C).

**Autumn and winter:** A temperature of about 50 deg F (10 deg C) is best; higher temperatures will cause the berries to fall prematurely. Keep the temperature even throughout the period. Put plants in a well-lit position with some direct sunlight. Water occasionally to prevent the compost from drying out completely. Do not feed.

# Parodia chrysacanthion

Desert cactus    Argentina

Parodias are grown for their brilliantly coloured spines but they also produce flowers, even when quite young. *P. chrysacanthion* is a globular cactus, usually just a solitary globe, reaching a diameter of about 5in (12.5cm) and a height of 3in (7.5cm). Many golden yellow spines grow from the areoles which cover the pale green

**Propagation:** By removing offsets in spring, but not until they are well developed. If the parent plant has died down and looks unattractive, cut it away and leave the offsets to grow.

**Autumn and winter:** Give the plant a rest at temperatures between 55–60 deg F (13–16 deg C), but no lower. A well-lit position, out of direct sunlight, is needed. Water occasionally to prevent the compost from drying out. During the resting period keep the centre of the rosette dry; water left there may cause the plant to rot. Do not feed.

to put the plant out of doors until the berries begin to form. Indoors the nertera will tolerate higher temperatures, but the effect is to make it grow quickly and produce dense foliage. For flowers and fruit a very well-lit position is essential, with some direct sunlight. Water frequently to keep the compost moist at all times. Both before and after flowering the plant should be sprayed frequently. Feed with a weak solution of fertiliser once a month; too much feeding produces lush growth of foliage at the expense of flowers and berries.

# Nertera granadensis

Bead Plant
Fruiting creeper    South America,
    New Zealand

The nertera's orange berries may be small, but their numbers make up for that, almost hiding the green foliage. The long stems, which creep along the surface of the compost, are covered with fleshy oval leaves. The plants are best displayed in wide shallow pots in which they will grow into a mound about 3in (7.5cm) high. In spring and early summer small white flowers appear followed by the orange berries, which last through the winter. Often the plant is discarded after the berries drop, but it can perfectly well be treated as the perennial it is.

**The year's care**

**Spring and summer:** A temperature about 60 deg F (16 deg C) is needed and it is a good idea

*Parodia sanguiniflora*

*Parodia chrysacanthion*

# Passiflora caerulea

Passion Flower
Flowering evergreen    Brazil

*P. caerulea* is a hardy plant often seen growing out of doors, but given cool conditions it will produce its fascinating flowers indoors, even on young plants. It grows quickly and can reach 10ft (3m); the stems are weak and need support. Use either stakes or a trellis to which the plant's tendrils can cling. The shiny dark green leaves, with five or more lobes, are up to 5in (12.5cm) across. The stunning flowers, which appear from summer to early autumn, have white petals with many purple and white filaments. They may be followed by orange fruits, but this is rarely so indoors.

### The year's care

**Spring and summer:** Temperatures between 55–60 deg F (13–16 deg C) are suitable, but if they go above 70 deg F (21 deg C) the plant will suffer. *C. passiflora* needs a very bright well-ventilated spot, with direct sunlight in the cooler parts of the day, to encourage flowering. If the plant is placed out of doors for a time so much the better. Water frequently to keep the compost always moist and feed

*Passiflora caerulea*

globe. There are funnel-shaped flowers about 1in (2.5cm) long in late spring and early summer. *P. sanguiniflora* is also globular at first but as it matures it becomes cylindrical, growing to a height of 5in (12.5cm) and a diameter of 4in (10cm). It will also throw out offsets. The pale green stem is covered with areoles from which protrude white spines with a few brown ones at the centre. Bright red flowers, 2in (5cm), across are produced in summer.

### The year's care

**Spring and summer:** A parodia will be all right in normal room temperatures at this time of the year. It requires a lot of light with plenty of direct sun to maintain its beautiful spine colouring. Water frequently but allow the compost to dry out between waterings. It is a very sensitive cactus and is likely to lose its roots if watered too much. Feed once a month.

**Potting-on:** In spring each year pot-on into a larger pot, until the cactus has reached its maximum girth – about 5in (12.5cm) – and thereafter repot into the same size pot. Use a mixture of one part of loam-based compost and one part grit. When replanting cut away any brown roots which have begun to rot.

**Propagation:** By sowing seed in spring or by removing offsets in late spring.

**Autumn and winter:** The plant should rest at temperatures between 48–54 deg F (9–12 deg C), but it must still be in a well-lit spot with direct sunlight. This will keep spine colouring up to the mark and encourage flowering. Very little water is needed when the plant is resting; once a month should be enough. Do not feed.

every two weeks. In spring when it comes out of its winter quarters, hard prune the stems to within six inches of the compost.

**Potting-on:** In spring every two years; it does better if somewhat potbound, for unrestricted roots will produce plants with plenty of foliage but few flowers. Use a loam-based compost.

**Propagation:** In summer with stem cuttings about 4in (10cm) long.

**Autumn and winter:** The passion flower needs a cool resting period at no more than 50 deg F (10 deg C), but should still have bright light and direct sunlight. Water about every two weeks to prevent the compost from drying out completely. Do not feed.

# Pelargonium

Geranium
Flowering shrubs; trailer,
climbers   South Africa

Most pelargoniums, more commonly known as geraniums, are grown for their flowers, produced over many weeks in summer and autumn, but some for their striking fragrant foliage. The regal pelargonium, *P. × domesticum*, with slightly serrated, rounded, mid-green leaves, grows up to 2ft (60cm). The showy flowers range from white through to pink, lavender and scarlet, and some are bi-coloured. The petals are also veined and marked with a slightly darker shade of the main flower colour. Each flower may be up to 2in (5cm) across, the clusters of them making a large head of bloom. They appear in great abundance from late spring to late summer. The flowering period of *P. × hortorum* is much longer, lasting from spring until late autumn; they may even produce flowers on and off through the year with only short intervals in between. These hybrids have been developed from *P. zonale*, so called because of the brownish red rings on the mid-green leaves. The flowers, from white to numerous shades of pink and red, are carried in thick clusters on long stalks. Some varieties of *P. × hortorum* may grow to 3ft (90cm), but there are many F1 hybrids which stay a compact 12in (30cm).

*Pelargonium × domesticum*

*Pelargonium peltatum*

*P. peltatum*, the ivy-leaved geranium, is shown to best advantage when grown in a hanging basket. The fleshy ivy-shaped leaves are carried on long trailing stems up to 2ft (60cm) long. The flowers appear in clusters on 6in (15cm) stalks from spring to autumn, and the colours are similar to those of *P. × hortorum*. Some are bi-coloured. One of the scented geraniums, *P.*

*crispum*, which grows to about 2ft (60cm), has crinkly and velvety leaves, and if gently rubbed they will give off a lingering fresh lemon scent. They are usually mid-green, but in some forms they are variegated with creamy white edges. From late spring until autumn pale pink flowers are produced. Another scented species is *P. tomentosum*, the peppermint geranium, which although a climber grows to only 2ft (60cm). Its large, velvety, lobed leaves smell strongly of peppermint. From late spring to autumn small insignificant flowers are produced.

### The year's care

**Spring and summer:** The ideal temperature is about 60 deg F (16 deg C), but pelargoniums will adjust to higher temperatures. For prolonged flowering they need a very well-lit spot with plenty of direct sunlight. Poor light will result in few flowers and straggly, etiolated growth. Plants need an abundance of fresh air; indeed most of them do better out of doors, in window boxes, for example, than they do indoors. Water frequently to keep the compost moist, but take care that it does not become sodden. Overwatered plants are in danger of being attacked by a fungal disease called blackleg – the base of the stems turns black – and this quickly leads to total rot and death of the plant. Feed every two weeks. In early spring overwintered pelargoniums should be pruned back to within 6in (15cm) of the compost. Once new growth has been established growing tips should be pinched out. This will encourage bushiness and while the plant will lose some early flowers, it does mean that later there will be many more which last over a longer period.

**Potting-on:** In early spring each year, using either a loam or peat-based compost. The plant will do better if it is somewhat potbound. If the roots fill the whole pot, pot-on to a larger one, otherwise gently tease away some of the old compost and replant with new compost in the same pot.

**Propagation:** In summer, by taking stem cuttings about 4in (10cm) long. Do not allow the compost to become too wet or the cuttings may be attacked by blackleg. Plants of *P. × hortorum* can be easily raised from seed sown in winter, but they will not flower until early summer.

**Autumn and winter:** Pelargoniums do better if they have a rest period between 45–50 deg F (7–10 deg C), but no lower. Frost will certainly kill them. *P. × domesticum* should be overwintered in temperatures between 50–55 deg F (10–13 deg C). Even in

*Pellionia pulchra*

winter pelargoniums need a brightly lit position with the chance of direct sunlight. Water occasionally to prevent the compost from drying out completely. If the temperatures are low the need for watering will be infrequent. Do not feed.

## Pellionia pulchra

Trailer   China

Pellionias are good plants for hanging baskets or for trailing over the edges of a pot. *P. pulchra* has purple stems up to 18in (45cm) long, covered with oval, light green leaves, purple veined on the upper surface and with lighter purple colouring underneath. *P. daveauana* has slightly longer stems with round to oval bright green leaves, the edges marked with bronzy green.

### The year's care

**Spring and summer:** Normal seasonal room temperatures are satisfactory. While the plant needs good light to maintain its bright colouring, choose a slightly shaded spot out of direct sunlight. Water frequently to keep the compost always moist but do not let it become waterlogged. Never leave the pot standing in water in its saucer – the sure way to rot the roots. Feed every two weeks.

**Potting-on:** In spring if the roots have filled the pot. Use a peat-based compost.

**Propagation:** In spring by taking stem tip cuttings about 3in (7.5cm) long.

**Autumn and winter:** Pellionias will tolerate a minimum temperature of 55 deg F (13 deg C), but no lower, and they will still be at home if it rises to 65 deg F (18 deg C). Water occasionally to prevent the compost from drying out altogether. The higher the temperature the more frequent the waterings will have to be. Do not feed.

## Philodendron

Foliage   Central and South America

Philodendrons are of two types – climbing and erect non-climbing. All are grown for their luxuriant glossy foliage; flowers rarely appear on those grown indoors and are unremarkable. Philodendrons will grow up to 8ft (2.4m) or more and the climbers will need strong support. They produce aerial roots which in the wild twine themselves round tree trunks and take up food and water. Indoors these roots are best pushed into a moss stick which must be kept constantly moist.

Of the climbing philodendrons, *P. scandens*, the heartleaf philodendron, is

*Philodendron scandens*

the most popular since it is easy to care for and remains reasonably compact. It can be trained as a climber or planted in a hanging basket with the stems hanging down. The 6in (15cm) long leaves are heart-shaped, dark green and glossy. *P. andreanum* (syn. *P. melanochryson*), the velour philodendron, has heart-shaped leaves, 6in (15cm) long when young, but as they mature they gradually elongate to 24in (60cm).

They are particularly handsome – velvety dark green on top and with purplish undersides. *P.* 'Burgundy', a hybrid, is a comparatively slow grower but tends to spread because the leaves are carried on almost horizontal red stalks up to 10in (25cm) long. The leaves are lance-shaped, about 12in (30cm) long, bright red when young, turning dark green as they mature, but retaining a rich burgundy colour on the underside. *P. erubescens*, called the blushing philodendron because the new leaves are pink, has arrowhead leaves up to 10in (25cm) long. As they age they turn dark green with a coppery sheen, but the undersides are red. *P. panduraeforme*, the fiddle leaf, is a fast grower with dark green heart-shaped leaves when young, later becoming fiddle-shaped and about 12in (30cm) long.

Of the erect growing philodendrons *P. bipinnatifidum* reaches about 5ft (1.5m), with 18in (45cm) leaves, heart-shaped when young, but becoming divided into many lobes. *P. selloum* is similar, but the leaves are larger, up to 3ft (90cm), and more deeply dissected, almost to the central rib. Yet another

*Philodendron erubescens*

different shape of leaf is found on *P. wendlandii*; leaves are narrow and lance-shaped, dark green and glossy and about 12in (30cm) long; they grow in rosette formation.

### The year's care

**Spring and summer:** Temperatures should be in the range 65–75 deg F (18–24 deg C). All philodendrons need good light, particularly the highly coloured types, but in a slightly shaded position and certainly not exposed to direct sunlight. Water frequently to keep the compost moist and feed every two weeks.

**Potting-on:** In spring when the roots have filled the pot, using a peat-based compost. Eventually they will grow too big to be moved, and the only thing to do is to renew the top 2in (5cm) layer of compost.

**Propagation:** Take 4in (10cm) stem tip cuttings in summer for the climbing types. More successful results are achieved by sowing seed of the erect growing types.

**Autumn and winter:** While philodendrons like warmth during active growth lower temperatures are needed to encourage the plant to rest; in the range 60–65 deg F (16–18 deg C) is ideal. However, they will tolerate a temperature of 55 deg F (13 deg C), but no lower. Keep plants in a slightly shady spot out of direct sunlight. Water occasionally, say once a week, to prevent the compost from drying out completely. Philodendrons do not need feeding when they are resting.

## Pilea cadierei

Aluminium Plant
Foliage   Vietnam

These beautifully coloured and patterned small plants make a splendid display of dense foliage and are cheap to buy. *P. cadierei* has dark green oval leaves with a silvery quilted effect. It usually grows no more than 10in (25cm), but then, losing its lower leaves, becomes leggy and straggly. There is a cultivar *P.c.* 'Nana' with smaller leaves which grows to around 6in (15cm). *P. spruceana*, the friendship plant, has rounded leaves with bronzy red markings and purple undersides.

*Pilea cadierei*

# Plumbago capensis

Cape Leadwort
Flowering climber    South Africa

*P. capensis* (syn. *P. auriculata*) has
straggly stems, up to 4ft (1.2m) long,
and they need support; they probably
look their best when trained round a
hoop. The oval green leaves are about
2in (5cm) long. Clusters of pale blue
flowers with five petals appear from
spring until autumn. *P.c.* 'Alba' has
white flowers and mixtures of the two
forms in the same pot look
particularly attractive.

## The year's care

**Spring and summer:** Plants do
better between 50–55 deg F (10–13
deg C), but they will adjust to higher
temperatures. Plumbagos need very
bright light and direct sunlight if they
are to go on flowering and not
become even more straggly than they
naturally are. Water frequently,
always keeping the compost moist.
Feed every two weeks. Plants should
be pruned every year in spring,

*Plumbago capensis*

## The year's care

**Spring and summer:** The plant
should be in a temperature between
55–65 deg F (13–18 deg C). It needs
bright light to maintain the brilliant
colouring, but must not be exposed to
direct sunlight. Water frequently to
keep the compost moist, not soaking
wet. Feed every two weeks. Pileas are
self-branching, but can be induced to
grow more bushy by pinching out the
growing tips. However, after about 18
months they will nonetheless become
straggly.

**Potting-on:** As plants become leggy
they are not worth keeping, so neither
potting-on nor repotting is necessary.

**Propagation:** A plant nearing the
end of its attractive life should be
propagated by taking tip cuttings in
late spring and summer. Use either a
loam or peat-based compost.

**Autumn and winter:** The ideal
range of temperature is the same as
that for spring and summer – 55–65
deg F (13–18 deg C) – but the plant
will stand a temperature down to 50
deg F (10 deg C). Keep it in a shaded
spot. Water occasionally to prevent
the compost from drying out
completely. Do not feed.

*Raphis excelsa*

**Potting-on:** When young and small the palm should be potted-on every year in spring, using two parts of peat compost to one part of sand. As it matures it will need potting-on only every other year, until it is too big to move.

**Propagation:** By sowing seed in spring, but considerable bottom heat – 75 deg F (24 deg C) – is required, as well as your patience for a long time until the plant reaches a reasonable size.

**Autumn and winter:** Give the palm a resting period with a temperature no higher than 55 deg F (13 deg C); it will tolerate a temperature as low as 45 deg F (7 deg C). Place the pot in a bright light and some weak winter sun will do no harm. Water occasionally to keep the compost just moist. It should not be fed.

cutting back to a third of their size. Flowers are produced only on new growth, not on the previous year's, so pruning is vital.

**Potting-on:** In early spring every year, in a loam-based compost.

**Propagation:** In early summer, by taking stem cuttings. They should be about 4in (10cm) long.

**Autumn and winter:** A resting period with a temperature not below 50 deg F (10 deg C) is necessary for a good show of flowers the following year. The plants need bright light with as much winter sun as possible. Water occasionally to prevent the compost from drying out. Do not feed.

# Raphis excelsa

Little Lady Palm
Palm   China and Japan

*Raphis excelsa* is a slow growing, reasonably compact palm, eventually reaching about 5ft (1.5m). The fan-shaped leaves, carried on 9in (22.5cm) stems, are divided into several segments, about 8in (20cm) long. As the plant matures the segments become more pronounced. *R. humilis* is similar in appearance, but will grow to about 7ft (2.1m) and the leaves are divided into many more segments which are narrower and a little longer than those of *R. excelsa*.

**The year's care**

**Spring and summer:** A Raphis palm will do best if the temperature is about 65 deg F (18 deg C). It needs a bright light, but shaded from direct sunlight. Water frequently to keep the compost always moist. In very warm weather spray the leaves daily. Feed only once a month. This palm is prone to attacks from red spider mites and scale insects; watch out.

# Rhoeo spathacea

Boat Lily
Foliage   Mexico

The lance-shaped leaves of *R. spathacea* grow in rosette formation from a central stem which becomes more apparent when the lower leaves die down. The leaves, up to 12in (30cm) long are olive green on the upper surface and purple underneath; fortunately both sides can be seen

*Rhoeo spathacea*

because the leaves grow erect. At the base of the leaves purple, boat-shaped bracts appear, bearing clusters of white flowers from late spring to summer. The flowers do not last long but the vivid bracts will show colour for many months. There is a variegated form *R.s.* 'Vittata' which is even more striking because the upper surface of the leaves is striped with yellow.

### The year's care

**Spring and summer:** Temperatures around 60 deg F (16 deg C) are suitable, but the rhoeo will adjust to higher summer temperatures. On warm dry days it should be sprayed or the pot can be stood on a tray of wet pebbles to increase humidity. The plant, while needing a bright light, should be shaded from direct sunlight. Water often to keep the compost moist. Feed every two weeks.

**Potting-on:** Rhoeos do not make much root growth so potting-on will be necessary only every two years. In alternate years repot into new compost into the same size of pot, after gently removing the old compost from around the roots, not disturbing them too much. Use either a loam or peat-based compost.

**Propagation:** When repotting, by removing offsets produced from the base of the plant. Take care that you remove them with enough roots to sustain them.

**Autumn and winter:** The rhoeo will not tolerate a temperature below 50 deg F (10 deg C) and a somewhat higher temperature is desirable. Keep the plant in a well-lit position to maintain its high colour. Water occasionally to prevent the compost from drying out completely. Do not feed.

# Rhoicissus capensis

Cape Grape
Evergreen climber    South Africa

This easy-to-grow vine will need support for its tendrils to cling to. It will quickly grow to 6ft (1.8m) but it can be cut back to keep it in check with no ill effect. The woody stems carry rounded glossy bright green leaves up to 6in (15cm) across.

*Rhoicissus capensis*

### The year's care

**Spring and summer:** Temperatures in the range 55–65 deg F (13–18 deg C) are ideal. *R. capensis* requires good light, but not direct sunlight which tends to burn the leaves and make them fall. Water frequently to keep the compost moist. Feed every two weeks. If the plant starts to get out of hand cut back the stems as much as you want. New growth will soon appear from the cut stems.

**Potting-on:** In spring every year, using a loam-based compost.

**Propagation:** In summer, by taking stem tip cuttings about 4in (10cm) long.

**Autumn and winter:** Give *R. capensis* a rest period at 50 deg F (10 deg C), but keep it in a well-lit place. It will tolerate a higher temperature, but it will thrive better for having had a rest. If kept at a low temperature it needs watering only occasionally to prevent the compost from drying out. The higher the temperature the more water it will need and the better the

light must be if the plant is not to become etiolated. It does not need feeding.

# Sansevieria trifasciata
## 'Laurentii'

Mother-in-law's Tongue
Succulent    West Africa

This succulent is tough, virtually indestructible and often neglected – and shows it. With a little attention it will stop looking dowdy. *S.t.* 'Laurentii' throws up its narrow sword-like leaves from a rhizome and, depending on how well the plant is looked after, they will grow to 18in (45cm) or more. They are mid green with darker horizontal wavy bands and yellow edges. In contrast, *S.* 'Hahnii' forms a low growing rosette of triangular-shaped leaves up to 4in (10cm) long, mid green with darker horizontal bands. There are variegated forms, one – *S.* 'Golden Hahnii' – having yellow edged and striped leaves. Sansevierias do produce unnoteworthy yellowish flowers carried on long stems, but seldom indoors.

### The year's care

**Spring and summer:** Sansevierias like warmth – temperatures above 60 deg F (16 deg C). They should be in bright light, including direct sunlight to maintain their markings, although they will grow in slight shade. They grow slowly in any event, but if they are in gloom they will virtually come to a standstill. Watering once a week will probably be enough to keep the compost just moist. If they are watered too much, and the compost becomes soggy and waterlogged, the roots will rot and the leaves will collapse at the point where they join the rhizome. Avoid watering in the centre of the rosette-forming varieties, or they too will rot.

**Potting-on:** Sansevierias do better if their roots are restricted, so pot-on only every two or three years, in spring. The tall growing types will need moving into larger pots not so much because their roots have filled the pot but because they become top heavy and keel over. When replanting these it is better to use a clay pot rather than a light plastic one and the

them in compost, making sure that they are planted bottom end down. New plants will grow, but even if you take cuttings from a variegated plant the new plants will be plain green.

**Autumn and winter:** Temperatures should not fall below 50 deg F (10 deg C) and they are better approaching 60 deg F (16 deg C). Keep the pot in a bright light, with direct sunlight. Water about once a month if the plant is in the cool; a little more frequently in the warmth. Do not feed.

# Saxifraga stolonifera

Mother of Thousands
Foliage    China

From the centre of its rosette of leaves *S. stolonifera* (syn. *S. sarmentosa*) sends out many runners bearing small replicas of itself – an interesting plant for a hanging basket. The rounded, slightly hairy leaves, up to 3in (7.5cm) across, are dark green with silver veins on the top surface and red underneath. The whole plant will be no more than 8in (20cm) in height, but the runners bearing the plantlets can grow to 2ft (60cm). White star-like flowers are produced in clusters in summer. There is a variegated, slower growing form, *S.s.* 'Tricolor', which has leaves edged with cream and tinted pink.

*Sansevieria trifasciata* 'Laurentii'

*Sansevieria* 'Golden Hahnii'

*Saxifraga stolonifera*

heavier loam-based compost rather than peat.

**Propagation:** Either by removing offsets when repotting or from leaf cuttings taken in summer. Divide a leaf into 2in (5cm) sections and plant

## The year's care

**Spring and summer:** This saxifrage does better in a cool temperature – between 50–60 deg F (10–16 deg C). In warm weather the plant should be mist-sprayed frequently. It needs bright light with a little direct sunlight, but not fierce sun. Water frequently to keep the compost always moist. Feed once a month.

**Potting-on:** In spring each year in a loam-based compost.

**Propagation:** Plantlets can be removed from the runners and potted up in summer in a rooting compost. A more reliable method is layering. Pin down the plantlet, still attached to the runner, in a pot of rooting compost. When roots have developed sever it from the parent plant.

**Autumn and winter:** The saxifrage will benefit from a winter rest and will tolerate a temperature as low as 45 deg F (7 deg C). In warm centrally heated rooms it will suffer. Good light is essential, with as much winter sun as possible. Water about once a week to prevent the compost from drying out completely. Do not feed.

# Sedum morganianum

Burro's Tail
Succulent   Mexico

The long fleshy 'tails' of this succulent can grow to 3ft (90cm) and are best displayed from a hanging basket. Each stem is covered with small pale green overlapping leaves which curve inwards. Take care when handling them because they easily break off. Clusters of pink flowers may appear in summer, but usually do not on plants grown indoors. *S. sieboldii* 'Medio-variegatum' has arching stems up to 8in (20cm) long, and the rounded green leaves have red edges and are blotched with yellow. *S. pachyphyllum* is commonly called Jelly Beans because of the pale green capsules, tipped with red, carried on its 12in (30cm) stems. *S. rubrotinctum* is similar in appearance but the stems are only 8in (20cm) long and its capsule-like green leaves turn red if the plant gets enough sunlight.

## The year's care

**Spring and summer:** Sedums will adjust to living in warm or even hot

*Sedum morganianum*

rooms, but they must have good ventilation and bright light with plenty of direct sunlight. They could do well out of doors in full sun. Water frequently to keep the compost always moist, but overwatering will make the leaves go soft. Feed once a month.

**Potting-on:** In spring each year, using a loam-based compost.

**Propagation:** By taking stem cuttings in summer, about 4in (10cm) long. Allow the cuttings to dry out for a few days before potting up.

**Autumn and winter:** Give sedums a rest period in a temperature between 45–50 deg F (7–10 deg C), but keep them in a bright light with as much sun as possible. Water about once a month. Do not feed them when resting.

# Senecio rowleyanus

String of Beads
Succulent   South Africa

*S. rowleyanus* does indeed look like a string of beads – an oddity best seen with its stems trailing over the sides of a hanging basket. The stems, between 2–3ft (60–90cm) long, are covered with green globular leaves, each with a pointed tip. Every leaf has a vertical translucent band through which the plant absorbs sunlight. White and purple fragrant flowers, carried on short stems, appear in early autumn. The stems tend to root on the surface of the compost, forming a thick mat, so if they are grown in a hanging basket they have to be discouraged from doing this and trained over the sides instead.

## The year's care

**Spring and summer:** Temperatures should be in the range 60–65 deg F (16–18 deg C). Senecios need plenty of light and some direct sun, but not hot midday sun. Water frequently to keep the compost always moist. Feed once a month.

**Potting-on:** In spring each year in a mixture of one part sand to two parts of loam-based compost.

**Propagation:** In summer, by taking stem cuttings. For a good display plant several cuttings in a single pot. Plants may also be raised from seed in spring.

*Senecio rowleyanus*

**Autumn and winter:** *S. rowleyanus* needs a resting period at around 50 deg F (10 deg C), but do not allow the temperature to drop much lower or the leaves will fall. Keep the plants in a good light with some weak direct sunlight. Water occasionally; once a month should be enough. Do not feed.

## Solanum capicastrum

Winter Cherry
Flowering shrub   Brazil

The colourful berries of *S. capicastrum* contribute a little cheer to the gloom of winter. The plant grows to about 18in (45cm) and the spread is about the same. There is a main stout stem branching into short stems which are covered with densely packed dark green oval leaves. Small white flowers appear in summer and are followed by green berries, gradually turning yellow and then red. The ripe berries will last for many weeks if the plants are kept cool, with good light. *S. pseudocapsicum*, the Jerusalem Cherry, is similar in form to *S. capicastrum* but is more vigorous. Its berries may be a little larger and last longer, given the right conditions.

### The year's care

**Spring and summer:** Normal room temperatures are fine for these solanums, but they would do better with a good spell outside as long as there is shelter from fierce sun. If they have to stay indoors keep them on a window-sill which does not get the midday sun. Water frequently so that the compost is always moist. When the flowers appear give a light spray now and again to help to set the fruit. Feed every two weeks. In spring when fruiting has finished cut back the plants to a third of their size. When new growth is underway pinch out growing tips to encourage bushiness.

**Potting-on:** In spring each year in a loam-based compost, although indoors it does not last for many years.

**Propagation:** By sowing seed in early spring. Flowers and fruit should appear later the same year.

**Autumn and winter:** Plants which have spent the summer out of doors should be brought indoors again before there is any risk of frost. A resting period temperature of around 50 deg F (10 deg C) is best to make the berries last as long as possible, but the plants will tolerate a temperature up to 60 deg F (16 deg C). While the berries are still on the plant give it what sunlight there is; they fall more quickly in poor light. Water occasionally to keep the compost just moist. Do not feed.

## Sparmannia africana

African Hemp
Evergreen shrub   South Africa

*S. africana* is a fast growing shrub, which will quickly reach 6ft (1.8m), though it can be held in check by hard pruning. It is notable more for its foliage than its flowers; the leaves are large, about 8in (20cm) long, bright green, heart-shaped and hairy and they are carried on short stalks branching from rigid stems. Clusters of white flowers with yellow and purple stamens appear in late spring and early summer. They do not last long, but are produced over a period of weeks.

### The year's care

**Spring and summer:** The plant should be in a temperature between 60–65 deg F (16–18 deg C) and it needs a well-lit, slightly shaded spot if it is to flower. In a poor light the leaf colour tends to fade to yellow, while

*Solanum capicastrum*

*Sparmannia africana*

higher temperature it will, of course, need more frequent watering. Do not feed.

# Tolmiea menziesii

Piggyback Plant
Foliage   North America

*Tolmiea menziesii* is a very hardy, easy-to-grow plant, needing the minimum of attention. Its maximum height is about 12in (30cm), with a similar spread. The fresh bright green leaves, carried on short stalks, are hairy and heart-shaped, some 3in (7.5cm) wide. The novel attraction of this plant is the plantlet which grows on each leaf at the junction with the stalk – explaining the plant's nickname of piggyback. Greenish brown undistinguished flowers may be produced.

## The year's care

**Spring and summer:** The best summer temperature is around 55 deg F (13 deg C) and if it gets hotter a well-ventilated position is desirable

*Tolmiea menziesii*

in direct sunlight the leaves scorch. Water frequently to keep the compost moist at all times. Feed once every two weeks. Pinch out growing tips in spring to encourage bushiness. If the plant gets out of hand cut it down to half its size when flowering has finished.

**Potting-on:** Because sparmannias grow so rapidly a young plant may need potting-on twice in the first year. After that pot-on every year when flowering is over, in a loam-based compost.

**Propagation:** In late spring by taking stem cuttings about 6in (15cm) long.

**Autumn and winter:** Give the plant a rest period at about 50 deg F (10 deg C) if at all possible. It will tolerate a higher temperature, but an enforced rest will encourage sturdy new growth and flowers the following year. Always keep the plant in a bright light, but shaded from direct sunlight. If the light is good all the year round flowers may appear in early winter. Water occasionally to keep the compost just moist when the plant is overwintered at a low temperature. If it has to be kept at a

to diminish possible attacks by red spider mites. Also mist-spray frequently. The plant needs a bright spot, out of direct sunlight. It will grow in shade, but the growth tends to be weak and the foliage pale. Water often to keep the compost always moist. If the plant does not get enough water the leaves will go limp and shrivel. Feed every two weeks.

**Potting-on:** In spring each year in a peat-based compost, but it is best to replace them before they age.

**Propagation:** In spring and summer by removing a leaf with a well-developed plantlet growing from it. Shorten the stem a little, leaving about 2in (5cm) attached to the leaf and insert it in rooting compost. Alternatively, pin down a leaf stalk in compost at the point where the stalk joins the leaf. The plantlet will soon develop roots and when it is well-established sever the leaf stalk from the parent plant.

**Autumn and winter:** Give the plant a rest period at around 50 deg F (10 deg C), but it will adjust to a higher temperature. A well-lit, slightly shaded spot should be provided. Water occasionally to keep the compost just moist. Do not feed.

# Tradescantia fluminensis

Wandering Jew
Trailer   South America

Tradescantias look best in a hanging container, at least if they are not allowed to become unkempt. The trouble is that as the stems get longer they lose their older leaves and grow lanky. These stems then need to be

cut away and replaced by newly rooted cuttings. The decline can be delayed by pinching out the stems when they are about 15in (37.5cm) long, so increasing the bushiness of the plant. *T. fluminensis* has bright green oval leaves, shaded pale purple underneath. There are two popular varieties, *T.f.* 'Quicksilver', the leaves of which are striped green and white, and *T.f.* 'Variegata', with similar colouring but broader stripes. *T. albiflora* 'Tricolor' has green leaves striped with white and purple. *T. blossfeldiana* grows more erect, and in the variety *T.b.* 'Variegata' the leaves are striped with green, cream and purple. All tradescantias produce unremarkable white or pink flowers in spring and summer.

### The year's care

**Spring and summer:** The temperature should be around 65 deg F (18 deg C). A tradescantia requires bright light with some direct but not scorching sun, to maintain the richly variegated foliage. Weak colouring and straggly growth come with poor light. Water frequently to keep the compost moist. If the plant is kept too dry, greenfly are likely to be a problem. Feed every two weeks. Remember to pinch out growing tips to encourage bushiness and cut off any bare stems down to compost level. If any shoots appear with plain green leaves cut those also to compost level or the whole plant may revert to plain green.

**Potting-on:** Every two or three years in spring, in either loam or peat-based compost. It may not be worth while with old plants, and these should be thrown away and a fresh start made with new cuttings.

**Propagation:** By taking cuttings in spring or summer. They can either be planted in compost or rooted in water and then potted up.

**Autumn and winter:** Tradescantias will tolerate temperatures as low as 50 deg F (10 deg C), but keep them in a bright light with some direct sunlight. Water occasionally to keep the compost just moist. Do not feed.

# Vanda cristata

Orchid   Nepal

Even in the hands of a beginner this epiphytic orchid is not too difficult to care for. It grows no more than 12in (30cm) high with opposite pairs of bright green strap-shaped arching leaves, some 6in (15cm) long. On mature plants aerial roots grow from the stem. In early summer flower spikes appear, bearing two or three blooms about 2in (5cm) across. The petals are yellow-green with a white lip, striped and spotted with maroon. They last for several weeks.

### The year's care

**Spring and summer:** *V. cristata* will do all right in normal seasonal temperatures, but in very warm weather it should be sprayed daily, except when in flower. It must have bright light with some direct sun, but should be kept away from fierce midday sun. Water frequently, so that the compost is evenly moist, but not sodden. Feed once a month.

**Potting-on:** Every other year in spring in a mixture of peat, osmunda fibre and sphagnum moss. However, the orchid should be repotted into fresh compost in alternate years.

*Tradescantia fluminensis*

*Tradescantia fluminensis* 'Quicksilver'

*Vanda cristata*

**Propagation:** By removing offsets in spring.

**Autumn and winter:** Give the plant a rest at a temperature between 50–55 deg F (10–13 deg C) to ensure flowering the following season. *V. cristata* will tolerate a drop in temperature to 45 deg F (7 deg C) but if kept at this temperature for any length of time it will stop growing. It still needs bright light and some direct sun. Water only occasionally to prevent the compost from drying out completely. Do not feed in the resting period.

# Yucca aloifolia

Spanish bayonet
Foliage   USA, Mexico, West Indies

Yuccas are dramatic architectural plants which eventually need plenty of room. *Y. aloifolia* grows a thick trunk up to 4ft (1.2m) long, with rosettes of sword-shaped leaves at the top. The leaves, some 2ft (60cm) long, are dark green and edged with fine teeth. *Y. elephantipes* is similar in appearance, but the leaves are without the menacing teeth. Unfortunately, yuccas grown indoors seldom produce the staggering flower spikes, up to 2ft (60cm) long, covered with creamy white flowers.

A fairly recent introduction is the so-called yucca cane plant. These are

*Yucca aloifolia*

grown from stems of the plant – usually *Y. elephantipes* – imported from countries where they grow in the wild. They arrive stripped of leaves and seemingly dead, and they are cut up into various lengths by nurserymen and rooted. The resulting plants are then sold in various heights ranging from 12in (30cm) to 6ft (1.8m) or more. The taller they are the more expensive they become. The stems of the yucca cane plants never grow any taller, so when you buy one you know how tall it is always going to be.

*Yucca cane plant*

## The year's care

**Spring and summer:** Yuccas are happy with a temperature of 55 deg F (13 deg C) and will adjust to normal seasonal temperatures. They need excellent light and direct sunlight, and do better if they can spend summer outdoors, increasing the chances that they will flower. Water frequently to keep the compost moist all the time. Feed every two weeks.

**Potting-on:** In spring every other year, in a mixture of one part sand to two parts of loam-based compost. It may be necessary to move a plant into a larger pot not because the roots have filled the old pot but because the plant is becoming top heavy. It is advisable to use a clay pot, less likely to be overturned.

**Propagation:** In summer by removing offsets which may appear at the base of the plant, or from seed sown in spring. Alternatively if a plant has grown leggy you can produce a do-it-yourself cane plant. Cut up the stem into sections and plant them in rooting compost, making certain that you plant the bottom end down. However, you will have to provide considerable bottom heat of 75 deg F (24 deg C) to induce the stem to root and sprout.

**Autumn and winter:** Give yuccas a rest at between 45–50 deg F (7–10 deg C). They still must have bright light and direct winter sun. Water occasionally to keep the compost just moist. Do not feed.

# Zebrina pendula

Wandering Jew
Trailer   Mexico

*Zebrina pendula* is related to the tradescantia, and is often mistaken for it. One variety, however, is considerably more attractive than a tradescantia – *Z. pendula* 'Quadricolor' – because in addition to the tradescantia-like variegation the undersides of the leaves are purple, very striking when seen from below in a hanging basket. The oval 2in (5cm) leaves are carried on 15in (37.5cm) stems, and the upper surface is green, striped with cream, pink and silver. Puny pink flowers appear in spring and summer. To keep this zebrina in good condition it needs a slightly higher temperature than a tradescantia.

## The year's care

**Spring and summer:** A temperature around 65 deg F (18 deg C) is best. Zebrinas need bright light, with direct sunlight, to preserve the flamboyant colouring. The plants will continue to grow in slightly shaded spots, but the colours will be duller and the growth straggly. On the other hand, keep the plants out of the hot midday sun, which may turn the leaves brown. Water fairly frequently but allow the surface of the compost to dry out before watering again. This treatment seems to heighten leaf colour. Feed every two weeks. Regularly pinch out growing tips to encourage bushiness and remove completely any lanky stems which have few leaves.

**Potting-on:** In spring in a peat-based compost to which a little sand has been added. However, after two years zebrinas are hardly worth keeping. It is better to raise new plants from cuttings.

**Propagation:** By taking stem tip cuttings about 4in (10cm) long. Plant them straight into compost, several to a pot for a bushier display, or root them in water before potting up.

**Autumn and winter:** Do not allow the temperature to fall below 55 deg F (13 deg C) and somewhat higher is better. To maintain the variegations bright light, with some direct sunlight, is even more vital during the short hours of winter daylight. Water only occasionally to keep the compost barely moist. Do not feed.

*Zephyranthes grandiflora*

*Zebrina pendula*

# Zephyranthes grandiflora

Zephyr Lily
Bulb    Central America, West Indies

Although *Z. grandiflora* flowers for a comparatively short period and looks unattractive for the rest of the year it is still a desirable houseplant. The narrow green leaves appear either when the plant is flowering or immediately after the flowers die down. They bloom in late summer and autumn, borne on 8in (20cm) stems, and are pink and funnel-shaped, gradually spreading wide their six petals.

## The year's care

**Spring and summer:** In early spring plant four or five bulbs in a peat based compost. The tips of the bulbs should be level with the surface of the compost. Overwintered and newly planted bulbs should be kept in a temperature of 50 deg F (10 deg C) and in the light. In late spring bring the pots into a warm room but keep them out of direct sunlight. Water occasionally so that the compost is just moist until shoots appear, then water more frequently to make the compost thoroughly moist at all times. Feed every two weeks from the time the shoots appear until flowering is over. When the flowers have finished the foliage should die down, but it may need some encouragement to do so by drastically reducing watering.

**Potting-on:** In early spring each year to replace the old compost with fresh. If you replant the bulbs with their bulblets still attached you will eventually have to replant into a bigger pot. This may be necessary only every three years, for zephyranthes appear to do better if somewhat potbound.

**Propagation:** By removing bulblets, if you wish to, when repotting.

**Autumn and winter:** During their dormant period the bulbs should be kept around 55 deg F (13 deg C) and in a light position. Once the foliage has died down do not water until early spring. No feeding is necessary.

# Difficult plants for cool rooms

The plants in this section of the A–Z, like those in the preceding easy-cool section, need to be in the cool either all the year round or during the resting period, but for one reason or another they are a little more demanding. In general this extra attention is needed in autumn and winter, and for more than half the plants the emphasis then is on ensuring that the plant is kept at the right temperature during the resting period. For some that may mean not letting it fall too low; for example, two desert cacti *Myrtillocactus geometrizans* and *Opuntia microdasys* need higher winter temperatures than most cacti or their stems will grow discoloured.

The other major call for attention is providing as good a light as possible in winter. This is not easy, but moving it nearer to a window is some help.

Exceptionally, there are reminders that a few plants need bountiful watering. These are three carnivorous plants and *Cyperus alternifolius* (Umbrella Plant); in the growing period especially they almost need to be swimming in it.

To identify easily what is the particular attention each plant should receive the relevant sentences are enclosed between arrow heads, thus: ►◄. The 28 entries cover 38 plants.

The entries in this section are listed here according to the type of plant they are.

**Flowering**
*Bougainvillea buttiana*
*Callistemon citrinus*
*Cyclamen persicum*
*Hoya carnosa*
*Rhododendron simsii*
*Stephanotis floribunda*

**Fruiting**
*Ardisia crenata*
*Capsicum annuum*
*Citrus mitis*
*Duchesnea indica*
*Fortunella margarita*

**Foliage**
*Cyperus alternifolius*

**Cacti**
*Aporocactus flagelliformis*
*Cephalocereus senilis*
*Epiphyllum* 'Ackermannii'

*Myrtillocactus geometrizans*
*Opuntia microdasys*
*Rebutia miniscula*
*Rhipsalidopsis gaertneri*
*Schlumbergera truncata*

**Succulent**
*Ceropegia woodii*

**Carnivorous**
*Dionaea muscipula*
*Drosera rotundifolia*
*Sarracenia flavia*

**Fern**
*Adiantum capillus-veneris*

**Orchids**
*Cymbidium* 'Peter Pan'
*Dendrobium nobile*

**Bulb**
*Veltheimia viridifolia*

# Adiantum capillus-veneris

Maidenhair Fern
Fern   Britain, USA

The lace-like foliage of the maidenhair fern needs a humid atmosphere to stay in tip-top condition. Once you have decided on a suitable place for it, it is advisable to let it stay there and not to move it round the room. *A. capillus-veneris* will grow no more than 12in (30cm) high,

*Adiantum cappillus-veneris*

but fronds can reach 2ft (60cm) and when they have grown so long they are best displayed in a hanging basket. The triangular leaflets are carried on black wiry stems. *A. cuneatum* (syn. *A. raddianum*), the delta maidenhair fern from Brazil, grows to about 18in (45cm) with a spread of about 2ft (60cm). The leaflets on the fronds are somewhat coarser than those of *A. capillus-veneris*. *A. tenerum*, the fan maidenhair fern from the West Indies, has one variety 'Farleyense' with fronds up to 3ft (90cm) long, bearing crimped and frilled leaflets.

## The year's care

**Spring and summer:** In general, adiantums do best in the temperature range of 60–65 deg F (16–18 deg C), but *A. capillus-veneris* is at the lower end of that scale. They all need bright light but not direct sunlight, which will cause the leaves to pale and wither. ►A high degree of humidity is vital, especially in hot weather. Place the pot on a tray of wet pebbles or surround it with moist compost. Daily spraying overhead for plants in hanging baskets will help, but the effect is not as long lasting as with the other two methods.◄ Water frequently

*Adiantum cuneatum*

to keep the compost moist at all times. If leaves turn brown, shrivel and fall this suggests lack of water, or of humidity, or both. Feed once every three to four weeks. Any old or damaged fronds should be cut off at compost level. New fronds will soon appear. ►Never leave adiantums in a draught.◄

**Potting-on:** In spring when roots have filled the pot. Use a free-draining mixture of equal parts of peat, loam and sand, or a peat-based compost.

**Propagation:** By division in spring when repotting, but this may spoil the symmetry of the plant and it will take time for it to grow to a rounded shape again. Plants can be raised from the spores on the undersides of the leaves, but this is a complicated process and requires bottom heat of 70 deg F (21 deg C).

**Autumn and winter:** Give the plant a rest at 55 deg F (13 deg C), never falling below 50 deg F (10 deg C). A light but shaded spot is necessary and humidity is just as important in winter as in summer. Water occasionally to keep the compost just moist. Do not let it dry out completely or the plant will shrivel. If by a mishap that should happen cut back all the stems to compost level and spray the stubble daily. New fronds will appear in time. Do not feed the plant when it is resting.

# Aporocactus flagelliformis

Rat's Tail Cactus
Desert Cactus   Mexico

The cascade of stems of the rat's tail cactus look best falling over the side of a hanging container; they grow to 3ft (90cm), and are ½in (1.75cm) in diameter. The stems are green but covered with brown spines which protrude from the areoles along the edges of the twelve or so ribs. The beautiful deep pink tubular flowers appear from varying points on the stems in spring and early summer and last for several days. Even young plants will bloom.

## The year's care

**Spring and summer:** In early spring bring *A. flagelliformis* into a

*Aporocactus flagelliformis*

warm room with a temperature around 65 deg F (18 deg C). ▶Place it in a good light with direct sunlight. If the light is poor flower buds will drop and stems will become weak and spindly.◀ Water frequently to keep the compost moist at all times. Feed once a month.

**Potting-on:** Repot each year when flowering is over, in either a peat-based compost or a mixture of one part of sand to three parts of a loam-based compost. Pot-on only when the roots fill the pot or basket.

**Propagation:** By taking stem tip cuttings about 6in (15cm) long in summer. Leave the cutting to dry out for a few days before potting-up.

**Autumn and winter:** ▶If the plant is to flower the following spring it needs a cool rest period at about 50 deg F (10 deg C), in a good light with direct sun. Do not let the temperature fall below 45 deg F (7 deg C) or flowering will be affected.◀ Water occasionally to prevent the compost from drying out completely. If the cactus is overwatered in winter the stems are likely to rot. Cut away the rotting area and brush over the cut with a fungicide powder. Do not feed.

## Ardisia crenata

Coral Berry
Fruiting    East Indies

*Ardisia crenata* is usually on sale around Christmas when it is covered with bright red berries. To prevent them from falling prematurely the plant has to be kept in a cool, well-lit room. It will grow to about 2ft (60cm), but slowly, producing flowers and fruit even when small. The 6in (15cm) long narrow leaves are a glossy dark green with wavy edges. The berries can last for six months and are followed in summer by small fragrant red flowers. When they fade berries develop, gradually turning red, completing the cycle.

### The year's care

**Spring and summer:** Temperatures should be in the range 55–65 deg F (13–18 deg C). Place the shrub in a light position, but out of direct sun. A period out of doors will do no harm, as long as the plant is shaded. Water frequently to keep the compost always moist, but gradually increase the periods between watering as the resting season approaches. In summer spray the leaves with lukewarm water. Feed every two weeks. If the plant becomes leggy cut back the stems to within 3in (7.5cm) of the compost. New shoots will grow from the cut-down stems.

**Potting-on:** Each year in spring in a loam-based compost, with added leaf

*Ardisia crenata*

mould. The plant is best replaced when it ages.

**Propagation:** From seed sown in spring, but it may be three years before the plants flower and fruit. Cuttings with a heel can be taken in summer, but plants raised from seed will be more vigorous.

**Autumn and winter:** ▶A temperature about 50 deg F (10 deg C) ensures that the berries last as long as possible. With higher temperatures they are likely to drop.◀ Keep the plant in a bright light, but out of direct sun. Berries tend to drop if the atmosphere is too dry and an overhead spray now and again will help to prevent this. Water occasionally so that the compost is just moist. Do not feed.

## Bougainvillea buttiana

Paper Flowers
Flowering    Brazil

Bougainvilleas are not easy to keep looking their best, because they need so much sun as well as warmth in the growing season. Neither the small oval leaves nor the small creamy flowers are particularly interesting; it is for the bracts, like highly coloured tissue paper, that the plant is grown. They appear, enveloping the flowers, between early spring and early autumn, in a multitude of colours according to the varieties – white, yellow, pink, red, orange and purple – and they last for many weeks. Many hybrids have been developed, the most popular from *B. buttiana*, which has bright crimson bracts. *B.b.* 'Kiltie Campbell' has orange bracts, and *B.b.* 'Mrs Butt', also known as 'Crimson Lake', has rose-crimson bracts. These hybrids have been bred for compactness and should stay a manageable size of about 18–24in (45–60cm). *B. glabra*, on the other hand, is a great climber and can reach 10ft (3m). Its leaves are bright green with masses of deep purple bracts surrounding yellow flowers. *B.g.* 'Variegata' has leaves edged with white or cream.

### The year's care

**Spring and summer:** Bougainvilleas will be happy with normal seasonal temperatures. ▶They need good light, with as much direct sun as they can

*Callistemon citrinus*

*Bougainvillea buttiana*

get, or there will be few flowers or none at all. The leaves also fall in poor light.◄ To prevent the plant from sprawling all over the place it is best to train the branches round a hoop of plastic-coated wire. Push both ends of a piece of wire into the compost and thread the stems round the hoop, tying them to it if necessary. Water frequently but allow the compost to become fairly dry before watering again. Feed every two weeks.

**Potting-on:** Each spring in a loam-based compost, until an 8in (20cm) pot is reached.

**Propagation:** From cuttings, 4–6in (10–15cm) long, taken in the spring, but bottom heat of about 75 deg F (24 deg C) is required.

**Autumn and winter:** A bougainvillea should have a rest period with a temperature around 55 deg F (13 deg C). If it falls below 50 deg F (10 deg C) the plant is likely to lose its leaves. ►A well-lit spot with as much winter sun as possible is essential.◄ Water occasionally to keep the compost just moist. Do not feed.

To induce bushiness prune the plant in late winter. Prune the main stems by a third, making cuts just above a leaf. Then cut back all remaining side shoots to within 1in (2.5cm) of the main stems.

## Callistemon citrinus

Bottle Brush
Flowering   Australia

The attraction of *C. citrinus* is in its novel flowers, similar in shape to bottle brushes, but unless the plant has cool winter conditions flowering will be poor. The stems of the plant, which can grow to 6ft (1.8m), are covered with silky hair but that wears off as they mature. The tight clusters of long narrow leaves, up to 3in (7.5cm) long, are a copper colour when young, turning bright green as they develop fully. The flowers, from early to late summer, are carried on 6in (15cm) stems. They have no petals, but large tufts of bright red filament-like stamens tipped with yellow. The cultivar *C.c.* 'Splendens' is probably the best form.

### The year's care

**Spring and summer:** The ideal temperature is between 60–65 deg F (16–18 deg C). ►A callistemon must have good light and some direct sun.◄ When flowering has finished the plant should be placed out of doors in good sunlight, but must be brought indoors before there is any danger of evening ground frosts. Water frequently so that the compost is always moist. Feed every two weeks. When flowering has finished cut back the foliage by about half to keep the plant in good shape and under control.

**Potting-on:** Every spring in loam-based compost. In time when the plant has been potted on to a 10in (25cm) pot stop repotting and instead remove the top 3in (7.5cm) of compost and replace it with fresh compost.

**Propagation:** In spring from stem cuttings taken with a heel – that is, a cutting with some of the old hard stem from which it was taken. Cuttings should be about 4in (10cm) long; avoid any with flowers.

**Autumn and winter:** ►A rest period with temperatures between 45–50 deg F (7–10 deg C) is essential to ensure good flowering the following year. The plant must also have good light with as much winter sun as possible.◄ Water occasionally to keep the compost barely moist. Do not feed.

*Capsicum annuum*

## Capsicum annuum

Chili Pepper
Fruiting    South America

Capsicums are perennial plants treated as annuals because it is difficult to make them fruit the second year. Nevertheless they are worth growing for their brightly coloured red and green fruits. Most of the ornamental peppers are a compact and bushy 9in (22.5cm), but some can reach a height of 18in (45cm). The 2in (5cm) lance-shaped leaves are carried on branches from the main woody stem. White flowers appear from early summer to early autumn, but most plants are sold late in the year when the fruits have already appeared. Various cultivars bear different shaped multi-coloured fruit. The tomato or cherry-shaped fruits are bright red, about 1in (2.5cm) in diameter. The long pointed cone-like fruits, up to 2in (5cm) long, change colour from green to yellow to orange and finally red. Another hybrid forms clusters of pointed red fingers up to 3in (7.5cm) long, and they may also change colour as they mature.

### The year's care

**Spring and summer:** Temperatures in the range 55–65 deg F (13–18 deg C) are best. Plants need good light and direct sun, but they should be protected from fierce sun. Regular overhead spraying will increase humidity. Alternatively plants can be placed on a tray of wet pebbles or surrounded with moist peat. A dry atmosphere encourages red spider mites and aphids. Water frequently to keep the compost always moist; if it dries out the leaves will turn yellow. Feed once a week when the flowers appear, and stop feeding when the fruit begins to form.

**Potting-on:** Not necessary, as the plant is usually discarded after fruiting.

**Propagation:** From seed sown in spring, with the temperature kept at an even 65 deg F (18 deg C).

**Autumn and winter:** ►The problem is to find a place cool and light enough to ensure that the fruit does not fall prematurely. That means a temperature between 55–60 deg F (13–16 deg C), and nearer 55 deg F (13 deg C) is better. Good light is especially important in the short hours of winter daylight. In poor light the fruit drops at an alarming rate.◄ Water occasionally to keep the compost just moist. Do not feed.

## Cephalocereus senilis

Old Man Cactus
Desert cactus    Mexico

The single fleshy columnar stem of *C. senilis*, unlikely to grow more than 12in (30cm) high, is covered with fine hairs up to 5in (12.5cm) long which grow from the areoles. Take care when handling the plant since the hairs conceal short spines which also grow from the areoles. As the plant matures the hair changes colour from silvery white to dull grey and the column starts balding from the base upwards. By this time its attractiveness and novelty are rapidly dwindling. In the wild *C. senilis* will produce white flowers but only when it has reached the considerable height of about 18ft (5.4m). It will not flower indoors. ►Hairs may become matted with dirt and grease. They can be washed with soapy water, and then with clear water to rinse away all traces of soap. Then comb out the hairs. Washing should be tackled only on warm days. A less harsh, but

*Cephalocereus senilis*

effective treatment is to give the hairs a regular gentle brush with a very soft brush so that the dirt does not accumulate.◄

## The year's care

**Spring and summer:** *C. senilis* will adjust to normal room temperatures and great heat will do no harm. ►The cactus should be in good light with full sun.◄ Water frequently so that the compost is always moist, but not soaking wet. Feed every two weeks. ►Pests such as red spider mites and mealy bugs hide in the long hairs, but regular brushing should reveal whether anything has taken up residence there.◄

**Potting-on:** When young the old man cactus should be potted-on each spring in either a loam-based or peat-based compost to which a third part of sand has been added to make the mixture more porous. As the plant matures less frequent potting-on is necessary. Tap the compost ball out of the pot and if the roots fill it, pot-on.

**Propagation:** From seed sown in spring, a simple operation.

**Autumn and winter:** The plant should have a rest period at about 50 deg F (10 deg C), but do not let the temperature fall below 45 deg F (7 deg C). ►It must have a good light with direct sun, otherwise the stem tends to elongate.◄ Keep it out of draughts. Water very occasionally, about once a month. If the plant is overwintered at low temperatures, as it should be, but then given too much water, it is likely to rot. Do not feed.

## Ceropegia woodii

String of Hearts, Heart Vine
Succulent   South Africa

*C. woodii* is one of the more unusual looking succulents and one of the few succulent trailers, suitable for a hanging container. It is a tuberous rooted plant and the woody tuber is often partly exposed through the surface of the compost. From this tuber the thin trailing purple stems emerge and grow to some 3ft (90cm). Pairs of fleshy, heart-shaped leaves are carried along the stem at intervals of about 3in (7.5cm). The grey-green leaves are marked with silvery grey on the upper surface and purple

*Ceropegia woodii*

underneath. Small purple lantern-shaped flowers, about 1in (2.5cm) long, appear in summer and last through to autumn.

## The year's care

**Spring and summer:** *C. woodii* adjusts to the usual seasonal temperatures. ►Good light is necessary; if there is not enough, leaf colour will be affected and the intervals between the pairs of leaves will get wider. The best place for the plant is in a hanging basket in a window where it can get direct, but not scorching, sunlight each day.◄ Water occasionally so that the compost is just moist. At no stage should it become waterlogged. Feed once a month.

**Potting-on:** When young in spring each year in a loam-based compost with the addition of coarse sand. Later they will not need to be potted-on, merely repotted. Repot the tuber with its upper surface exposed above the level of the compost.

**Propagation:** In spring detach the small tubers which grow on the trailing stems. It is better to cut off a piece of stem along with the tuber to avoid damaging it. Roots may take up to three months to develop.

**Autumn and winter:**
►Temperatures should be low but never below 45 deg F (7 deg C) and a little warmer is better. If the plant is not given a rest at these low temperatures it will begin to grow straggly and unattractive. Good light with direct sun is also essential.◄ Water about once a month to prevent the compost from drying out too much. Do not feed.

## Citrus mitis

Calamondin Orange
Fruiting   Philippines

The appeal of *Citrus mitis* is in the flowers and orange fruits which are produced by even young small shrubs. The Calamondin Orange will rarely grow to more than 3ft (90cm) and growth is very slow. It is a much branching shrub with glossy oval leaves about 3in (7.5cm) long. The fragrant white flowers usually appear in summer, but the plant can flower off and on throughout the year. When flowering is over the small fruits, about 1in (2.5cm) in diameter, take over, at first green but becoming orange. The fruit takes a considerable time to ripen and once ripe it will stay on the bush for many months.

## The year's care

**Spring and summer:** The temperature should be about 65 deg F (18 deg C) and the plant should be in a well-ventilated spot. ►Bright light

*Citrus mitis*

with direct sun is vital and plants will do better if they spend the summer out of doors. For fruit to develop the flowers need to be pollinated, and this will be done by insects if the plant spends the summer outside. Indoors pollinate by drawing a fine soft brush over the blooms.◄ Pinch out growing tips for bushy growth and lightly prune to maintain good shape. Water fairly frequently to keep the compost moist, especially when the fruit is developing. Overhead spraying of the plants when in flower will help the fruit to set. Feed every two weeks.

**Potting-on:** Since they are slow growing, pot-on every other year in spring in a loam-based compost with some added bone meal.

**Propagation:** In spring, by sowing seed, or taking cuttings about 4in (10cm) long. Bottom heat of 70–75 deg F (21–24 deg C) is necessary to germinate seed and for cuttings to strike.

**Autumn and winter:** The ideal temperature is around 55 deg F (13 deg C) and should not fall below 50 deg F (10 deg C). If the atmosphere is too dry red spider mites will be encouraged. Either spray the plant regularly or stand the pot on a tray of wet pebbles or surround it with moist peat. ►Good light and direct sun are even more important at this time of the year.◄ Water very occasionally to keep the compost barely moist. Do not feed.

# Cyclamen persicum

Flowering   Eastern Mediterranean

Cyclamen are often believed to be too difficult to keep throughout the year and are thrown away after flowering, but with a little care, corms will last for several years. Heart-shaped light or dark green leaves marbled with silver grow on short stems. The flowers, shaped like shuttlecocks and appearing from autumn until late winter, are carried on 8in (20cm) stalks. There are many cultivars, giving a range of flower colour from white to pink and deep red. Cyclamen are usually on sale immediately before Christmas and many are given as presents. While it is only natural for the recipient to want to enjoy and show off the gift, the warmth of a centrally heated room spells death for

*Cyclamen persicum*

the plant. The leaves turn yellow and buds drop. Cyclamen need to be kept cool, with only limited watering.

### The year's care

**Spring and summer:** ►The ideal temperature range is between 45–55 deg F (7–13 deg C).◄ The plant needs bright light but not direct sunlight. When flowering is over in late winter it will continue to produce new leaves to build up the strength of the corm for the next season's flowering. ►Water the compost occasionally to keep it just moist. When the plant stops producing new leaves reduce further the frequency of watering. The leaves will eventually turn yellow and watering should then be stopped altogether. As the leaves and stems die remove them cleanly from the corm; any small bits of the stem left behind may cause the corm to rot. Put the corm away, still in its pot of dry compost, in a cool dark place. In summer bring out to a light position,

but out of direct sunlight, and water it a little. Increase the frequency of watering as the leaves start to appear, keeping the compost just moist – if too wet the corm will rot. Never water directly on to the corm, for that, too, will cause rotting.◄ Feed every two weeks after new growth has begun.

**Potting-on:** Every year in late summer, using a peat-based compost. The corm should be planted to show just above the surface of the compost.

**Propagation:** By sowing seed in autumn or spring.

**Autumn and winter:** ►Cyclamen need temperatures between only 45–55 deg F (7–13 deg C) during this period, otherwise leaves will yellow and buds and flowers drop.◄ The plant should be in bright light, but not direct sunlight. A humid atmosphere helps; either stand the pot on a tray of wet pebbles or surround it with moist peat. Do not spray a plant that is flowering, for that will mark the petals. ►Water occasionally

*Cymbidium* 'Peter Pan'

to keep the compost just moist. Do not water directly on to the corm. The safe method of watering is to immerse the pot in a bowl of shallow water. Never leave the pot standing in water in its saucer.◄ Continue to feed the plant every two weeks until flowering is over.

# Cymbidium 'Peter Pan'

Orchid   India and South-East Asia

A staggering show of these long lasting flowers is not beyond anyone as long as the plant can be kept cool. 'Peter Pan' is a hybrid, with narrow, bright green, pointed leaves, and it will grow no higher than about 15in (37.5cm). Each flower stem bears as many as a dozen flowers – greenish yellow with a deep crimson lip and about 3in (7.5cm) across – in late spring and early summer.

### The year's care

**Spring and summer:** ►Daytime temperatures should be between 60–65 deg F (16–18 C) and at night down to 50 deg F (10 deg C).◄ The orchid needs good light but should be shaded from direct sunlight. It also does better in a humid atmosphere. Stand the pot on a tray of wet pebbles or surround it with moist peat. Frequent overhead spraying helps. If possible give the plant a spell outdoors in summer, but out of the direct sun.

Water frequently to keep the compost moist, but not allowing it to become sodden – a sure way to rot the pseudo-bulb. The immersion method of standing the pot for a time in a bowl of shallow water is the best. Feed every two weeks.

**Potting-on:** Every other year in spring, in a mixture of peat, osmunda fibre and sphagnum moss.

**Propagation:** By detaching pseudo-bulbs with roots attached when replanting.

**Autumn and winter:** ►The plant should be given a rest at temperatures between 50–55 deg F (10–13 deg C) with a night temperature as low as 45 deg F (7 deg C).◄ A bright spot out of direct sun is needed. Continue to provide a humid atmosphere. Water only occasionally to prevent the compost from drying out completely. Do not feed.

# Cyperus alternifolius

Umbrella Plant
Foliage   Madagascar

*C. alternifolius* is a marsh plant found growing by the water's edge and is one of the few plants which perpetually needs to stand in water. The thin stalks of this sedge, about 4ft (1.2m) tall, carry loose rosettes of up to a dozen green, arching, leaflike bracts. Brownish green unexciting flowers appear from the centre of the

*Cyperus alternifolius*

rosette in summer. *C.a.* 'Variegatus' has green leaves striped with white. *C.a.* 'Gracilis', the dwarf umbrella plant, is much smaller – about 18in (45cm). The umbrella head of *C. diffusus* has many more bracts and the stems grow to about 15in (37.5cm).

### The year's care

**Spring and summer:** Temperatures should be between 55–65 deg F (13–18 deg C). An umbrella plant needs bright light, but is best shaded from direct sun. *C.a.* 'Variegatus' must have excellent light always to maintain its variegation. ►This plant can never be overwatered. Place the pot in a container with about 1in (2.5cm) of water in the bottom, topping it up to keep it around that level. If the compost is too dry the tips of the bracts will brown. If it is allowed to dry out completely the umbrellas turn yellow and wither within a day. If this should happen cut down all the stems to compost level, thoroughly soak the compost and new growth will soon appear, unless the roots themselves have been killed through the lack of water.◄ Feed every two weeks.

**Potting-on:** Every spring, using a loam-based compost.

**Propagation:** The easiest method is to divide the plant when repotting. Seed can be sown in spring, but it is slow to germinate.

**Autumn and winter:** In the rest period the temperature should be between 50–55 deg F (10–13 deg C). Keep the plant in a slightly shaded position. ►Make sure that the compost is always thoroughly moist, topping up the water in the container regularly.◄ Do not feed.

# Dendrobium nobile

Orchid   India

This is one of the most popular dendrobiums and is comparatively easy to look after as long as it can be kept warm in the spring and summer growing period and cool during the winter rest. The bamboo-like stems, which grow to 3ft (90cm), are in fact the pseudo-bulbs, and near the top of each one there appear in autumn narrow strap-shaped leaves, about 5in (12.5cm) long. In late winter the leaves begin to fall – an indication

*Dendrobium nobile*

that the pseudo-bulb is about to flower. The pink to purple flowers about 3in (7.5cm) across, have pale yellow tips with a maroon blotch in the centre.

### The year's care

**Spring and summer:**
▶Temperatures must be in the range 70–75 deg F (21–24 deg C).◀ *D. nobile* needs bright light, but shade from direct sun. When the leaves begin to fall and flower buds appear, frequent watering will be needed, but allow the compost almost to dry out between waterings. During hot weather spray the plant frequently; if the air is too dry red spider mites will be encouraged. Feed once a month. Cut away browning, dead pseudo-bulbs.

**Potting-on:** A dendrobium prefers to be somewhat potbound, so potting-on will be necessary only every three years, and should be done when flowering is over. However, repot each year to renew the compost, using a mixture of peat, osmunda fibre and sphagnum moss.

**Propagation:** By division when repotting, but make sure that each section of rhizome has about five pseudo-bulbs and that some of them have not already produced leaves.

**Autumn and winter:** ▶*D. nobile* must have a rest period if it is to flower successfully the following season. Temperatures should be between 50–55 deg F (10–13 deg C) and the plant can stand temperatures down to 45 deg F (7 deg C).◀ A bright light is necessary, but not

direct sunlight. Water very occasionally so that compost is barely moist. The resting plant must not be fed.

## Dionaea muscipula

Venus Fly Trap
Carnivorous    North and South Carolina

The bog plant *D. muscipula* is the most readily available carnivorous plant, and the way in which it traps and devours insects is a constant source of fascination, especially to children. The bright green triangular leaves, up to 2in (5cm), are carried in rosette formation, rising straight from the surface of the compost. On the end of each stem is a hinged trap, with teeth along the edges. These overlap when the trap shuts. The inside of the trap is bright red and the insects are attracted both by the colour and by the scent of the nectar at the base of the teeth. When an insect alights on the inside of the trap it touches the three trigger hairs on each of the lobes, and the trap snaps shut. Enzymes produced by the plant soften the insect's body and make it easy to digest. A few days later the trap opens, revealing the skeleton of the insect. It is not necessary to 'feed' the plant with insects or morsels of meat; it will catch its own. The temptation to fool the plant and trigger off the trap should be resisted because it weakens the plant. Clusters of white flowers appear in summer.

### The year's care

**Spring and summer:** Temperatures should be in the range 50–55 deg F (10–13 deg C). The plant needs bright light with direct sun and it does best on a sunny window-sill.

*Dionaea muscipula*

▶Water very frequently so that the compost is always moist. Pots can stand in saucers of water, kept topped up so that there is always a constant supply of moisture. This also provides the much-needed humidity. Use soft water, either rainwater or distilled water.◀ If the plant is catching insects it is not necessary to give it a liquid fertiliser feed. But if growth is poor a weak liquid feed can be given once a month.

**Potting-on:** Only every two to three years in spring, using a mixture of peat, sand and sphagnum moss.

**Propagation:** By dividing plants in spring or by sowing seed.

**Autumn and winter:** ▶The plant must have a rest period at temperatures between 45–50 deg F (8–10 deg C) if it is to flower in summer. Keep it on a bright sunny window-sill. Water frequently so that the compost is always moist, but during the resting period do not leave the pot standing in water. Press the surface of the compost with a finger and if moisture appears the compost is too wet. Allow it to dry before watering again.◀ Do not feed.

## Drosera rotundifolia

Sundew

Carnivorous    Europe, North America

The droseras trap their insect food in a sticky substance, which glistens in the sun, attracting the unsuspecting victim. The leaf stalks, about 1in (2.5cm) long are in the form of a rosette, radiating outwards like the spokes of a wheel. The rounded leaves, ½in (1.75cm) across, are covered with reddish hairs and these secrete the sticky substance at their tips. Once an insect alights on the leaf it is stuck, and its struggles to free itself bring into action other hairs nearby, which secure the insect firmly. The tips of the hairs then secrete the enzymes which digest the insect's body, leaving behind its skeleton. White flowers borne on stalks 2–5in (5–12cm) long are produced from the centre of the rosette in summer.

### The year's care

**Spring and summer:** *D. rotundifolia* requires a temperature between 50–55 deg F (10–13 deg C). The plant

*Drosera rotundifolia*

*Duchesnea indica*

should be placed in good light with direct sunlight; a window-sill is ideal. ▸Water frequently to keep the compost moist and place the pot in a saucer of water, which should be kept topped up. Use either rainwater or distilled water.◂ Do not feed the plant with insects; if there are any about it can catch its own. A weak liquid feed can be applied to the compost once a month, but there is a danger of overfeeding, which might lead to the death of the plant.

**Potting-on:** Only every two or three years in spring, using a mixture of peat, sand and sphagnum moss.

**Propagation:** By dividing plants in spring or by sowing seed.

**Autumn and winter:** ▸Plants should have a rest at temperatures between 45–50 deg F (8–10 deg C) for successful flowering the following summer.◂ In autumn the plant will put out closely packed new growth, which will remain in a state of suspension during the resting period. The old leaves die down leaving the new clump from which growth will appear the following year. The plant requires bright sunny light. ▸Water frequently to keep the compost always moist, but not waterlogged. During this period do not leave the pot standing in water.◂ Do not feed.

## Duchesnea indica

Indian Strawberry
Fruiting   India

*D. indica* is a vigorously growing trailer, or it can be trained as a climber. The stems, 2ft (60cm)

or more long, carry groups of three heart-shaped leaves along their length. From early summer to early autumn bright yellow flowers appear, followed by red fruits very similar in appearance to strawberries. They can be eaten, but they have no taste.

### The year's care

**Spring and summer:** ▸The Indian strawberry needs cool conditions during this period – around 55 deg F (13 deg C), although it will tolerate rather more warmth.◂ In warm weather the foliage should be sprayed frequently. The plant needs bright light, but not direct sun. Water frequently so that the plant is always moist. Feed every two weeks.

**Potting-on:** In spring each year in a loam-based compost. When the plant becomes straggly it is better to propagate it and to discard the old one.

**Propagation:** Either by dividing when replanting or, more successfully, by layering the runners. Pin down the stems, still attached to the parent, in compost. When roots have developed the runners can be severed from the parent plant.

**Autumn and winter:** ▸Cool conditions are vital if the plant is to flower and fruit in the following

season. The ideal temperature is about 45 deg F (7 deg C), but make sure that the plant is not exposed to frost.◂ In the resting period it still needs bright light, but not direct sun. Water occasionally so that the compost is barely moist. Do not feed.

## Epiphyllum
'Ackermannii'

Orchid Cactus
Jungle cactus   Central America

Most cacti grown indoors are from the desert, but the epiphyllums originate in jungle areas where they grow on trees. *E.* 'Ackermannii' is a hybrid with flattened stems which reach 2–3ft (60–90cm). At this length they will need some support or they can hang over the sides of the pot. The stems grow in clumps from compost level and have tiny bristles from the areoles. Large red blooms, perhaps 3in (7.5cm) across, appear in late spring from the upper areoles of the stems. On *E.* 'Cooperi' the white to yellow flowers grow from the base of the stems, and open at night.

### The year's care

**Spring and summer:** ▸Epiphyllums need warmth, between 65–70 deg F (18–21 deg C).◂ They also need good

*Epiphyllum* 'Ackermannii'

*Fortunella margarita*

light, with shade from direct sun, and they will do better if they are put outdoors in summer. In early spring flower buds will begin to appear, and while the plant remains in bud do not move the pot to a new position or the buds may fall. Water frequently from the time when the first buds appear, so that the compost is always moist. If it gets dry the buds are likely to drop, as they will if the cactus is left in a draught. Give a weak liquid feed once a month after the appearance of buds.

**Potting-on:** When flowering has finished in a porous loam-based compost, with added sand. The plant will do better if potbound and once it has been potted-on to a 6in (15cm) pot change the compost each year, but do not transfer the cactus to a larger pot.

**Propagation:** By taking cuttings 5in (12.5cm) long in summer. Leave them to dry out for a day or two before potting up. For a good display plant several in a pot.

**Autumn and winter:** ►A cool resting period is most important if the epiphyllum is to flower. The temperature should be between 45–50 deg F (7–10 deg C).◄ The cactus will

still require good light, but not direct sun. Water only occasionally, so that the compost does not dry out altogether. If stems become soft and shrivel it is getting too little water. Do not feed.

## Fortunella margarita

Kumquat
Fruiting   China

As with other fruiting plants, *F. margarita* will be shy to flower and fruit unless it has a cool winter rest. Indoors the kumquat will grow to a height of about 4ft (1.2m), putting out many branches of glossy green leaves up to 3in (7.5cm) long. Small, fragrant white flowers show in summer and are followed by fruits in autumn and winter. They ripen gradually to dark orange and will last for a few weeks before they fall.

### The year's care

**Spring and summer:** During this period the plant will be happy in normal seasonal temperatures, although very warm dry periods may attract red spider mites and scale. Keep the plant in a well-ventilated,

bright spot with direct sun. If it can go out of doors so much the better. Water frequently, but do not make the compost waterlogged. Spray the plant daily when flowers appear to help the fruit to set. Feed every two weeks.

**Potting-on:** Each year in spring in a loam-based compost to which leaf mould has been added.

**Propagation:** Seeds taken straight from the fruit and planted in seed compost should germinate readily. Cuttings, about 4in (10cm) long, can be taken in summer.

**Autumn and winter:** ►Give the plant a rest at a temperature around 55 deg F (13 deg C), but it should not fall below 50 deg F (10 deg C).◄ Continue to keep the plant in a bright position with as much winter sun as possible. Water occasionally to prevent the compost from drying out completely. Do not feed.

## Hoya carnosa

Wax Plant
Flowering   Australia

*H. carnosa* grows vigorously, putting out up to 18in (45cm) growth each year. However, flowers do not usually appear until the stems are about 3ft (90cm) or more long. Rather than having this rampant growth sprawling all over the place it is best to train the stems over a hoop of wire stuck into the compost. That way the plant will also look more bushy. The leaves are dark green and glossy, and up to 3in (7.5cm) long. Clusters of fragrant waxy whitish pink flowers with a red, star-shaped centre, appear in summer and the plant may continue flowering off and on through to the autumn.

*H.c.* 'Variegata' has the added attraction of leaves with edges flushed with pink.

### The year's care

**Spring and summer:** Temperatures should be between 60–65 deg F (16–18 deg C). A hoya needs very good light with some direct sun, but not scorching midday sun, which may damage the leaves. Place the plant in a well-ventilated spot and mist-spray regularly, except when in flower. The pot could be stood on a tray of wet pebbles or surrounded with moist peat to increase humidity. Water frequently, but allow the compost to dry out a little between watering. Feed every two weeks. ►Once the flower buds have begun to show do not move the plant or the buds may drop. When the flowers begin to fade let them fall from the plant of their own accord and do not touch the flowering spurs because new ones grow from there. If a spur is pruned away completely a flower will not be produced from that point again.◄ Aphids and mealy bugs can be a threat.

**Potting-on:** Every two years in spring in either a loam or peat-based compost.

**Propagation:** By taking 4in (10cm) stem cuttings in summer, but considerable heat (70 deg F, 21 deg C) and humidity are necessary.

**Autumn and winter:** Give the plant a rest at temperatures between 50–55 deg F (10–13 deg C), but keep it in a good light with direct weak winter sun. Water occasionally to prevent the compost from drying out completely. Do not feed.

# Myrtillocactus geometrizans

Desert cactus    Mexico

*M. geometrizans* is well worth growing for its lime green coloured columns, as seen on many a Western film, but it does need slightly higher winter temperatures than most cacti. Indoors the columns may grow to a height of 3ft (90cm), but this will take some time. They send out branches from a point about 8in (20cm) up the column. Each column has up to six ribs with short black spines protruding from the areoles along the rib edges. Small creamy flowers appear in summer, followed by blue berries, but you are unlikely to get flowers or berries indoors.

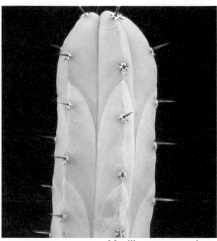

*Myrtillocactus geometrizans*

### The year's care

**Spring and summer:** *M. geometrizans* will do all right with normal seasonal temperatures and even great heat will not bother it. It needs a bright spot with as much direct sun as possible – on a window-sill, for instance. Water fairly frequently, but allow the compost to dry out a little between waterings. Feed every two weeks.

**Potting-on:** Each year in spring in a mixture of three parts of loam-based compost to one part sand.

**Propagation:** By sowing seed in spring.

**Autumn and winter:** ►This cactus needs a minimum temperature of 50 deg F (10 deg C) and one nearer to 60 deg F (16 deg C) is better. Lower temperatures cause brown patches to appear on the columns.◄ Keep the cactus in a good light, with direct sunlight. Water only occasionally, about once a month, to prevent the compost from drying out completely. Do not feed.

# Opuntia microdasys

Prickly Pear
Desert cactus    Mexico

*Opuntia microdasys*, like *Myrtillocactus geometrizans*, needs a slightly higher winter temperature than most other cacti, if its pads are to stay in good condition. It will grow to a height of about 12in (30cm) with a similar spread of branching stems, but it takes several years to reach that stage. The flattened stems, or pads, up to 3in (7.5cm) long, are covered with many areoles, bearing the tiny yellow bristles known as glochids, common in

*Hoya carnosa*

*Opuntia microdasys*

opuntias. Yellow flowers may be produced from areoles on the edges of the pads, but they are rarely seen on plants cultivated indoors.

### The year's care

**Spring and summer:** *O. microdasys* is tolerant of the normal temperatures of this time of the year. It requires good light with full sun; if in shade growth tends to become elongated. A well-ventilated spot is also important. Water frequently so that the compost is moist always. Feed every two weeks. Be on the look out for mealy bugs.

**Potting-on:** Each year in spring in a mixture of two parts of loam-based compost and one part of sand.

**Propagation:** From cuttings taken in summer. Cut off a pad and allow it to dry out for a few days before potting up.

**Autumn and winter:** ▶The prickly pear must be overwintered at a temperature above 50 deg F (10 deg C) and temperatures around 60 deg F (16 deg C) are to be preferred. Below 50 deg F (10 deg C) unsightly reddish brown patches will appear on the pads, marking them for ever.◀ At this time of the year the plant still needs good light, with direct sun. Water very occasionally to prevent the compost from drying out completely. A really dry compost is likely to make the pads shrivel and drop off. Do not feed.

## Rebutia miniscula

Red Crown
Desert cactus    Argentina

*Rebutia miniscula* is a must in any cacti collection since it remains reasonably compact and will produce masses of flowers when still young – always provided that it gets the necessary cool winter rest. It forms a clump of globe shaped stems, at most 2in (5cm) across. The whole ribless sphere is covered with areoles bearing short white spines. In late spring and summer bright red flaring trumpet-shaped flowers, about 2in (5cm) across, appear at the base and sides of the sphere, covering it almost completely. Without a rest period plants may still flower, but not so profusely.

### The year's care

**Spring and summer:** *R. miniscula* will get along all right in normal

*Rebutia miniscula*

seasonal temperatures. Give the plant a well-lit, sunny and well-ventilated spot. Water frequently, making the compost thoroughly moist, but letting it dry out a little between waterings. Feed every two weeks. An attack by mealy bugs can be a problem, because they hide among the densely packed clusters of spheres.

**Potting-on:** Each year in spring in a mixture of two parts of loam-based compost to one part of sharp sand to make a free-draining mix.

**Propagation:** By division of the offsets in summer, or by sowing seed in spring.

**Autumn and winter:** ▶This cactus must have a rest at a temperature of about 45 deg F (7 deg C) to produce plently of flowers the following season.◀ In winter it must still have good light, with as much sunshine as there is. Water only very occasionally, about once a month, to prevent the compost from drying out completely. Do not feed.

## Rhipsalidopsis gaertneri

Easter Cactus
Jungle cactus    Brazil

The Easter cactus, which may be sold under its other botanical name of *Schlumbergera gaertneri*, is an epiphytic cactus found growing on trees in tropical forest areas. The stems consist of flattened sections joined together, with areoles along the edges. They grow erect at first but as more sections appear and the stems reach about 12in (30cm) they begin to arch over, and are then suitable for planting in hanging baskets. In spring brick red flowers appear from the areoles at the end of the latest formed section. Each flower may not last long, but the plant continues to bloom for several weeks.

### The year's care

**Spring and summer:** After a cool rest period bring the cactus into the warmth when the buds first appear. Temperatures between 65–75 deg F (18–24 deg C) are best; the warmer it is the more quickly the flower buds will open. It needs bright light, but must be shaded from direct sun. It will do better if it has a spell out of

*Rhipsalidopsis gaertneri*

# Rhododendron simsii

Indian Azalea
Flowering    China

*R. simsii* is one of those unfortunate Christmas gift plants which rapidly dies because it is cossetted in a warm centrally heated room, whereas what it needs is a cool room. The oval, leathery, dark green leaves are about 1in (2.5cm) long but when the plant is in bloom they are almost obscured by the 2in (5cm) flowers, in shades of red, purple and white. The normal flowering period is late spring, but nurserymen get them ready to flower earlier in time for the Christmas trade – about the worst time to buy an azalea. A plant grows to about 12 in (30cm).

## The year's care

**Spring and summer:** ▶The ideal temperature is 65 deg F (18 deg C); if it is warmer the leaves will fall. Provide humidity by standing the pot on a tray of wet pebbles or by surrounding it with moist peat.◀ Azaleas kept indoors require bright light but not direct sunlight. They do much better spending a lot of time outdoors, but in shade. ▶Water

*Rhododendron simsii*

doors in summer. Once flower buds have appeared, water frequently to keep the compost always moist and spray the plant often during summer. Feed every three weeks with a weak solution of fertiliser, but do not start feeding until buds have formed.

**Potting-on:** Every year when flowering is over, in a free-draining mixture of two parts of loam-based compost and one part of sand.

**Propagation:** By taking stem cuttings in summer. Break off two to three of the stem sections and leave them to dry for a day or two before potting up.

**Autumn and winter:** ▶Give the Easter cactus a cool rest period to allow the buds to develop, at a temperature around 55 deg F (13 deg C). It will be harmed by temperatures below 50 deg F (10 deg C).◀ Keep it in a bright light, but out of direct sun. Water occasionally to prevent the compost from drying out completely. Shrivelled stems are usually a sign that the plant is not getting enough water. Do not feed.

*Sarracenia flavia*

frequently to keep the compost always moist. Use soft water; prolonged watering with hard water will turn the leaves yellow.◄ Feed every two weeks with an acid fertiliser. Remove all dead flowers and seed pods, and when flowering is over trim branches into shape.

**Potting-on:** Each year after flowering, in a peat-based compost.

**Propagation:** Take stem tip cuttings, about 3in (7.5cm) long, in summer, and root them in a heated propagator.

**Autumn and winter:** ►Plants which have been out of doors during the summer must be brought indoors before there is any danger of frost. Cool temperatures between 45–55 deg F (7–13 deg C) are required, and the cooler end of that range is better. In high temperatures the flower buds and leaves will rapidly drop; that is why there are so many post-Christmas disasters. A humid atmosphere is equally important at this time of the year. Place the plant in bright light, but away from direct sun. Water fairly

frequently to keep the compost moist, using rain water if the mains water is hard. If the plant has been brought into early flowering, cut the flowers off as they die, and the seed pods. Do not feed.

## Sarracenia flavia

Pitcher Plant
Carnivorous   North America

*S. flavia* is a carnivorous plant with tall elegant pitchers and their bright yellow-green colouring lures the prey. When an insect lands on the top of the pitcher it is enticed by the smell of nectar secreted inside the rim and ventures further. The nectar is very slippery, and insects, unable to get a foothold, fall to the bottom of the pitcher into a broth of enzymes in which the plant will digest them. Insects find it impossible to escape. Either their wing span is restricted in the confined space and they cannot fly out, or the downward pointing hairs lining the pitcher prevent them from crawling out. The tubular

shaped pitchers grow up to 2ft (60cm) high, with a lidded opening about 2in (5cm) wide. Yellow flowers, up to 4in (10cm) across, appear in summer, carried on long stems.

### The year's care

**Spring and summer:** *S. flavia* should have temperatures between 50–55 deg F (10–13 deg C) and should be in a bright sunny spot, perhaps a window-sill. ►It is a bog plant, so it will need watering frequently to keep the compost always moist. In fact, the pot can be left standing in a saucer of water, kept topped up, during this time of the year. Use either rainwater or distilled water.◄ The plant should not be fed with flies. A weak solution of fertiliser can be watered into the compost once a month, but if the plant is also catching files, even that may prove too rich a diet, which could be fatal.

**Potting-on:** In spring every two or three years, in a mixture of peat, sand and sphagnum moss.

**Propagation:** By dividing plants in spring or sowing seed.

**Autumn and winter:** ►If the plant is to flower the following year it will need a rest period at temperatures between 45–50 deg F (7–10 deg C).◄ In early autumn thick leaf stalks appear which last through to the following spring. By early winter the pitchers will die back. Keep the plant in a bright sunny spot. ►Water frequently so that the compost is moist, but do not leave the pot standing in water during this period.◄ Do not feed.

## Schlumbergera truncata

Crab Cactus, Christmas Cactus
Jungle cactus   Brazil

This epiphytic cactus, also known as *Zygocactus truncatus*, produces its striking flowers just before Christmas. Its popular name of crab cactus is derived from the appearance of the notched edges of the many segments forming the 12in (30cm) stems. Pink to dark red flowers are produced either singly or in pairs from the areoles on the tip of the latest formed section. The Christmas cactus most widely on sale is a hybrid of *S. truncata* – *S.* 'Buckleyi' (syn. *S.* 'Bridgesii') This also has segmented stems, but the notches are more rounded. Red flowers open around Christmas and through to mid or late winter.

### The year's care

**Spring and summer:**
Schlumbergeras need temperatures between 65–75 deg F (18–24 deg C) and should be placed in a good light but out of direct sun. If the plant can be placed out of doors during summer so much the better, but keep it out of the sun and bring it indoors before there is any risk of frost. Water frequently so that the compost is always moist. Feed every three weeks with a weak solution of fertiliser.

**Potting-on:** Each year in early spring when flowering is over, in a mixture of two parts of loam-based compost to one part of sand.

**Propagation:** By taking stem cuttings in summer. Break off a piece of stem which has two or three sections. Leave it to dry out for a day or two before potting up.

**Autumn and winter:** ▶This plant has a comparatively short rest period – it starts in early autumn and goes on to early winter. During that time the temperature should be down to between 55–60 deg F (13–16 deg C). Although the plant should be in a good light, but not direct sunlight, it will produce more and earlier flowers if in early winter the number of hours of daylight is restricted. At that time it should also spend the nights in an unlit room. When flower buds begin to appear remove the plant into the warmth (65–75 deg F, 18–24 deg C).◀ While the plant is resting water occasionally to keep the compost just moist. When flower buds appear increase the frequency of watering, but the compost must never become waterlogged. Too much water may cause buds to fall, as will moving the pot around or letting it stand in a draught. Do not feed.

*Schlumbergera truncata*

*Stephanotis floribunda*

# Stephanotis floribunda

Madagascar Jasmine
Flowering   Madagascar

This climbing shrub grows rapidly and can soon make growth of 10ft (3m). It is more manageable and more attractive if the stems are trained round a hoop of wire pushed into the compost. The leathery oval evergreen leaves, some 3in (7.5cm) long, grow in opposite pairs along the stems. Fragrant white waxy flowers appear in clusters in late spring and early summer, but there may be some flowers off and on until autumn.

## The year's care

**Spring and summer:** *S. floribunda* needs warmth in the growing season – around 70 deg F (21 deg C). It should be in bright light, but not direct sun. The plant will do better if the atmosphere around it can be kept humid. It can be sprayed frequently, but not when it is in flower. For more persistent humidity stand the pot on a tray of wet pebbles or surround it with damp peat. Water frequently so that the compost is always moist. Feed every two weeks. Watch out for scale insects.

**Potting-on:** Every year in spring, using a peat or loam-based compost.

**Propagation:** By taking 4in (10cm) stem cuttings in spring. Do not use stems which are developing flower buds. A temperature of about 70 deg F (21 deg C) is needed for cuttings to strike.

**Autumn and winter:** ▶The plant should be kept at cool temperatures – around 55 deg F (13 deg C). If the plant is kept in a warm dry room during the winter, when the light is poor, growth will be straggly and there will be long gaps between the pairs of leaves. Mealy bugs and scale will also be encouraged.◀ It needs bright light and direct sun in winter will do no harm. Water occasionally so that the compost is just moist. Do not feed.

# Veltheimia viridifolia

Forest Lily
Bulb   South Africa

*V. viridifolia* is only a part-time houseplant since the foliage dies down after flowering and the bulb is stored during its dormant period from early to late summer. The glossy, bright green, crinkly-edged leaves, about 10in (25cm) long grow in a rosette formation. The long flower stalk – as much as 18in (45cm) – carries clusters of pink tubular flowers which last for several weeks during the winter months.

## The year's care

**Spring and summer:** ▶In spring the temperatures should be no more than 55 deg F (13 deg C), but the light should be bright with some direct sun. Water fairly frequently at this stage so that the compost is moist throughout. In early summer the foliage wilts and turns yellow; stop watering, and let the compost dry out. If possible put the pot where the bulb can get a good baking in the sun. Keep it in the dried out compost during the dormant period from early to late summer.◀

**Autumn and winter:** ▶In early autumn break away the old compost from the bulb, taking care not to damage the roots and repot in fresh compost, peat or loam-based. Leave part of the bulb showing above the compost. Keep the plant in a temperature of 55 deg F (13 deg C) and no higher or the plant will not thrive. Put it in a well-ventilated spot, with direct sun, except when it is in flower. Water occasionally to keep the compost just moist until the foliage appears and then gradually increase the frequency of watering so that the compost is moist throughout.◀ Feed every two weeks when new growth has become well established, but stop feeding when flowering is over.

**Potting-on:** Once every two years in early autumn in either a peat or loam-based compost.

**Propagation:** By removing offsets from mature bulbs in early autumn when replanting.

*Veltheimia viridifolia*

# Easy plants for warm rooms

This section of the A–Z moves on to plants which need warmth; many of them originated in tropical regions. These are plants likely to be chosen for growing in homes which have central heating, probably throughout the whole house. Nonetheless, most of the plants need or benefit from a period of rest, and if they can be moved for a time in autumn and winter to any cooler rooms, so much the better.

By keeping a plant as warm in winter as in summer you run into two areas of trouble. The first is that in the warmth a plant goes on growing, but warmth without enough light means sickly growth. The second is that in winter the air in a centrally heated house, with windows closed, is desert dry and the plants suffer from lack of humidity. That is why the entries in this part are peppered with exhortations to place the pots on trays of wet pebbles or to surround them with moist peat. (For advice on humidity see pp. 26–27).

The section includes some of the most highly coloured foliage plants – *Begonia rex*, callisia, cordyline, dracaena – as well as a wide choice of ficus. Among the flowering plants are the ubiquitous flowering begonias and saintpaulias, as well as the exotic strelitzia. The 26 entries cover 58 species or varieties.

---

**Warning signs**
Leaves turn brown
Leaves curl and may fall
Leaves turn yellow during resting period
Leaves drop during resting period
Leaves translucent and shrivelled (touched by frost)

---

The entries in this section are listed here according to the type of plant they are.

**Flowering**
*Achimenes longiflora*
*Begonia tuberhybrida*
*Beloperone guttata*
*Brunfelsia calycina*
*Clerodendrum thomsoniae*
*Hippeastrum*
*Jacobinea carnea*
*Saintpaulia ionantha*
*Strelitzia reginae*

**Foliage**
*Begonia rex*
*Callisia elegans*
*Cordyline terminalis*
*Dieffenbachia picta*
*Dracaena marginata* 'Tricolor'

*Ficus*
*Hypoestes sanguinolenta*
*Maranta leuconeura* 'Erythrophylla'
*Peperomia argyreia*
*Scindapsus aureus*

**Bromeliads**
*Aechmea fasciata*
*Ananas comosus* 'Variegatus'
*Billbergia nutans*

**Palm**
*Howea forsteriana*

**Ferns**
*Blechnum gibbum*
*Nephrolepis exaltata*
*Pellea rotundifolia*

*Achimenes longiflora*

# Achimenes longiflora

Hot Water Plant
Flowering   Central America

The flowers of *A. longiflora* may be small but their number and the lengthy flowering season make up for that. The hairy dark green leaves, with toothed edges, are carried on trailing stems up to 20in (50cm) long. These can either be supported or left to trail in a basket. The blue or purple flowers with white centres appear from early summer to early autumn. When flowering has finished the stems die down and the rhizomes are stored dry until brought into growth again the following year. There are many cultivars with pink and blue flowers and one, *A.l.* 'Alba', which has white flowers with purple centres.

### The year's care

**Spring and summer:** In early spring repot the rhizome in fresh, peat-based compost and bring it into a temperature of 65 deg F (18 deg C) to start it into new growth. When shoots appear the plant will be happy in temperatures between 55–65 deg F (13–18 deg C), but not in great heat. It will need bright light, out of direct sun. Between the time of repotting the tuber and the appearance of new shoots water occasionally to keep the compost just moist. Thereafter water frequently so that the compost is well moistened always. Never let it dry out completely. Feed every two weeks.

**Potting-on:** Every year in spring in a peat-based compost.

**Propagation:** When repotting the plant divide the rhizome, or take stem cuttings about 4in (10cm) long, in early summer.

**Autumn and winter:** In early autumn when the plant has finished flowering, stop watering and allow the foliage to die down. When it has done so cut the stems off at compost level and either store the rhizome totally dry in the compost or remove it and store it in dry sand until it is time to start it into growth the following spring. The ideal storage temperature is 50 deg F (10 deg C) and it should never fall much lower since the rhizome is easily killed by frost.

# Aechmea fasciata

Urn Plant
Bromeliad   Brazil

In the wild *A. fasciata* (syn. *Aechmea* or *Billbergia rhodocyanea*) is an epiphytic, or air plant which anchors itself to rocks or tree branches. However, it does adapt itself to growing in a pot indoors. The urn plant forms a rosette of strap-shaped grey-green leaves marked with horizontal silvery bands. Individual leaves can grow to 2ft (60cm) long and the overall spread may be 3ft (90cm), so it needs plenty of room. The flower spike grows from the centre of the rosette, the top section a mass of bright pink bracts with small blue flowers emerging between. The flowers themselves do not last long, but the bracts will stay colourful for many months. Eventually the flower spike dies down, and then the foliage; each rosette flowers only once. Small offsets are thrown up from the base of the plant and these can be detached to make new plants.

### The year's care

**Spring and summer:** The temperature should be about 70 deg F (21 deg C). The plant must be in an airy place with bright light and some direct sun, but not scorching midday sun. Frequent mist spraying in hot weather is important. Water the compost fairly often, but if overwatered the plant and flower stalk may rot. Fill the central 'urn' of the rosette with water – rainwater if the mains supply is hard – and keep it topped up, emptying it occasionally so that it does not become foul. Feed once a month.

**Potting-on:** It is not necessary to pot-on as the plant will die down after flowering, leaving offsets to be potted up.

**Propagation:** By detaching offsets when the parent plant has died down, but let them get well established before cutting them away. Plant in a mixture of loam, peat and leaf mould. Avoid any compost which contains lime. It will be two or three years, possibly more, before these offshoots produce bracts.

**Autumn and winter:** The aechmea will do better if it has a rest period in temperatures between 55–60 deg F (13–16 deg C), but if need be it will tolerate normal room temperatures. Keep it in a good light with what weak direct sun there is. Water occasionally so that the compost is just moist; once a month should be enough. During this period keep the centre of the rosette dry. Do not feed.

# Ananas comosus variegatus

Variegated pineapple
Terrestrial bromeliad    Brazil

*Ananas comosus variegatus* is the houseplant version of the commercial pineapple. The shape of the leaves is similar – long and narrow with sharply serrated teeth – but the main difference is that the grey-green leaves have white to yellow margins, which turn a dusky pink if the plant has sufficient sunlight. The plant grows in a rosette formation, the arching leaves up to 3ft (90cm) in length, which means that it will need plenty of room. However, it is not a vigorous grower. After several years it may produce a spike of purple flowers from the centre of the rosette, followed by the familiar fruit, which is usually flushed with pink. When grown indoors the fruit is small and unfortunately uneatable. When flowering and fruiting are over the parent plant dies but does leave behind offsets at the base of the plant. These can be removed and potted up.

### The year's care

**Spring and summer:** Temperatures in the range 65–75 deg F (18–24 deg C) are ideal. Bright direct sunlight is also essential if the rich variegations are to be maintained. These plants like humid conditions and mist-spraying them twice a week in summer is beneficial. Dry, brittle, brown-tipped leaves indicate a lack of humidity. The brown tips may be cut off, but do not cut into the healthy green tissue – this is a sure way to kill the leaf completely. Water frequently to keep the compost thoroughly moist. Feed every two or three weeks.

**Potting-on:** In spring each year using a loam-based compost devised for use with bromeliads. Plants are usually sold when in fruit and when the parent subsequently dies the offsets will have to be potted up regardless of the time of the year.

**Propagation:** From offsets, using a loam-based bromeliad compost, which is very free-draining and lime free.

**Autumn and winter:** The ananas does not have an obvious resting period so during these months the temperature must be at least 60 deg F

*Aechmea fasciata*

*Ananas comosus variegatus*

(16 deg C) and the plant will certainly do better at a higher temperature. It must also have as much sunlight as possible. Spray once a week to provide humidity. Frequency of watering will depend on how warm the room is; do not allow the compost to dry out completely between waterings. Do not feed.

# Begonia rex

Painted Leaf Begonia
Foliage    Assam

Of all the plants grown for their foliage *Begonia rex* and its hybrids are the most colourful. They look good either in group plantings, contrasting with green plants, or singly. The heart-shaped leaves, up to 10in (25cm) long and 8in (20cm) wide, are carried on short leaf stalks from the underground rhizome. The overall height of the plant will be no more than 18in (45cm). The leaf colour varies tremendously – the basic green is overmarked with shades of pink, red, purple and silver, sometimes all together on the same leaf. The edges and undersides of the leaves and the stems are covered with red hairs.

From early summer to early autumn mature plants will produce pink flowers; these are far less interesting than the leaves and they are best nipped out so that the plant concentrates on producing its highly coloured foliage. *B. masoniana*, the iron cross begonia, so called because of the browny red cross in the centre of each leaf, grows to a height of about 9in (22.5cm). The puckered surface of the 6in (15cm) leaves is covered in small red hairs. As the plant matures the

*Begonia masoniana*

*Begonia rex*

leaves acquire a silvery sheen. Indoors it is unlikely to flower; if it should the flowers are greenish.

**The year's care**

**Spring and summer:** These begonias should be in a temperature between 65–70 deg F (18–21 deg C). They need bright light to maintain their colours, but must be shaded from direct sun. Water frequently to keep the compost always moist. Feed every two weeks.

**Potting-on:** In spring every year in a peat-based compost.

**Propagation:** By taking leaf cuttings in summer.

**Autumn and winter:** The temperature should be between 55–60 deg F (13–16 deg C). Bright light is needed, but not direct sun. Water occasionally so that the compost is barely moist. Do not feed.

# Begonia tuberhybrida

Flowering    South America

*Begonia tuberhybrida* is the most popular flowering tuberous begonia, and it is widely used as a bedding plant outdoors. These hybrids have 6in (15cm) long heart-shaped leaves with serrated edges. The overall height of the plant is no more than 15in (37.5cm). Flowers, which appear from early summer to early autumn may be single or double, up to 6in (15cm) across, and the colours are white, yellow, orange and crimson. After flowering the foliage dies down and the tubers are stored over winter to be replanted the following year. Among other readily available flowering begonias are the hybrids developed from *Begonia semperflorens*, a fibrous rooted begonia. This is a very compact bushy plant, growing to about 12in (30cm). The heart-shaped leaves may be green, red or purple, and the flowers, which appear from late spring to autumn, range from white to pink and red. Two other groups of hybrids, also fibrous rooted, are those referred to as 'Gloire de Lorraine' and 'Schwabenland'. 'Gloire de Lorraine' are bushy plants rarely growing more than 12in (30cm) high. The mid green leaves are rounded, and pink to red flowers are produced from autumn to late

*Begonia* 'Schwabenland'

*Begonia tuberhybrida*

growing shoot. All the other begonias mentioned can be propagated by taking stem cuttings in spring and summer.

**Autumn and winter:** When *B. tuberhybrida* has ceased flowering stop watering and allow the foliage to die down. Then cut it off, remove the tuber from the pot and store it in a dry place at a temperature of 45 deg F (7 deg C). Begonias which are still flowering, and also *B. semperflorens* hybrids which are about to come into flower, should be kept in a temperature at this time of the year between 65–70 deg F (18–21 deg C). If the plants stop flowering cut back the foliage to within 4in (10cm) of the compost and give them a rest period at temperatures around 60 deg F (16 deg C). They all need bright light and a little winter sun does no harm. Plants in flower should be watered frequently, but allow the compost to dry out a little between waterings. They also need a humid atmosphere. Resting plants should be watered only occasionally to prevent the compost from drying out completely. Do not feed.

# Beloperone guttata

Shrimp Plant
Flowering   Mexico

The attraction of this bushy plant is in its layered, pinky brown shrimp-shaped bracts, which remain colourful for many months, and sometimes the whole year. The oval, slightly shiny, mid-green leaves, about 2in (5cm) long, are carried on woody stems. The plant tends to sprawl, and unchecked will grow to 2ft (60cm). Therefore it needs to be pruned annually in spring to keep it to a bushy and compact 12in (30cm). White flowers appear from the bracts from late spring to late autumn.

### The year's care

**Spring and summer:** The temperature should be around 65 deg F (18 deg C). *B. guttata* needs a light airy spot to maintain good bract colouring and to encourage flowers. Some direct sun is desirable but not midday sun. Water frequently so that the compost is always moist, but never waterlogged. Feed every two weeks. In spring, prune back straggly stems

winter. Plants are usually on sale just before Christmas. The 'Schwabenland' hybrids have larger leaves and flowers, which are orange, red or yellow, but the plants will grow to no more than about 18in (45cm) high. They can be bought in flower at almost any time of the year and may flower off and on throughout the year.

### The year's care

**Spring and summer:** Overwintered tubers of *B. tuberhybrida* should be planted in early spring and brought into a temperature around 70 deg F (21 deg C) to encourage sprouting. Once they have sprouted, temperatures around 65 deg F (18 deg C) will be adequate, as they are for all other begonias. They must all have plenty of light, but not direct sunlight. A little added humidity around them is a great help. Stand the pots on trays of wet pebbles or surround them with moist peat. Do not spray the begonias when they are in flower because the water will mark the blooms. Water frequently, but let the compost dry out a little between waterings. If the compost becomes waterlogged plants are likely to rot following attacks by mildew and botrytis. Too little water causes the flowers to drop. Feed every two weeks.

**Potting-on:** In spring every year, using a peat-based compost.

**Propagation:** *B. tuberhybrida* in spring, by dividing the tuber, but make sure that each piece has a

*Beloperone guttata*

## The year's care

**Spring and summer:** Temperatures should be between 60–65 deg F (16–18 deg C). The plant needs bright light, with some direct, but not scorching, sun. Poor light affects the leaf colouring and the flowering of the plant. Water frequently, but allow the compost to dry out somewhat between waterings. Feed once a month.

**Potting-on:** Every year in spring in a peat-based compost.

**Propagation:** By removing offsets when potting-on. They should be left to grow to about 6in (15cm) before they are detached from the parent plant. Make sure that each offset has enough roots to support it.

**Autumn and winter:** As *B. nutans* seems to do well without a rest period it can be kept in temperatures between 60–65 deg F (16–18 deg C). It even thrives in dry centrally heated rooms. However, it must have a bright light with any winter sun available. Water fairly often so that the compost is just moist, but the frequency will obviously depend on how warm the room is. Do not feed during this period.

to within some 6in (15cm) of the compost, making cuts just above a leaf. When new growth shows pinch out growing tips to encourage bushiness.

**Potting-on:** In loam or peat-based compost in spring each year.

**Propagation:** By taking 4in (10cm) stem tip cuttings in spring.

**Autumn and winter:** This plant will do better with a rest period at a temperature about 60 deg F (16 deg C), but in a bright spot with winter sunshine. Water occasionally so that the compost is barely moist. Do not feed.

## Billbergia nutans

Queen's Tears
Bromeliad   Brazil

Billbergias are terrestrial bromeliads, growing on the ground instead of in the air as the epiphytic bromeliads do. They can produce flowers at any time of the year and seem to survive well without a winter rest period. *B. nutans* is the most popular and easily

obtained. The long and narrow arching dark green leaves, with a metallic sheen, are up to 20in (50cm) long. They grow in a rosette formation, giving the plant a spread of about 3ft (90cm). The delicate green and blue flowers emerge in clusters from pink bracts, carried on long stems.

## Blechnum gibbum

Fern   New Caledonia, West Pacific

Although this plant is a fern, as it grows older it begins to look like a palm; this is because the lower leaves die and drop off and a scaly trunk

*Billbergia nutans*

*Blechnum gibbum*

**Autumn and winter:** This fern must have a minimum temperature of 55 deg F (13 deg C) and temperatures around 60 deg F (16 deg C) are better. It still needs good light, but shade from direct sun. Water fairly frequently so that the compost is just moist. It is important not to let the compost dry out completely or the fronds will shrivel. Do not feed.

# Brunfelsia calycina

Yesterday, Today and Tomorrow
Flowering   Brazil

This is an evergreen shrub which grows to about 2ft (60cm). The shiny green leaves, about 4in (10cm) long, have a leathery look. The sweet-scented, five-petalled flowers are curious, for they change colour daily, from purple to pale lavender to white, and by the fourth day they are dead; hence the plant's common name. Although each flower is short lived, in the right conditions the plant can bloom all year round – the most prolific period is between early summer and autumn. The secret of such prolonged flowering is good light. Probably the best form is *B.c.* 'Macrantha', which has showy flowers up to 3in (7.5cm) across, with white eyes.

develops. From this grows the broad shuttlecock of shiny light green fronds, which are deeply divided into graceful tapering leaflets. The fern requires room to spread itself as the fronds can grow 3ft (90cm) long. A bushy specimen makes an excellent focal-point plant.

**Propagation:** From spores stored in cases on the undersides of leaves, but this is usually considered a specialist operation. Plants sometimes produce offsets, and these can be detached when repotting.

### The year's care

**Spring and summer:** A temperature range between 65–75 deg F (18–24 deg C) is ideal. As with all ferns *B. gibbum* will do better in a humid atmosphere. Either surround the pot with moist peat or stand it on a tray of wet pebbles. The foliage can be sprayed frequently, but if the tap water is hard use rain water, for limy water will ruin the shiny appearance of the leaves. Place the plant in a good light, but shaded from direct sunlight. Plenty of air is important; during the summer put the fern near an open window, or, if possible, outside on a balcony. Water frequently so that the compost is moist always. Feed every two weeks.

**Potting-on:** Each year in spring, in a peat-based compost, or preferably a combination of equal parts of peat, loam and sand.

*Brunfelsia calycina*

## The year's care

**Spring and summer:** Temperatures should be in the range 60–70 deg F (16–21 deg C). Good light is essential to ensure continuous flowering, but with shade from hot direct sunlight in summer. *B. calycina* does best in a humid atmosphere, which can be achieved by surrounding the pot with moist peat or standing it on a tray of wet pebbles. A regular very light mist spraying would help, but avoid soaking the flowers. Water frequently so that the compost is always moist. Feed every two weeks. Older plants should be cut back to half their size in spring each year and the growing tips of the new shoots, when they have grown a few inches, should be pinched out to encourage bushiness. If the air is dry and warm watch out for infestations of greenfly.

**Potting-on:** Since they are not fast growers the plants will need to be potted-on only every two or three years, in spring, in a peat-based compost with some leaf mould added. However, repot in other years to renew the exhausted compost.

**Propagation:** By taking stem cuttings about 5in (12.5cm) long, but a temperature of around 70 deg F (21 deg C) will be needed for them to strike.

**Autumn and winter:** Lack of a rest period does not seem to affect these plants, so temperatures in the range of 60–70 deg F (16–21 deg C) can be maintained. If plants do stop flowering an enforced rest period, by reducing the temperature to 55 deg F (13 deg C) for a few weeks, will do good. Bright light with weak winter sun will help to encourage winter flowering. Resting plants should be watered occasionally so that the compost is barely moist. Plants still growing and in flower will need to be watered more frequently. Do not feed.

# Callisia elegans

Striped Inch Plant
Foliage   Mexico

Callisias closely resemble tradescantias in both appearance and creeping habit, and are equally suitable for planting in a hanging basket. There the purple undersides of the leaves will be seen to best advantage. The upper surface of the

*Callisia elegans*

1in (2.5cm) oval leaves is dark green, marked with white stripes converging at the tips. The stems, densely packed with leaves, grow upright to begin with but when they are about 4in (10cm) long they start to arch over the edge of the pot and then grow to about 2ft (60cm). Small white flowers are produced from late spring to autumn, but they are undistinguished.

## The year's care

**Spring and summer:** Temperatures should be between 60–65 deg F (16–18 deg C). *C. elegans* needs good light with some direct sunlight, but it has to be shielded from really hot sun. Water often when growth is active so that the compost is moist always. If the callisia is growing in a pot ensure that after watering all the excess water has drained away before putting the pot back on its saucer. Feed every two weeks. In spring cut back any bare stems to compost level to encourage new growth.

**Potting-on:** Callisias are usually worth keeping for only two years so they will be potted-on only once, in spring, in either a peat or loam-based compost.

**Propagation:** From basal or stem tip cuttings, about 4in (10cm) long, taken in spring or summer. (Basal shoots are the new growth which appears from the base of the plant.) Plant them in compost or put them in water until

roots have developed and then pot them up.

**Autumn and winter:** Give the plant a short rest for a few weeks in winter at a temperature around 55 deg F (13 deg C). A plant not allowed to rest tends to put out lanky growth because of the combination of high temperature and poor light. To maintain the variegations a light position is vital, with direct weak winter sun. Water occasionally so that the compost is just moist. No feeding.

# Clerodendrum thomsoniae

Bleeding Heart Vine
Flowering   West Africa

This vine grows rapidly, easily reaching a height of 6ft (1.8m) or more, but it can be kept in check by hard pruning every year and regular pinching out. The glossy heart-shaped leaves, about 4in (10cm) long, are carried on upright branches, but they look better if trained round some kind of framework. From early summer to early autumn there are clusters of red star-shaped flowers, each surrounded by a white calyx.

## The year's care

**Spring and summer:** The temperature should be between 65–70 deg F (18–21 deg C). *C. thomsoniae* must have bright light, but shaded

*Clerodendrum thomsoniae*

from direct sun, if it is to flower successfully. It will also benefit from regular mist-spraying of the leaves before it comes into flower. Water frequently so that the compost is always moist. Feed every two weeks. In early spring cut back the stems to about a quarter of their size and later pinch out the growing tips to keep the plant bushy.

**Potting-on:** Every year in spring, using either a loam or a peat-based compost.

**Propagation:** By taking stem cuttings, about 4in (10cm) long, in spring and by sowing seed.

**Autumn and winter:** *C. thomsoniae* should have a rest period, but the temperature should not fall below 55 deg F (13 deg C); around 60 deg F (16 deg C) is ideal. Bright light is necessary if the plant is to flower next season. Keep the compost just moist with occasional watering. Do not feed.

# Cordyline terminalis

Hawaiian Ti Plant
Foliage   Polynesia

The cultivars of *Cordyline terminalis* provide the most vivid coloured foliage and so look best alongside plain green plants. They will grow at the most to 2ft (60cm) with a loose rosette of arching leaves, spreading about 18in (45cm). The lance-shaped leaves of *C.t.* 'Red Edge' are bright

*Cordyline terminalis* 'Lord Robertson'

*Cordyline terminalis* 'Prince Albert'

green, edged with red and they may also be red streaked. *C.t.* 'Lord Robertson' has green leaves marked with red and cream. The green leaves of *C.t.* 'Prince Albert' are marked with varying shades of red.

### The year's care

**Spring and summer:** The ideal temperature is a constant 70 deg C (21 deg C). Cordylines should have a bright light, but must be shaded from direct sunlight, which can mark the leaves. Water frequently to keep the compost always moist, but not waterlogged. Brown tips to the leaves indicate that the compost is too dry. Feed every two weeks.

**Potting-on:** Every two years in spring, using a peat-based compost.

**Propagation:** By detaching the suckers which are sometimes thrown up at the base of the plant; this is done when repotting. Older plants in time become leggy and unattractive; the growing tip can then be cut off and induced to root, but a heated propagator will be needed. The remainder of the stem can be cut into 3in (7.5cm) sections, each with a growing point, and planted bottom down in compost.

**Autumn and winter:** The temperature should be no lower than 60 deg F (16 deg C). Cooler conditions will make the leaves soften and rot. Keep the plant in good light, but out of direct sun. Water occasionally so that the compost is barely moist; once a week will usually be enough. Do not feed during this period.

## Dieffenbachia picta

Dumb Cane
Foliage   Brazil

Dieffenbachias have very showy, boldly marked, colourful leaves of green and cream or yellow. As the plant grows older the lower leaves die and fall leaving a bare stem, but the drooping habit of the leaves above usually hides its nakedness. There are many cultivars of *D. picta*, the lance-shaped leaves of which are up to 8in (20cm) long, but the overall height of the plant will be no more than 2ft (60cm). When stems reach this height they need strong support or they are

*Dieffenbachia picta*

likely to snap at the base. The leaves are green with irregular cream or yellow markings, which in some cultivars may cover almost the whole leaf. *D. amoena* does not have such striking or prominent markings, but makes up for that in the sheer size of its oval leaves – up to 18in (45cm) long, and 10in (25cm) wide. This plant will grow to 5ft (1.5m) or more, with a spread of leaves 3ft (90cm) or more. The sap of dieffenbachias contains calcium oxalate which causes pain and swelling of the tongue if any accidentally gets into your mouth. Take care when removing dying leaves or when taking cuttings.

### The year's care

**Spring and summer:** The temperature should be about 65 deg F (18 deg C). Bright light, but shade from direct sun, is necessary to maintain the rich variegations. Humidity around the plant will help to keep the leaves in good condition. Either stand the pot on a tray of wet pebbles or surround it with moist peat. Water fairly frequently, but allow the compost to dry out a little

between waterings. Feed every two weeks. Leggy stems can be cut down to within 5in (12.5cm) of the compost and new growth will sprout from the stump. The cut-off part of the stem can be used for propagating.

**Potting-on:** Each year in spring in a loam-based compost.

**Propagation:** By taking stem tip cuttings or cutting up pieces of stem into 4in (10cm) sections. Whole stems which have broken off will also root quickly in water. Remove most of the leaves from the lower part of the stem and submerge the larger part of it in water. When roots have appeared cut the stem into sections, each with roots, and plant them in compost, bottom end down.

**Autumn and winter:** The minimum temperature must be 60 deg F (16 deg C) otherwise the lower leaves may turn yellow. Dieffenbachias need bright light and direct winter sun will do no harm. If the plant is in a warm room it will have to be watered fairly frequently. Too dry compost makes the leaf edges turn brown. Avoid keeping it in draughts – the leaves drop. Do not feed.

# Dracaena marginata
## 'Tricolor'

Dragon Tree
Foliage    Madagascar

The dracaenas are many and
infinitely varied, in leaf shapes,
markings and colouring. *D. marginata*
'Tricolor', easy to grow, reaches a
height of 5ft (1.5m). Leaves grow
from compost level on a young plant
but as it matures the lower leaves fall
leaving a bare thin stem with a rosette
of stems at the top. The narrow-
pointed arching leaves, attractively
striped with green, pink and cream,
grow to 18in (45cm). *D. deremensis*
'Bausei' has sword-shaped green
leaves, 18in (45cm) long, with a white
stripe down the centre. The overall
height of this plant is about 4ft
(1.2m). Another cultivar, 'Warneckii',
is much the same size but the leaves
have several white stripes. *D. fragrans*
'Massangeana' grows to about 5ft
(1.5m), in time forming a stout trunk
topped with a rosette of sword-shaped
leaves, striped with yellow. The leaf
shape of *D. godseffiana*, known as gold
dust, is a complete contrast and the
plant itself is much more compact.
The oval green glossy leaves, no more
than 3in (7.5cm) long, are thickly
spotted with yellow. The plant grows
slowly, branching freely, and reaches
only about 18in (45cm).

## The year's care

**Spring and summer:** Temperatures
between 65–75 deg F (18–24 deg C)
are ideal for these tropical plants.
They all require bright light for good
leaf colour, but must be shaded from
direct sun. Plants will stay in far
better condition if the atmosphere
around them is humid. Stand pots on
trays of wet pebbles or surround them
with moist peat. Water frequently so
that the compost is always moist. Feed
every two weeks.

**Potting-on:** *D. godseffiana* once every
two or three years in spring, since it
grows slowly. All the others should be
potted-on each year. Use a loam-
based compost.

**Propagation:** By stem tip cuttings, or
sections of the stem 3in (7.5cm) long,
each with a growing point. This is
done in summer. *D. godseffiana* is
propagated by stem tip cuttings only.

*Dracaena godseffiana*

*Dracaena marginata* 'Tricolor'

*Dracaena fragrans* 'Massangeana'

*Ficus benjamina*

*Ficus elastica* 'Robusta'

**Autumn and winter:** The temperature should be no lower than 60 deg F (16 deg C) and nearer to 65 deg F (18 deg C) is better. Keep the plants in a bright light, but shaded from the sun, and maintain humidity. Water occasionally so that the compost is just moist. If it is too dry leaves will turn brown. Do not feed.

# Ficus

Foliage   India, China, West Africa

Among the ficus species there are shrubs, small trees, climbers and trailers – all from warm areas of the world. They readily adapt themselves to life indoors and as long as they are kept warm enough they are relatively undemanding.

*Ficus benjamina*, the weeping fig, from India, is the most graceful and elegant of all the ficus. The woody stems are fairly pliable, so plants can either grow upwards with support or be left to arch over the side of the pot. Stems grow to 6ft (1.8m) or more, but this will take some years. Plants which have been allowed to spread may in time be taking up so much room that they have to be staked to grow upwards. The oval pointed leaves, about 4in (10cm) long, are a light glossy green when they first unfurl, but gradually turn dark green. *F. diversifolia* (syn. *F. deltoidea*), the mistletoe fig from India and Malaya, has attractive yellow berries against a background of pear-shaped, leathery leaves, about 2in (5cm) long. This ficus grows slowly to 3ft (90cm) at the most, but it puts out many branches. *F. elastica*, the ubiquitous rubber plant from India, has several forms, some with plain green leaves, others strikingly variegated. *F.e.* 'Decora' and *F.e.* 'Robusta' have glossy, leathery, dark green elliptical leaves up to 12in (30cm) long. Among the variegated cultivars *F.e.* 'Tricolor' has green leaves with pink and cream patches and *F.e.* 'Schrijveriana' has green leaves with pale green, almost yellow, patches. All these *Ficus elastica* forms will grow to 6ft (1.8m) or more with ease, but the growing tip can be cut back to induce branching. *F. lyrata* (syn. *F. pandurata*), the fiddle leaf fig from West Africa, will grow as tall as *F. elastica* in a short time. The glossy, tough, fiddle-shaped leaves, up to 18in (45cm) long and 10in (25cm) wide, are carried on a single stem. *F. pumila*, the creeping fig, from China, puts out trailing stems up to 4ft (1.2m) long which spread over wide areas, but they can be kept in check by pruning. The heart-shaped leaves are tiny, about 1in (2.5cm) long, but they are numerous and closely packed.

## The year's care

**Spring and summer:** Temperatures should be in the range 65–75 deg F (18–24 deg C). All these ficus, except one, require good light, but not direct sun. The exception is *F. pumila*, one plant that is happy in a shady part of the room. Direct sun often scorches the leaves, especially those just opened. Variegated ficus need a better light if they are to maintain their colour. Keep the plants in an airy part of the room, but out of draughts. The glossy leaves of ficus are the major attraction so sponge them regularly. Water frequently, but let the compost dry out a little between waterings; overwatering may make the leaves fall. However, *F. pumila* must have moist compost all the time, or the leaves are likely to shrivel and fall. Feed ficus every two weeks. Prune the stems of *F. pumila* in the spring if they have become lanky.

*Ficus pumila*

This will also encourage bushy growth. If either *F. elastica* or *F. lyrata* loses many of the lower leaves and looks absurd the plant need not be thrown away but can be given a new lease of life and a new look. Cut back the stem in spring to within 6in (15cm) of the compost. New side shoots will soon appear from the dormant leaf buds of the stump.

**Potting-on:** Ficus will do better if the plants are restricted, so pot-on every two years in spring in either a peat-based compost or a mixture of equal parts of loam, peat, leaf mould and sharp sand. When in time a ficus has grown too large to be moved from its pot carefully remove the top layer of compost each spring and replace it with fresh.

**Propagation:** *F. pumila*, *F. diversifolia* and *F. benjamina* are propagated by taking stem cuttings, about 4in (10cm) long, in summer. *F. elastica* and *F. lyrata* can be air layered but with the loss of the original plant, so it is done only when a plant is past its best and has lost its lower leaves.

**Autumn and winter:** The ideal temperature is about 60 deg F (16 deg C) to give ficus a winter rest. In higher temperatures the plants will continue to grow but suffer from the lack of adequate light for healthy growth. Even resting they need good light, especially the variegated forms, but shade them from direct sun. Plants in low temperatures should be watered occasionally so that the compost is just moist. In warmer rooms they will need more frequent watering. Do not overwater, since this is likely to cause browning of leaf edges and eventual dropping of leaves. Do not feed.

# Hippeastrum hybrids

Bulb   Brazil and Mexico

The life of the flowers of hippeastrums is comparatively short, up to two weeks in the warmth and a month in a cool room, but they are an exciting sight when they do appear, and several bulbs can be induced to bloom at different times in winter and early spring. It is best to choose large bulbs, about 5in (12.5cm) across, because these are most likely to produce more than one flower stem, each with four or sometimes five individual flowers. The first sign of life from a bulb after it has been planted is usually the tip of the flower bud slowly emerging and then shooting up rapidly on a hollow stem which may reach 20in (50cm). The trumpet-shaped flowers, up to 6in (15cm) across, are available in shades of pink, orange, red, plain white or white streaked with pale pink or red. They flower from mid winter to early spring, and the time of flowering is hastened by higher temperatures and delayed by lower, within the recommended range. Often the narrow strap-shaped leaves appear only after the bulb has finished flowering, but sometimes the leaves appear along with the flower stem. Bulbs are usually offered for sale in late autumn and early winter.

## The year's care

**Spring and summer:** The temperature should be between 55–60 deg F (13–16 deg C). It needs a bright light with direct sunshine for good leaf growth and a spell out of doors during the summer will help the bulb to build up its reserves for flowering next year. Water frequently so that the compost is always moist, and feed every two weeks.

**Autumn and winter:** In early autumn the leaves will start to yellow

*Hippeastrum hybrids*

and wither of their own accord and water should then be withheld. If the foliage is still green stop watering and it will soon die down. Cut off the dead foliage and store the bulb, still in its pot of compost, at a temperature around 50 deg F (10 deg C). Dormant bulbs should not be watered and they do not need to be in a light position. Watch the bulb for signs of activity and as soon as a glimmer of new growth is seen take the bulb from the pot and gently tease away some of the old compost without disturbing the roots too much. On no account cut them away. Return the bulb to the same pot planting it in fresh compost with about 1in (2.5cm) of its shoulder above the compost. Bring it into a temperature between 65–70 deg F (18–21 deg C). Water occasionally so that the compost is just moist and gradually increase the frequency of watering when the plant is in flower and the leaves appear. When the flowers have faded cut away the flower head with its seed pods, but leave the hollow stem to shrivel before removing it.

**Potting-on:** Hippeastrums prefer to be pot bound so moving them into a larger pot may not be necessary for three years or so, until the bulb has obviously outgrown its pot. If it does not have a chance to build up its strength in summer it is more likely to grow smaller each year, and cease to flower. Pot-on into a loam-based compost when new growth first shows.

**Propagation:** By removing offsets when repotting, but it will be several years before they grow to flowering size.

# Howea forsteriana

Kentia Palm
Palm   Lord Howe Island, Pacific

This is probably the most popular large palm and is blessedly undemanding. The fronds of a young howea are held erect but gradually arch over with age. It can grow to a height of 7ft (2.1m) and in time spread its fronds over a similar span. Long stems carry deeply divided dark green leaflets which may be up to 18in (45cm) long. *H. belmoreana* is similar to *H. forsteriana* in general appearance, but the stems tend to arch over slightly more. Both are equally graceful.

## The year's care

**Spring and summer:** The ideal range of temperature is 55–65 deg F (13–18 deg C). While this palm will tolerate a certain amount of light shade it does better in good light, but not in direct sunlight. Water

frequently to make the compost always moist, but never soggy. Feed every two weeks.

**Potting-on:** Every other year in a loam-based compost. When the palm has at last been moved to a 12in (30cm) pot, stop potting-on; instead remove the top 3in (7.5cm) of compost every year and replace it with fresh compost.

**Propagation:** By sowing seed in spring, but considerable bottom heat of 75–80 deg (24–27 deg C) is needed. Seed can take up to nine months to germinate and anything recognisable as a howea a further five years to develop.

**Autumn and winter:** This plant requires a minimum temperature of 55 deg F (13 deg C), and nearer 60 deg F (16 deg C) is preferable. A slightly shaded spot is acceptable, but do not keep the palm in deep gloom during the short winter days. Water occasionally, keeping the compost barely moist. Do not feed.

*Howea forsteriana*

*Hypoestes sanguinolenta*

# Hypoestes sanguinolenta

Pink Polka Dot, Freckle Face
Foliage   Madagascar

*H. sanguinolenta* is prized for its
brightly marked foliage; the dark
green oval leaves about 2in (5cm)
long, are spotted with shocking pink.
The plant grows no more than 12in
(30cm) tall, but it must be pinched
out to make bushy growth. Left to
itself the stems become straggly and
the general appearance very untidy.
Recently developed cultivars are not
so much spotted as splashed with
large areas of pink, sometimes
covering almost the whole leaf.

### The year's care

**Spring and summer:** The
temperature should be between 65–70
deg F (18–21 deg C). Good light with
some direct but not scorching sun is
essential to maintain the rich pink
variegations. The plant will still grow
in a shaded part of the room but the
markings will be sparse and less
prominent. Regular spraying of the
plant, especially during warm
weather, will keep it in good
condition. Water frequently so that
the compost is always moist; if
allowed to dry out the lower leaves
will rapidly fall. Feed every two
weeks. Pinch out the growing tips for
bushy growth and if the stems have
become bare and straggly over the
winter cut them down to within 4in
(10cm) of the compost. New growth
will soon appear.

**Potting-on:** In spring each year in a
peat-based compost.

**Propagation:** By taking stem
cuttings, about 4in (10cm) long in
summer. They will need a
temperature around 70 deg F (21
deg C) to strike.

**Autumn and winter:** The hypoestes
needs a minimum temperature of 55
deg F (13 deg C), and closer to 60
deg F (16 deg C) is preferable. During
the short winter days this plant needs
bright light and all available sunshine
for good colouring. Water
occasionally to keep the compost
barely moist. Not to be fed.

# Jacobinia carnea

King's Crown
Flowering   Brazil

The feathery plume-shaped flowers of
*J. carnea* are particularly beautiful,
but unfortunately do not last long.
This shrub will grow to 5ft (1.5m), its
stems covered with oval, pointed,
glossy, dark green leaves, up to 6in
(15cm) long. The plume of pink to
red flowers appears in late summer.
*J. pauciflora* is much more compact,
growing to only 2ft (60cm) and has
tiny oval bright green leaves less than
1in (2.5cm) long. Clusters of red
flowers with yellow tips appear in late
autumn and may continue to open
well into winter.

### The year's care

**Spring and summer:** Jacobinias
will do all right in temperatures
between 60–65 deg F (16–18 deg C),
with bright light. Some direct sun will
do no harm but shield the plant from
hot midday sun. Water frequently to
keep the compost moist throughout.
Feed every two weeks. Pinch out
growing tips in spring for bushy
growth and cut back any leggy stems
to within 4in (10cm) of the compost.
This is done once only, in the plant's
second year; after that it is best replaced
by a new plant raised from cuttings.

**Potting-on:** If the plant is to be kept
for a second year pot-on in spring in
peat-based compost.

*Jacobinia carnea*

*Jacobinia pauciflora*

**Propagation:** By taking stem cuttings, about 4in (10cm) long, in spring.

**Autumn and winter:** When the plant has finished flowering give it a rest at temperatures around 55 deg F (13 deg C). It needs bright light and some direct sun to encourage and maintain flower production. Continue to water frequently when the plant is in flower, but reduce watering considerably when the plant is resting, keeping the compost just moist. Do not feed.

# Maranta leuconeura
## 'Erythrophylla'

Prayer Plant
Foliage    Central and South America

Every evening at dusk the leaves of marantas are raised to become erect, each pair folded together, so hiding their richly marked upper surfaces but revealing the red undersides. The following morning they open again. *M.l.* 'Erythrophylla' has dark green oval leaves about 4in (10cm) long and the main veins are picked out in crimson – therefore, as well as prayer plant, it has another common name of red herring bone. *M.l.* 'Kerchoveana', also called rabbit's foot, has oval leaves with dark brown blotches when they first unfurl, gradually turning to dark green. The spread of leaves can be about 15in (37.5cm) but these plants will not grow more than 12in (30cm) high.

## The year's care

**Spring and summer:** The ideal temperature range is between 65–70 deg F (18–21 deg C). Marantas need a bright light but should be shaded from direct sun, which makes the tips of the leaves turn brown and papery. Create a humid atmosphere round the plant by standing the pot on a tray of wet pebbles or surrounding it with

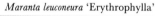
*Maranta leuconeura* 'Erythrophylla'

moist peat. While it will survive without this humidity the leaves are unlikely to remain in good condition. In warm weather spray regularly. Water frequently so that the compost is always moist, and feed every two weeks.

**Potting-on:** Every year in spring, using a peat-based compost.

**Propagation:** The easiest method is to divide the plant when repotting but make sure that there are enough roots to support each divided portion.

**Autumn and winter:** Give the plant a rest at temperatures between 60–65 deg F (16–18 deg C) but keep it in a bright position out of direct sun. Water occasionally, keeping the compost just moist. Do not allow it to dry out altogether – this causes the leaf tips to turn brown. Do not feed.

# Nephrolepis exaltata

Boston Fern
Fern    Throughout the Tropics

This tough but attractive fern with its graceful arching fronds looks good in a hanging basket, but it can eventually become so large as to block light out of the room. The fronds of *N. exaltata* are divided into many pinnae, growing in opposite pairs from the central rib, and they may be up to 3ft (90cm) long. It is rarely the species plant which is offered for sale, but one of the numerous cultivars developed from it. *N.e.* 'Rooseveltii' has pinnae with wavy edges, while *N.e.* 'Whitmanii' has very dense lacy pale green pinnae.

## The year's care

**Spring and summer:** Temperatures should be between 55–65 deg F (13–18 deg C). This fern will do better in bright light, away from direct sun, but it will tolerate a certain amount of shade. Water frequently to keep the compost moist always. Do not allow the root ball to dry out or fronds will quickly shrivel. If this should happen cut away the dead fronds at compost level and new growth should soon appear. Spray the foliage often, using rain water if the mains water is hard, to avoid marking the pinnae. Feed every two weeks.

**Potting-on:** Since this fern grows quite rapidly and roots soon fill the

*Nephrolepis exaltata*

pot, pot-on every year in spring in a peat-based compost.

**Propagation:** By dividing the plant when replanting, but this often destroys the overall symmetry of the fern until new growth has been established. It can also be propagated by rooting the tiny plantlets on the runners which the fern puts out. Pin a few runners down in a pot of compost and once the plantlets have developed roots sever them from the parent plant along with a piece of the runner. Transplant them when they are well established.

**Autumn and winter:** A rest period at temperatures between 55–60 deg F (13–16 deg C) will benefit the fern. Keep it in a good light, but out of direct sun. Water fairly frequently to keep the compost just moist; the lower the temperature the less water the plant requires. Do not let the compost become waterlogged – the roots will rot. Do not feed when resting.

## Pellaea rotundifolia

Button Fern
Fern   New Zealand

*P. rotundifolia* looks altogether different from other ferns because its pinnae are rounded rather than narrow and pointed. It will stay compact with the dark brown stems growing no longer than 12in (30cm). Each stem has a dozen or more opposite pairs of leathery dark green glossy pinnae with downy undersides. They are round when they first appear, but become oval as they age.

**The year's care**

**Spring and summer:** This fern will do well in normal seasonal temperatures between 55–65 deg F (13–18 deg C). Give it good light, but not direct sun, in a well-ventilated spot. Water frequently so that the compost is always moist. Feed every two weeks.

**Potting-on:** *P. rotundifolia* does not make much root so it will need potting-on only every other year in spring in a peat-based compost.

**Propagation:** The stems grow from a rhizome which can be divided in spring. Make sure that each piece has sufficient roots to support it.

**Autumn and winter:** The ideal temperature is around 55 deg F (13 deg C). Keep the fern in a good light, away from direct sun. Water fairly frequently to prevent the root ball from drying out completely. Do not feed.

## Peperomia argyreia

Watermelon Plant
Foliage   Central and South America

Peperomias are compact plants, rarely growing more than 12in (30cm) high and most reaching only 8in (20cm) with a similar spread of leaves. Several species grouped in a container look particularly attractive. *P. argyreia* (syn. *P. sandersii*) has broad, fleshy, dark green oval leaves up to 3in (7.5cm) long, banded with silver and carried on stalks rising from compost level. *P. caperata* 'Emerald Ripple' has leaves 1in (2.5cm) long, heart-shaped and dark green with purple-grey areas, and they are carried on pink stems. The surface of the leaves looks puckered and quilted. *P. hederifolia* has leaves of similar shape and appearance to those of *P.c.* 'Emerald Ripple', but they are larger – about 2½in (6.25cm) – and the colour is a striking silvery grey with dark green markings on the veins. Among the taller species *P. magnoliifolia* 'Variegata' has mid green leaves with areas of yellow-green, carried on green stems with red markings. All produce unremarkable white flower spikes from spring until early autumn.

*Pellaea rotundifolia*

*Peperomia argyreia*

*Peperomia magnoliifolia* 'Variegata'

## The year's care

**Spring and summer:** Peperomias should be kept in temperatures between 60–65 deg F (16–18 deg C). If the temperature goes much higher stand the pot on a tray of wet pebbles or surround it with moist peat to provide humidity. Or spray the leaves daily. All need good light, but all the plain green species should not have direct sun. The colour of the leaves of the variegated species will be richer with some sunshine. These plants are semi-succulent and need only fairly frequent watering. The compost should be allowed almost to dry out between waterings. Overwatering may cause rotting of roots, loss of leaves and death. Feed once a month.

**Potting-on:** Since they do not make much root growth they should be potted-on every two or three years in spring, but repot them each year into fresh compost. Use a porous peat-based compost.

**Propagation:** By taking stem cuttings about 3in (7.5cm) long in spring and early summer.

**Autumn and winter:** It is best if plants are kept close to the temperature they have had in spring and summer – between 60–65 deg F (16–18 deg C) – but they can stand temperatures as low as 50 deg F (10 deg C). Humidity is not as important in these months. They need bright light with shade from the sun, except the variegated forms which need all the winter sun available. Water occasionally to prevent the compost from drying out completely. Do not feed.

## Saintpaulia ionantha

African Violet
Flowering    East Africa

African violets are often thought of as difficult plants to grow and bring into flower, but with adequate heat and good light they will produce flowers through much of the year. The green, heart-shaped, hairy leaves, velvety looking on the upper surface, are carried on fleshy stems from compost level, but as the plant grows older it develops a small scaly trunk. It will rarely grow more than 6in (15cm) high, but it may spread to 9in (22.5cm) across. Flowers are

a bright light, but out of direct sun. A humid atmosphere is still needed. Water fairly frequently so that the compost is always moist. Do not feed.

# Scindapsus aureus

Devil's Ivy
Foliage    Solomon Islands

*S. aureus* is a climber chosen for its brightly coloured variegated foliage. It grows rapidly, reaching 6ft (1.8m) with no trouble at all, and needs stout support. The green leaves, splashed with yellow, are oval when they first appear, turning to heart-shaped as they mature. In a young plant leaves are about 6in (15cm) long but on an older plant they may grow to 12in (30cm) or more. One cultivar, *S.a.* 'Marble Queen', has green leaves marked with a creamy white, which sometimes covers almost the whole leaf. The leaves of *S.a.* 'Tricolor' have combinations of both dark and pale green, white and yellow.

## The year's care

**Spring and summer:** *S. aureus* needs temperatures between 65–70 deg F (18–21 deg C). If the leaves are to keep their bright variegation the plant must have good light, but shaded from hot direct sunlight. If it is put in a very shaded part of the room it may

*Scindapsus aureus*

*Saintpaulia ionantha*

produced in abundance between spring and early autumn, but they can be induced to continue throughout the year. There are many cultivars available, with either single or double flowers, in colours ranging from white, pink and red to deep purple. Several plants grouped in a large container look effective, and their closeness and the moisture from the peat around them provides a micro-climate of humidity to keep the plants in tip-top condition.

## The year's care

**Spring and summer:** The temperature should be between 60–70 deg F (16–21 deg C), otherwise the plant will flower poorly, or not at all, and may eventually die. It needs bright light, but not direct sunlight, which can cause yellow patches on the leaves, and on occasion scorch both foliage and flowers. The plant does better in a humid atmosphere and if it is not planted in a group the humidity can be achieved by standing the pot on a tray of wet pebbles or surrounding it with moist peat. However, the leaves must never be

sprayed. Water fairly frequently so that the compost is moist all the time, but not sodden. Watering should be done with great care. A single plant in a pot is best watered by standing the pot in about 2in (5cm) of water for half an hour or so. After removing the pot from the water let any excess water drain away before replacing the pot on the saucer. If the plant is watered from the top the leaves are likely to get wet and be permanently marked. Watering from the top is also the quickest way of making the fleshy stems rot, hastening the death of the plant. Plants in a group can be watered by holding the watering can so that the long spout is held close to the level of the compost, watering from the side rather than from above. Feed once a month.

**Potting-on:** In spring every two to three years using a peat-based compost, but repot the plant every year in spring to renew the compost.

**Propagation:** By taking leaf cuttings in spring.

**Autumn and winter:** Maintain a temperature between 60–70 deg F (16–21 deg C), and keep the plant in

even revert to plain green. In hot weather a humid atmosphere is desirable; stand the pot on a tray of wet pebbles or surrround it with moist peat. Keep the compost always moist with frequent watering. Feed every two weeks. Growing tips should be pinched out to encourage bushy growth. Cut back stems to keep the plants under control.

**Potting-on:** In spring only every other year since they prefer to be somewhat potbound. However, the old compost should be replaced by fresh in the years when the plant is not being potted-on. Use a peat-based compost.

**Propagation:** By taking stem tip cuttings, about 4in (10cm) long, in summer.

**Autumn and winter:** The minimum winter temperature is 55 deg F (13 deg C), but the ideal temperature for the resting period is around 60 deg F (16 deg C). Bright light is especially important in the short dull winter days to maintain leaf colour. If plants are kept at a low temperature they will not need a humid atmosphere. Water fairly frequently to keep the compost just moist. Do not feed.

# Strelitzia reginae

Bird of Paradise
Flowering    South Africa

If *S. reginae* is raised from seed it may be six years before the unusual and astonishingly beautiful flowers appear, but even that wait will have been worthwhile. The spear-shaped, leathery, green leaves are carried on the end of long stalks and the plant will grow up to 4ft (1.2m). The blue and orange flower petals emerge from a green bract with red edges. The bracts, some 6in (15cm) long, or carried on 3ft (90cm) stems. The flowering period is from spring to early summer and each flower lasts for several weeks.

## The year's care

**Spring and summer:** The temperature should be between 60–70 deg F (16–21 deg C). The plant needs bright light with some direct sunlight, but it should be shaded from very hot sun. Water frequently, allowing the compost to dry out a little between waterings. Feed every two weeks.

**Potting-on:** Each year in spring when the plants are young, but older plants resent being disturbed and may stop flowering for a year or two. Instead of repotting replace the top few inches of stale compost with fresh. Use a peat-based compost.

**Propagation:** The strelitzia forms clumps and it can be propagated by division in spring. It can also be raised from seed but considerable bottom heat (70 deg F, 21 deg C) and years and years of patience are needed.

**Autumn and winter:** The plant must have a longish rest period at a temperature between 55–60 deg F (13–16 deg C), but it will still require bright light during this time, with direct sun. Water occasionally to prevent the compost from drying out. Do not feed.

*Strelitzia reginae*

# Difficult plants for warm rooms

This section's 32 entries cover 57 plants, and as in the preceding section most of them are from the Tropics. Many of them are outstandingly attractive, but some can be tricky. With this selection the limit is virtually reached of plants which are both fairly readily available and feasible to grow in a warm house. The next step would be with plants from the equatorial zone and the conditions they need would be intolerable for us to live in.

The foliage plants listed are particularly beautiful – the highly coloured caladiums, calatheas, codiaeums, fittonias and geogenanthus (Seersucker Plant) and the graceful dizygotheca. Also there are three attractive palms, three ferns, four orchids and a couple of outstanding bromeliads. There is also one which you will not be able to buy but could grow yourself from an avocado pit (*Persea gratissima*).

The arrowheads ► ◄ point to the extra attention demanded by the plants in this section. Almost without exception they need high humidity and unless the house has an electric humidifier this involves standing the pots on trays of wet pebbles or surrounding them with moist peat, as well as mist-spraying the plants. (For advice on increasing humidity, see pages 26–27).

Another general need for plants in this section is for good light in both the growing and the resting season. While tropical plants will go on growing if the room is warm enough they should, if possible, be induced to rest; their resting temperatures are on the whole much higher than for plants in the cool section of the A–Z.

Two popular plants – poinsettias and kalanchoes – have a specific need. They are short-day plants, so in autumn they must be moved to a room where they can spend the following eight weeks in ten hours of daylight and fourteen hours of complete darkness. Without that treatment the poinsettia will not produce its bracts or the kalanchoe its flowers.

The entries in this section are listed here according to the type of plant they are.

### Flowering
*Acalypha hispida*
*Anthurium scherzerianum*
*Aphelandra squarrosa* 'Louisae'
*Columnea microphylla*
*Euphorbia pulcherrima*
*Hibiscus rosa-sinensis*
*Pachystachys lutea*
*Sinningia speciosa*
*Smithiantha zebrina*
*Spathiphyllum wallisii*

### Foliage
*Aglaonema crispum* 'Silver Queen'
*Caladium hortulanum*
*Calathea makoyana*
*Codiaeum variegatum pictum*
*Dizygotheca elegantissima*
*Fittonia verschaffeltii*
*Geogenanthus undatus*
*Persea gratissima*
*Schefflera actinophylla*

### Succulent
*Kalanchoe blossfeldiana*

### Bromeliads
*Guzmania lingulata*
*Vriesea splendens*

### Palms
*Chrysalidocarpus lutescens*
*Microcoelum weddellianum*
*Phoenix canariensis*

### Ferns
*Asplenium nidus*
*Platycerium bifurcatum*
*Pteris cretica* 'Albolineata'

### Orchids
*Cattleya bowringiana*
*Miltonia vexillaria*
*Odontoglossum grande*
*Paphiopedilum callosum*

*Aglaonema crispum* 'Silver Queen'

Still keep the air around it humid and a good light with direct sun.◄ Water fairly frequently to keep the compost just moist. Do not feed.

## Aglaonema crispum
'Silver Queen'

Chinese Evergreen
Foliage   South East Asia

This is one of the few plants which will tolerate a shady part of the room, but it must have high humidity and warmth. The leathery oval leaves, which grow up to 10in (25cm) long, are dark green with silvery markings. The overall height of the plant will be no more than some 15in (37.5in) since the leaves are carried on short stems. *A. commutatum* 'Treubii' is another very compact plant, with lance shaped leathery leaves about 5in (12.5cm) long, borne on 3in (7.5cm) stems. The dark green of the leaves is marked with yellow. *A.c.* 'Pseudobracteatum' has somewhat larger leaves in two shades of green with cream to yellow markings.

### The year's care

**Spring and summer:** The ideal temperature range is between 65–75 deg F (18–24 deg C). ►The plant requires a slightly shaded spot and should not be exposed to direct sun. A humid atmosphere is also important. The basic choice, as with all humidity-loving plants, is either to

*Acalypha hispida*

## Acalypha hispida

Chenille Plant
Flowering   New Guinea

*A. hispida* is grown both for its velvety foliage and its long tassels of flowers. The 6in (15cm) long, oval, pointed leaves are bright green and hairy. The plant grows quite quickly to 6ft (1.8m) and more, but it can be kept smaller by cutting back stems every year. The red tassels of flowers, up to 15in (37.5cm) long, appear from late spring to early autumn. *A. wilkesiana* is grown more for its striking foliage than for its flowers. The oval leaves, about 6in (15cm) long, are mottled with copper, red and pink. This species also grows to about 6ft (1.8m) and more, but it too can be pruned back every year.

### The year's care

**Spring and summer:** ►Acalyphas require warmth and humidity. The temperature should be between 65–70 deg F (18–21 deg C). Humidity can be provided by standing the pot on a tray of wet pebbles or surrounding it with moist peat. Daily spraying will also help, but do not spray when the plant is in flower. If the air is too dry the leaves will curl and there is always the danger of an attack by red spider mites and aphids. The plant requires bright light with some direct sunlight if it is to flower well, or for *A. wilkesiana* to maintain its rich leaf colour. Always give shade from fierce sun.◄ Water frequently to keep the compost always moist. Feed every two weeks. Cut back the plant in early spring to within 12in (30cm) of the compost if growth has become straggly.

**Potting-on:** Every year in spring, using a peat-based compost.

**Propagation:** By taking stem tip cuttings, about 4in (10cm) long, in spring, but a temperature of 75 deg F (24 deg C) is needed for the cuttings to strike.

**Autumn and winter:** ►The plant can stay in similar temperatures to those of spring and summer – 65–70 deg F (18–21 deg C) – or it can be given a rest, with a temperature not falling below 60 deg F (16 deg C).

*Anthurium scherzerianum*

stand the pot on a tray of wet pebbles or to surround it with moist peat.◄ Water frequently so that the compost is moist always. Feed every two weeks.

**Potting-on:** Every other year in spring, using a peat-based compost, and repot in the intervening years to renew the compost.

**Propagation:** By dividing when replanting, or by taking stem tip cuttings in summer.

**Autumn and winter:** Maintain similar temperatures to those of spring and summer – 65–75 deg F (18–24 deg C). It will tolerate lower temperatures, but not below 60 deg F (16 deg C). ►Humidity is very important during these months because the air in centrally heated rooms is likely to be very dry. Keep the plant shaded from direct sun.◄ Water fairly frequently to make the compost just moist. Do not feed.

# Anthurium scherzerianum

Flamingo Flower
Flowering    Central and South America

Although *A. scherzerianum* is a flowering plant it is the large bright red spathes surrounding each spadix which provide the major interest and colour. For an anthurium to stay in top condition it needs warmth and humidity. The dark green, leathery lance-shaped leaves, about 6in (15cm) long, are carried on stalks of about the same length – a highly desirable compact plant. The fleshy, curling flower spike, or spadix, which is orange-red, appears from early spring to summer, emerging from the centre of the 4in (10cm) spathe (a form of bract). The cultivars of *A. andreanum*, the painter's palette, have elongated heart-shaped dark green leathery leaves about 8in (20cm) long, carried on 8in (20cm) stems. Glossy heart-shaped pink to red spathes surround the yellow spadix.

## The year's care

**Spring and summer:** ►The temperature should be between 65–70 deg F (18–21 deg C). Keep the plant in a bright light, but not direct sun. Anthuriums need a humid atmosphere; stand the pot on a tray of wet pebbles or surround it with moist peat. Dry air may cause leaves to curl and become papery, as well as encouraging red spider mites. Regular spraying will also help, but use rainwater if the mains water is hard – the lime makes unattractive white marks on the foliage.◄ Water often so that the compost is always moist, preferably with rainwater in hard water areas.

**Potting-on:** Every year in spring using a peat-based compost with added sphagnum moss.

**Propagation:** By dividing when potting-on in spring. Plants can be raised from seed, but considerable bottom heat is required, plus a long wait for a plant to reach a respectable size.

**Autumn and winter:** ►Anthuriums need similar temperatures in this period to those in spring and summer – 65–70 deg F (18–21 deg C). They will tolerate a slightly lower temperature, but it should certainly not go below 60 deg F (16 deg C). Maintain a humid atmosphere, especially if the room is centrally heated.◄ Water fairly frequently to keep the compost just moist. Do not feed.

# Aphelandra squarrosa 'Louisae'

Zebra Plant
Flowering   Brazil

The variegated foliage of *A.s.* 'Louisae' is striking enough, but there are also unusual bright yellow bracts from which the small flowers emerge. The bright green shiny elliptic leaves, some 8in (20cm) long, have veins picked out in white. The leaves tend to droop, so do not assume that the plant is short of water and start overwatering it. In summer flower spikes appear at the top of the plant, consisting of overlapping layers of yellow bracts, tipped with orange. The yellow flowers emerge from between the bracts and last about

*Aphelandra squarrosa* 'Louisae'

three weeks. When flowering is over the bracts turn green. This species will grow to no more than 18in (45cm), and *A.s.* 'Brockfeld' is even more compact – about 12in (30cm). Its dark green oval leaves are more distinctively marked with cream and held more erect, but the bracts and flowers are similar to those of *A.s.* 'Louisae'. Plants of both species are often sold when in flower and thrown away when flowering is over, but there is no reason why they should not be kept for a second year.

**The year's care**

**Spring and summer:** The ideal temperature is between 65–70 deg F (18–21 deg C). The plant should be in a bright spot, but out of direct sun. ▶Humidity is very important; if the air is too dry the edges of the leaves are likely to turn brown and red spider mites may attack. Either stand the pot on a tray of wet pebbles or surround it with moist peat.◀ Water frequently to keep the compost moist always; if it dries out the leaves will fall. Feed every two weeks.

**Potting-on:** In spring, using a peat-based compost.

**Propagation:** Take stem tip cuttings, about 4in (10cm) long, in late spring.

**Autumn and winter:** Give the plant a rest at temperatures between 60–65 deg F (16–18 deg C). It will tolerate a temperature as low as 55 deg F (13 deg C) during this period, but certainly nothing lower. ▶Maintain a humid atmosphere and keep the plant out of draughts.◀ It still requires bright light, but shade from direct sun. Water occasionally so that the compost is just moist. When the bracts

have turned green cut back the stems by a quarter, just above a pair of leaves, to encourage new growth for the following year. Do not feed during this period.

# Asplenium nidus

Bird's Nest Fern
Fern   Asia, Africa, Australia

*A. nidus* is an epiphytic fern found growing on the branches of trees in areas of tropical rain forest, but it has adapted to life in a pot of compost. The bright green and glossy broad lance-shaped fronds can grow up to 4ft (1.2m) long and 8in (20cm) wide. They are carried in shuttlecock formation and the central rosette consists of short brown tufts from which new fronds emerge and unfurl. This is one of the more difficult plants to keep in good condition because it requires high humidity and stable temperatures if the fronds are not to turn brown at the tips.

**The year's care**

**Spring and summer:** ▶*A. nidus* requires temperatures between 65–70 deg F (18–21 deg C)◀ Keep the plant in a good light but out of direct sun. It will tolerate a slightly shady spot.

▶Provide a humid atmosphere, either by standing the pot on wet pebbles or surrounding it with moist peat. Regular spraying will also help, but not with hard water which marks the leaves with unsightly lime deposits. Use rainwater instead.◀ Water frequently so that the compost is always moist and water into the centre of the rosette; in the wild the fern collects water there. If the leaves go badly brown and the general appearance of the plant is poor, drastic treatment can save it. Cut off all the fronds at their base in spring and during the summer new growth will appear.

**Potting-on:** Every year in spring in a peat-based compost, or a mixture of loam, peat and sand.

**Propagation:** From the spores found on the undersides of the leaves. This is a long process, not always successful, and the young ferns will take a long time to mature.

**Autumn and winter:** ▶This fern requires temperatures between 65–70 deg F (18–21 deg C) – similar to those in spring and summer. Continue to maintain a humid atmosphere around the plant.◀ Provide good light, but not direct sun. Water fairly frequently so that the compost is just moist. Do not feed.

*Asplenium nidus*

# Caladium hortulanum hybrids

Angel Wings
Foliage   Tropical America, Brazil

Caladiums are showy house plants for the enthusiast with a fondness for leaves with coloured variegations. These tuberous rooted members of the arum family do flower, but it is for the leaves that they are grown. They are not the easiest plants to keep going from year to year; the plant dies down in autumn and the tubers have to be stored through the winter at high temperatures. Many cultivars have been raised from *C. hortulanum*, and it is these, usually unnamed, which are on sale rather than the species plant. The average height of a caladium is about 2ft (60cm) and the individual arrowhead-shaped leaves are about 12in (60cm). Leaf colour is varied, ranging from white to green to pink and red. The veins are picked out in green and red, so there are combinations of green on white, red on green, and green and white mottled leaves with brilliant red veins.

### The year's care

**Spring and summer:** ▶Start the tuber into growth in early spring by bringing the pot into a temperature of 70 deg F (21 deg C). When the leaves have appeared and the plant is well-established it can be moved to a room with a very slightly lower temperature, but not below 65 deg F (18 deg C); on the other hand, it can stand temperatures up to 75 deg F (24 deg C) as long as there is adequate humidity. To help to create this during the period of growth stand the pot on a tray of wet pebbles or surround the pot with moist peat.◀ A good light is vital to maintain the beautiful variegations, but they must not be exposed to direct sunlight. Keep the plant out of draughts, which cause the leaves to curl. Water fairly frequently so that the compost is moist throughout. When the leaves begin to die down in late summer reduce the frequency of watering and stop it altogether when the leaves are dead. Feed every two weeks from the time when the leaves are growing well until they begin to die down.

**Potting-on:** In early spring remove the soil ball from the pot and gently break away the compost, trim any

*Caladium hortulanum hybrid*

*Caladium hortulanum hybrid*

dead roots and repot in fresh compost. Plant the tuber to the equivalent of its own depth beneath the surface of the compost.

**Propagation:** Parent plants often produce offsets which can be detached when repotting.

**Autumn and winter:** ▶When the leaves have died down cut them off and store the tuber in the compost at a temperature of 60 deg F (16 deg C), preferably in a dark place. The tuber should be allowed to dry out, but the compost should not be allowed to become as dry as dust. Watering once a month will be enough.◀ Do not feed in the dormant period.

# Calathea makoyana

Peacock Plant
Foliage   Brazil

Calatheas are close rivals to caladiums for the brilliance of their foliage, but they are rather more subtle. One notable advantage that they have over caladiums is that they do not die down; there is a wonderful show of colour throughout the year. The broad oval green leaves have a central vein from which appear to spring tiny leaflets, but this is only a pattern that looks as though it had been embossed there and heightened with fine silvery brush strokes. The underside of the leaf is shaded purple. The leaves are about 10in (25cm) long, carried on stems of a similar length. *C. insignis* (syn. *C. lancifolia*), the rattlesnake

*Calathea makoyana*

plant, has tall erect lance-shaped leaves which can reach a height of 2ft (60cm). The light green of the leaf is overlaid with olive markings on either side of the central vein and the underside is shaded purple. *C. picturata* has oval leaves, green round the edges and silvery grey in the centre, about 6in (15cm) long, carried on short stems. *C. zebrina*, the zebra plant, is more restrained than the rest, with emerald green leaves, broken up by lighter shading of the midrib and veins, and a purple underside. It will rarely grow more than 18in (45cm) in height, arching its leaves gracefully over the side of the pot.

### The year's care

**Spring and summer:** A temperature between 60–70 deg F (16–21 deg C) is best. Higher temperatures will be tolerated but only if humidity is increased considerably. ▶A humid atmosphere is vital; stand the pot on wet pebbles or surround it with moist peat. A daily spray of the foliage will also help, but use rainwater and not hard tap water, to avoid staining the leaves. If the air is too dry the leaves

*Calathea zebrina*

will turn brown at the tips and red spider mites can become a menace.◀ Calatheas will be happy with a somewhat shady position, but do not put them in deep gloom. Water frequently to keep the compost moist. Soft tepid water should be used at all times. Feed every two weeks.

**Potting-on:** Every year in early summer in a peat-based compost.

**Propagation:** In spring the plant can be divided, but only if there is bushy growth, otherwise the result will be two spindly plants which will take months to grow into a good shape again.

**Autumn and winter:** Temperatures should be the same as for spring and summer – 60–70 deg F (16–21 deg C) – and should not fall below 60 deg F (16 deg C). If the temperature is too low the leaves will brown and curl. ▶Maintain a humid atmosphere, and keep the plant in a good light to maintain leaf colour. ◀ Water occasionally so that the compost is just moist; more frequently if the plant is kept in higher temperatures. Do not feed.

## Cattleya bowringiana

Cluster cattleya
Orchid   Central America

Given sufficient warmth and humidity *C. bowringiana* will produce an abundance of flowers in autumn. For the rest of the year it looks unprepossessing. The pseudo-bulbs protrude about 8in (20cm) above the level of the compost, and they carry one or perhaps two leathery strap-shaped leaves some 5in (12.5cm) long. The mass of purple flowers with a darker shaded lip are borne on a long flower stalk. They should last for several weeks.

### The year's care

**Spring and summer:** ▶The daytime temperature should be between 65–75 deg F (18–24 deg C), with a lower night temperature, but not falling below 60 deg F (16 deg C). *C. bowringiana* needs excellent light but must not be exposed to scorching sun. Provide good ventilation and a humid atmosphere by standing the pot on a tray of wet pebbles or by surrounding the pot with moist peat. Mist-spray the plants regularly, especially in very warm weather.◄ Water frequently so that the compost is always moist. Feed once a month.

**Potting-on:** The plant will need moving into a larger pot every two or three years in late spring, using a mixture of peat, sphagnum moss and osmunda fibre. In the intervening years the plant should be repotted to replace the exhausted compost with fresh.

**Propagation:** By dividing the rhizome when repotting. Make sure there are sufficient roots to support each pseudo-bulb.

*Cattleya bowringiana*

**Autumn and winter:** ►The orchid requires similar temperatures throughout this period to those of spring and summer – 65–75 deg F (18–24 deg C) by day and a few degrees lower at night. It still needs good light, but shade it from direct sun, especially when it is in flower, or the flowers will quickly fade. Continue to provide a humid atmosphere.◄ Water frequently until flowering has stopped and then water occasionally. Allow the compost almost to dry out between waterings, but if the pseudo-bulbs begin to shrivel water is needed. Do not feed.

*Chrysalidocarpus lutescens*

# Chrysalidocarpus lutescens

Areca Palm, Yellow Butterfly Palm
Palm    Mauritius

Although *C. lutescens* grows only a few inches each year it can eventually reach a height of 10ft (3m) or more, with a spread of several feet. This is a palm for large rooms with high ceilings. Warmth and humidity are essential to keep the fronds in good condition. Yellow stems of about 2ft (60cm) bear elegantly arching fronds, which in a medium-sized palm will be about 4ft (1.2m) long. The fronds are divided into almost opposite pairs of yellow-green leaves of about 8in (45cm).

## The year's care

### Spring and summer:
►Temperatures of 65–75 deg F (18–24 deg C) are a must for this palm and the atmosphere around it should also be humid. Stand the pot on wet pebbles or surround it with moist peat in a larger container. If the air is dry the tips of the leaves will brown.◄ Give the plant bright light,

including some direct sun, but not hot fierce midday sun. Water frequently to keep the compost moist at all times. Feed once a month.

**Potting-on:** Every year in spring in a mixture of half peat and half loam. When a pot size of 12in (30cm) has been reached instead of potting-on remove the top 3in (7.5cm) of compost and replace it with new.

**Propagation:** The palm can be raised from seed sown in spring, but it will be many years before it reaches a decent size. Mature plants throw up suckers and these can be removed and potted up. Make sure that you remove enough roots with each sucker to support its growth.

**Autumn and winter:** ►The ideal temperature range is the same as for spring and summer – 65–75 deg F (18–24 deg C) – but the plant will tolerate one as low as 60 deg F (16 deg C). Maintain a high degree of humidity.◄ Also provide bright light with direct sun. Water frequently to keep the compost always moist. If the palm is kept at a lower temperature water less frequently, to prevent the compost from drying out. Do not feed.

*Codiaeum variegatum pictum*

# Codiaeum variegatum pictum

Croton
Foliage    Malaysia

Many cultivars have been developed from *C.v. pictum* with different leaf shapes and colourings, some of them very gaudy. They grow to a height of 3ft (90cm) with a similar spread. The leaves may be broad or narrow, oblong, long thin fingers, or lobed, depending on the cultivar. Leaf colour may be yellow, green, pink, brown, orange and black in combinations of two, three or more colours. The veins of some are picked out in contrasting colour; in others the leaves are spotted or blotched with colour. Warmth and good light are two requirements for sturdy growth.

## The year's care

**Spring and summer:** ▶The temperature should be between 60–70 deg F (16–21 deg C). Aim for an even temperature since sudden changes make the leaves drop. Keep the plants out of draughts. Bright light, with direct sun, is necessary if the leaves are to retain their brilliant colouring. However, protect the plant from scorching sun. Provide a humid atmosphere around the plant by standing the pot on wet pebbles or by surrounding it with moist peat. Dry air often brings infestations of red spider mites. ◀ If the plant has become leggy the stems can be cut back in early spring to within 6in (15cm) of the compost, just above a node. New growth will soon appear.

**Potting-on:** Each year in spring in a peat-based compost.

**Propagation:** By taking stem tip or basal cuttings, 4in (10cm) long, in summer. This is a plant that can also be air layered.

**Autumn and winter:** ▶Codiaeums do best in temperatures similar to those of spring and summer – 60–70 deg F (16–21 deg C) – but they will tolerate a temperature as low as 55 deg F (13 deg C). Maintain a humid atmosphere and keep the plant in a bright light. Direct sun is even more important at this time of the year for good leaf colour. Poor light will cause the leaves to pale or even revert to plain green. If lower leaves fall check that the plant is not in a draught. ◀ Water fairly frequently to prevent the compost from drying out. Do not feed.

# Columnea microphylla

Goldfish Vine
Flowering    Costa Rica

The long trailing stems of *C. microphylla*, densely covered with small dark green leaves, make a contrasting background for the beautiful, curiously shaped red flowers. The plant looks best in a hanging container. Reddish hairs cover the 3ft (90cm) long stems and the leaves. The red-tipped flowers with yellow throats appear in large numbers in spring and last for about a month. Two other columneas which grow to much the same length are *C. banksii*, with fleshy leaves, and *C. gloriosa*, the leaves of which are covered with purplish hairs. They both normally bloom in spring, but often they can be bought in flower throughout the year.

## The year's care

**Spring and summer:** ▶A columnea must have steady warmth, around 65 deg F (18 deg C) if it is to do well. For prolific flowering it needs bright light, with shade from the direct summer sun. Humidity is also important, and if the plant is in a hanging basket container this can be provided by daily misting. A plant grown in a pot should be stood on wet pebbles or surrounded by moist peat. ◀ Water fairly frequently so that the compost stays just moist; if it becomes waterlogged the stems are likely to rot. Feed every two weeks.

**Potting-on:** Every second year when flowering has finished, in a peat-based

*Columnea microphylla*

compost. But repot in the other years to replace the old compost.

**Propagation:** Take stem tip cuttings, about 4in (10cm) long, when flowering is over.

**Autumn and winter:** ▶Give the plant a rest period at about 60 deg F (16 deg C) to build up its strength for flowering in spring. Maintain a humid atmosphere and keep the plant in good light, but out of direct sun.◀ Water occasionally to prevent the compost from drying out completely. Too much water at this time of the year can affect the spring flowering. Do not feed.

# Dizygotheca elegantissima

False Aralia
Foliage   New Hebrides

*D. elegantissima* is a truly elegant plant. Each leaf is made up of several narrow glossy leaflets with serrated edges, a coppery colour when they first appear, darkening to green as they age. It grows to about 5ft (1.5m). Most of the plants offered for sale are small, single stem specimens, but three or four of them planted in one pot have far greater effect, because of their bushiness in a group. *D. veitchii* is similar to *D. elegantissima*, but the leaflets are broader with deep red undersides.

## The year's care

**Spring and summer:** ▶If at all possible keep *D. elegantissima* in a constant temperature of around 65 deg F (18 deg C). Provide a humid atmosphere by standing the pot on a tray of wet pebbles or by surrounding

*Dizygotheca elegantissima*

the pot with moist peat. Frequent spraying of the leaves in warm weather will also help, but do not use hard water.◀ The plant needs good light but shade from direct sun. Water frequently so that the compost is evenly moist. Feed every two weeks. A plant which has developed a long, bare stem and looks odd can be cut back in spring to within about six inches of the compost, just above a node – the knobbly protuberance is easily recognisable on the stem of the plant. New growth will sprout from this point.

**Potting-on:** A dizygotheca does not grow very quickly, so potting-on every two years, in spring, will be enough. Use a peat-based compost.

**Propagation:** By sowing seed in spring.

**Autumn and winter:** ▶Give the plant a rest at a temperature of 60 deg F (16 deg C), but not below or the lower leaves will fall. Maintain a humid atmosphere.◀ Water occasionally so that the compost does not dry out completely. Do not feed.

# Euphorbia pulcherrima

Poinsettia
Flowering   Mexico

*E. pulcherrima* is usually on sale just before Christmas, providing vivid

winter colour of red bracts against bright mid-green leaves. Unlike the other popular Christmas gift of an azalea, which needs cool to retain its flowers, the poinsettia will thrive in centrally heated rooms. When the bracts begin to fall the plant is often discarded, but with the right care they can be induced to appear year after year. The trick is strict control of how many hours of daylight and how many of darkness it has for a two month period starting in autumn. The oval, toothed leaves are about 4in (10cm) long, and the plant will grow to no more than some 18in (45cm). There are several cultivars with different coloured bracts – red, pink or white – surrounding small undistinguished yellow flowers.

## The year's care

**Spring and summer:** ▶When the bracts have faded prune the stems to within 6in (15cm) of the compost and keep the plant in a temperature around 65 deg F (18 deg C). It will need bright light, but not direct sunlight. Water occasionally to prevent the compost from drying out completely until new growth appears; frequent watering will then be necessary.◀ Feed every two weeks when sturdy growth has been established.

**Potting-on:** Each year in late spring after the stems have been cut back;

*Euphorbia pulcherrima*

*Fittonia verschaffeltii*

but give the plant time to recover from this pruning before potting-on. Use either a loam-based or a peat-based mixture.

**Propagation:** By taking stem tip cuttings of about 4in (10cm) in early summer.

**Autumn and winter:** ►A poinsettia requires a temperature around 65 deg F (18 deg C). To make the plant produce bracts it must have strictly controlled hours of darkness and light during this time of the year. In mid autumn put it in a room where it will get no more than ten hours of daylight and fourteen hours of darkness, and that means total darkness. After eight weeks of that treatment bring the plant back into normal light, but not direct sunlight, and the red bracts should appear shortly afterwards.◄ Water fairly frequently to keep the compost just moist. The leaves will begin to drop if the plant is not getting enough water. Do not feed.

# Fittonia verschaffeltii

Red Net Leaf
Foliage   Peru

Fittonias are creeping plants spreading their stems over an area of 12in (30cm) or more. They are demanding because they need warmth and high humidity if they are not to grow into a straggly mass of bare stems. *F. verschaffeltii* has oval, dark green leaves about 3in (7.5cm) long, with the veins picked out in carmine. The leaves of *F. argyroneura*, the silver net leaf, have silvery white veins. There is a smaller version, *F.a.* 'Nana', with leaves no more than 1in (2.5cm) long and this is a slightly less demanding plant.

**The year's care**

**Spring and summer:** ►The ideal temperature range is between 65–70 deg F (18–21 deg C). Provide high humidity by standing the pot on wet pebbles or surrounding it with moist peat.◄ A fittonia prefers a slightly shaded spot at this time of the year, and should certainly never be exposed to direct sunlight, which damages the leaves. Water frequently to keep the compost evenly moist, but not sodden. If the compost is too wet stems and roots will rot. Feed every two weeks.

**Potting-on:** In spring each year. Use a shallow, wide pot, and plant in a mixture of two parts of peat-based compost to one part of sharp sand.

**Propagation:** Either by taking cuttings, about 3in (7.5cm) long, in early summer or by layering.

**Autumn and winter:** ►Give the plant a rest, with a temperature not below 60 deg F (16 deg C). Continue to provide a humid atmosphere.◄ Keep the plant out of draughts. In the poor winter light move the plant to a brighter part of the room, but do not expose it to direct sun. Water occasionally so that the compost is just moist. Do not feed.

# Geogenanthus undatus

Seersucker Plant
Foliage   Peru

*G. undatus* is a compact, low growing plant, no more than 12in (30cm) high. The broad oval leaves, about 4in (10cm) long, have a puckered and quilted look, with wavy lines in various shades of green. The upper surface of the leaf has a metallic sheen, while the underside is shaded purplish-red. In summer clusters of blue flowers appear on short stems, but they last less than a day. Warmth is essential to keep the plant in tip top condition.

**The year's care**

**Spring and summer:** ►The ideal temperature is a steady 70 deg F (21 deg C) and high humidity is vital. Stand the pot on a tray of wet pebbles or surround it with moist peat. Regular spraying of the leaves will also help.◄ Bright light is necessary to maintain the leaf colour, but not direct sun. Water frequently so that the compost is moist always. Feed every two weeks.

**Potting-on:** In spring, using either a loam or peat-based compost.

*Geogenanthus undatus*

**Propagation:** By taking stem tip cuttings, about 3in (7.5cm) long, in spring, or by division when repotting.

**Autumn and winter:** ▶*G. undatus* requires a constant temperature of 70 deg F (21 deg C), as in spring and summer, although it does tolerate temperatures as low as 65 deg F (18 deg C). Continue to provide a humid atmosphere. Dry air will encourage infestations of red spider mites and mealy bugs.◀ Bright light is especially important in the short winter days, but even so do not expose the plant to direct sun. Water fairly frequently so that the compost is just moist. Do not feed.

# Guzmania lingulata

Scarlet Star
Bromeliad   Central and South America, West Indies

Guzmanias are for the most part epiphytic bromeliads, with either green or variegated foliage. Their main attraction is the central flower stalk which has highly coloured, long-lasting bracts, surrounding flowers which are short-lived. *G. lingulata* forms a rosette of narrow, sword-shaped, green leaves often tinged with red, about 18in (45cm) long. The flower stalk carries bright red bracts which remain in good colour through autumn and into winter when the yellow flowers usually appear. Many cultivars have been developed with orange or deep red bracts and the most popular is *G.l.* 'Minor', which has leaves no more than 12in (30cm) long, with red bracts. *G. zahnii* has delicate translucent leaves, about 20in (50cm) long, which are striped with red along their length on both upper and lower surfaces. The bracts are deep red, with brilliant white flowers emerging in between them.

## The year's care

**Spring and summer:** ▶Keep a guzmania in a temperature between 65–70 deg F (18–21 deg C). To flower it needs bright light, but shade from hot midday sun. Provide the vital humidity by standing the pot on a tray of wet pebbles or surrounding it with moist peat.◀ Water frequently so that the compost is moist all the time and top up the central rosette with water. Feed monthly.

**Potting-on:** Every two years in spring in a peat-based compost. When flowering is over the parent plant dies, but offsets will have developed.

*Guzmania lingulata*

**Propagation:** By removing offsets after the parent plant has died. Wait until they are well-established and at least 3in (7.5cm) high before removing them.

**Autumn and winter:** ▶If possible give the plant a rest at a temperature between 60–65 deg F (16–18 deg C). Bright light is essential to keep the bracts a good colour and to ensure flowering. Continue to provide a high degree of humidity; leaf tips will turn brown in dry air.◀ Water fairly frequently so that the compost is just moist. Do not water into the rosette during this period. Do not feed.

# Hibiscus rosa-sinensis

Rose of China
Flowering   China, Tropics

This fast growing, evergreen shrub can rapidly reach 6ft (1.8m) unless it is pruned back hard every year. The oval, dark green and glossy leaves, up to 3in (7.5cm) long, have serrated edges. Showy funnel-shaped flowers, some 5in (12.5cm) across, have prominently protruding stamens. The flowers may be single or double, in shades of yellow, orange, red and pink, depending on the cultivar. They appear from early summer to autumn and though each flower lasts only just over a day, so many are produced on mature plants that this hardly matters. *H. r-s.* 'Cooperi' has dark green leaves with red and cream markings. Warmth and humidity are needed to prevent leaf and bud drop.

## The year's care

**Spring and summer:** ▶The temperature should be between 60–65 deg F (16–18 deg C). Spray the plant

*Hibiscus rosa-sinensis*

*Kalanchoe blossfeldiana*

moist; given too much water the leaves bloat and rot. Feed every three or four weeks.

**Potting-on:** In spring, in a loam-based compost.

**Propagation:** By taking stem tip cuttings, about 3in (7.5cm) long, in spring, or by sowing seed.

**Autumn and winter:** Give the plant a rest at a temperature between 55–60 deg F (13–16 deg C). ►To induce the flower to bloom again the following year place it in mid autumn in a room where it will get no more than ten hours of daylight with fourteen hours of total darkness. After eight weeks bring it back into normal light and put it on a window-sill where it will get the sun. Flowers should soon appear.◄ Water very occasionally to prevent the compost from drying out completely; the leaves will shrivel if the plant is not getting enough water. Do not feed.

# Microcoelum weddellianum

Coconut Palm
Palm   Brazil

*M. weddellianum* is usually on sale when it is no more than 12in (30cm) high, but given time it will grow to about 5ft (1.5m). In its early stages the delicate-looking fronds are about 10in (25cm) long with many narrow pinnae, arranged almost opposite

*Microcoelum weddellianum*

regularly in warm weather.◄ Good light is necessary for prolific flowering and some sunshine does no harm as long as the plant is shaded from fierce midday sun. Water frequently so that the compost is moist all the time. Feed every two weeks. To keep growth in check cut back the stems to within 6in (15cm) of the compost in early spring.

**Potting-on:** Each year in spring in a loam-based compost.

**Propagation:** By taking tip cuttings, about 4in (10cm) long, in summer.

**Autumn and winter:** ►Give the hibiscus a rest at a temperature between 55–60 deg F (13–16 deg C) – if it is any lower leaves are likely to fall. Spray every two or three days.◄ Keep the plant in a good light with direct sunlight. Water occasionally to prevent the compost from drying out completely. Do not feed.

# Kalanchoe blossfeldiana

Succulent   Madagascar

These succulents with their clusters of delicate flowers are often thrown away when they stop flowering, because their foliage is not

particularly attractive and they can be difficult to bring into flower again the following year. However, it can be done if the daylight it gets in the autumn is restricted. Plants in bloom are usually on sale before Christmas and flowers will go on appearing until early spring. The fleshy, circular, dark green leaves, tinged with red, are about 2in (5cm) long. The flowers grow in clusters on short stalks, their colours ranging from yellow to orange and red, according to the cultivar. Most kalanchoes grow no more than 12in (30cm) high and there are dwarf forms half that size. *K. pumila* has oval leaves with serrated edges covered with whitish powder, producing a pinkish-grey effect, which sets off the pink to violet flowers. *K. tomentosa* rarely flowers and is grown for its attractive rosette of fleshy oval leaves, covered with white down and edged with brown patches. They are carried on tall stems up to 18in (45cm) high.

### The year's care

**Spring and summer:** ►The ideal temperature range is between 60–65 deg F (16–18 deg C). The plant needs bright light, but should be shielded from hot midday sun.◄ Water fairly frequently to keep the compost just

each other along the central rib. As they mature the fronds reach about 3ft (90cm), but since they are held fairly erect the spread of the palm will be no more than 30in (75cm). To keep healthy the plant must have warmth and humidity.

**The year's care**

**Spring and summer:** ▶The temperature should be between 65–70 deg F (18–21 deg C). The palm needs good light but shade from direct sun. To make the air around it more humid stand the pot on a large tray of wet pebbles or surround it with moist peat. Daily spraying will also help.◀ Water frequently so that the compost is always moist, and if the tap water is hard it is better to save and use rainwater. Feed every two weeks.

**Potting-on:** Every two years in spring in a loam-based compost. Take great care when handling the roots since they are easily damaged.

**Propagation:** By sowing seed in spring, but it is a tedious business waiting for them to germinate, let alone grow to a decent size.

**Autumn and winter:** ▶The palm will do better if it has a rest at a temperature between 60–65 deg F (16–18 deg C), in bright light but out of direct sun. Humidity is also necessary throughout this period.◀ Water occasionally to keep the compost just moist, but do not let it dry out completely or the leaves will turn brown. Using hard water may also have the same effect. Do not feed.

# Miltonia vexillaria

Pansy Orchid
Orchid   Colombia

The attraction of this orchid is the pansy-like flowers which appear in late spring and last through summer. *M. vexillaria* is an epiphyte with short pseudo-bulbs, carrying 10in (25cm) strap-shaped stems. The flowers, are carried on 24in (60cm) stalks and each pseudo-bulb may throw up several stalks. The flowers, about 3in (7.5cm) across, are deep pink to red with prominent yellow markings. Carefully regulated temperatures and high humidity are vital if this orchid is to flower well.

**The year's care**

**Spring and summer:** ▶The ideal temperature is between 65–70 deg F (18–21 deg C), with night temperatures towards the lower end of the scale. Bright light is needed, but shade from direct sun, which bleaches out the delicate foliage. A well-ventilated spot with humidity is a must. Stand the pot on a tray of wet pebbles or keep the pot buried in moist peat. Spray the plant daily.◀ Water frequently, so that the compost is moist throughout, but not sodden, which causes the roots to rot. Feed once a month.

**Potting-on:** In summer when flowering is over, in a mixture of peat, osmunda fibre and sphagnum moss.

**Propagation:** By dividing the rhizome when potting-on. Each section should have two or more pseudo-bulbs.

**Autumn and winter:** ▶Slightly lower temperatures, between 60–65 deg F (16–18 deg C), are required with night temperatures at the lower end of the scale. Bright light is even more important at this time of the year in the build up to flowering. The plant may even be allowed spells of weak winter sun. Maintain a humid atmosphere.◀ Water occasionally to keep the compost fairly moist. Do not feed.

# Odontoglossum grande

Tiger Orchid
Orchid  ·Guatemala

The large spectacular striped flowers of *O. grande* make it a must for the orchid enthusiast and it can be successfully grown in the home. Each short pseudo-bulb produces two strap-shaped, bright green leaves about

*Miltonia vexillaria*

*Odontoglossum grande*

10in (25cm) long. The flowers, bright yellow with reddish brown bands, are about 6in (15cm) across, and several are borne on each of the 12in (30cm) flower stems. The flowers appear in the autumn and last for many weeks.

**The year's care**

**Spring and summer:** ▶The daytime temperature should be a constant 60 deg F (16 deg C), with a night temperature dropping to 50 deg F (10 deg C). The orchid will tolerate higher day temperatures, but no higher than 70 deg F (21 deg C). It requires bright light, but shade from direct sun. Even though it likes cool temperatures it must also have humidity, so this is another plant that needs to be in a pot standing on wet pebbles or surrounded by moist peat. Spray the plant daily.◀ Water frequently so that the compost is moist always. Feed once a month.

**Autumn and winter:** ▶O. grande requires the same even temperatures as for spring and summer – 60 deg F

(16 deg C) by day and 50 deg F (10 deg C) at night. It needs bright light, with some direct sun. Continue to provide humidity.◀ Water occasionally, but allow the compost almost to dry out between waterings. Do not feed.

**Potting-on:** Every year when flowering has finished, in a mixture of peat, osmunda fibre and sphagnum moss.

**Propagation:** By division when repotting. Each piece of the divided rhizome should have four or more pseudo-bulbs showing signs of fresh healthy growth.

# Pachystachys lutea

Lollipop Plant
Flowering   Peru

The interest in this once popular and recently resurrected indoor plant is the bright yellow bracts which bear a marked similarity to those of *Aphelandra squarrosa*. Once the flowers

*Pachystachys lutea*

and bracts have died down it is usually discarded, but if it is pruned every year in spring it should last for several years. The erect stems, up to 18in (45cm) long, carry opposite pairs of lance-shaped, dark green leaves. Between late spring and early autumn the bright yellow cone of overlapping bracts appears, with white-tipped flowers protruding in between. The flowers last for a few days only, but the bracts remain colourful for up to three months.

**The year's care**

**Spring and summer:** *P. lutea* requires temperatures between 60–65 deg F (16–18 deg C) and a brightly lit spot, but it should be shaded from direct sun. ▶Provide a humid atmosphere by standing the pot on a tray of wet pebbles or surrounding it with moist peat. Spraying the plant daily will also help, but the effect of this is not as long lasting.◀ Water frequently so that the compost is moist throughout, but not sodden. Feed once every two weeks. Prune back the shoots each spring to within 6in (15cm) of the compost to induce bushy growth.

**Potting-on:** Each year in spring in a loam or peat-based compost.

**Propagation:** By taking stem tip cuttings about 4in (10cm) long, in spring.

**Autumn and winter:** Give the plant a rest period at a temperature between 55–60 deg F (13–16 deg C). To ensure flowering the following year the plant will still require bright light, but shade from the sun. ▶Maintain a humid atmosphere.◀ Water occasionally to keep the compost just moist. The resting plant should not be fed.

# Paphiopedilum callosum

Slipper Orchid
Orchid   Nepal, Assam

The beauty of orchids lies in their flowers; the foliage is of little interest. *P. callosum* is an exception, with dark green, strap-shaped leaves attractively mottled with light green. They are about 2in (5cm) long, growing in overlapping opposite pairs. The flowers, appearing in spring on 12in

*Paphiopedilum callosum*

*Persea gratissima*

# Persea gratissima

Avocado Pear
Foliage   Central and South America

(30cm) stems are white with maroon and green stripes and light purple lips. *P. insigne* has narrow, strap-shaped, bright green leaves, about 10 in (25cm) long. Its flowers, on 10in (25cm) stems, are a yellowy green with purple-brown spots and the yellow lip is tinged with brown. Flowers usually appear in late winter and on both plants last for several weeks.

### The year's care

**Spring and summer:** ▶The temperature should be between 60–65 deg F (16–18 deg C). The orchid needs a slightly shaded spot and must never be exposed to direct sun, which turns the leaves yellow. Provide humidity by standing the pot on wet pebbles or surrounding it with moist peat. Humidity is especially important if temperatures rise much above those recommended.◀ Water frequently to keep the compost moist all the time, but not waterlogged. Too much water makes the sensitive roots rot. Feed once a month.

**Potting-on:** Every two to three years when flowering has finished. Use a mixture of peat, osmunda fibre and sphagnum moss. Use the same mix when repotting each year to renew the compost.

**Propagation:** By dividing the plant when repotting. Make sure that each piece of the rhizome has several leaves and enough roots to support it. Take care when disentangling the roots since they are easily damaged.

**Autumn and winter:** ▶Maintain daytime temperatures between 60–65 deg F (16–18 deg C) as in spring and summer, but the night temperature should drop to between 55–60 deg F (13–16 deg C) to ensure that the plant will flower. It should be in a slightly shaded spot, out of direct sun, and in a humid atmosphere.◀ Before and during flowering, water frequently to keep the compost always moist, but immediately after flowering water only occasionally for about ten weeks while the plant is resting. Do not feed.

*P. gratissima* is a do-it-yourself plant, for it will never be found on sale in a shop. It is raised from the pit (or stone) of an avocado, but not all pits will root because they may not be fertile. Some of the best looking plants come from the jumbo-size pits of a Californian avocado. Pits can be induced to root at any time of the year given enough warmth, but the best time is in spring and summer so that the plant has a good chance of becoming well-established before winter. Indoors an avocado can grow to 6ft (1.8m) or more, but the only way of getting a bushy plant is by cutting it back when it is still very young; the alternative is a long stem with a few leaves at the top. The bright green leaves are elliptical in shape and anything up to 12in (30cm) long.

### The year's care

**Spring and summer:** ▶*P. gratissima* should have a temperature between 60–70 deg F (16–21 deg C) and bright light with some direct – but not fierce – sun. To prevent the leaf tips, and eventually the whole leaf, from turning brown provide a humid atmosphere, putting the pot on a tray of wet pebbles or surrounding it with moist peat. ◂ Water frequently so that the compost is moist throughout. Feed every two weeks. Pinch out the growing tips to promote bushy growth.

**Potting-on:** Each year in spring in a peat-based compost, or a mixture of peat, loam and sharp sand.

**Propagation:** By inducing the pit to root. Take a pit freshly removed from a ripe pear and place it on the top of a narrow necked container filled with water; a bulb glass of the kind used for growing a hyacinth is fine if the top is large enough to take the pit. The pit, blunt end down, must be only just touching the surface of the water, which will have to be topped up as it evaporates, but only enough to keep the base of the pit wet. It is likely to rot if more is kept standing in water. Keep it in a temperature between 70–75 deg F (21–24 deg C), preferably in the dark. It may take weeks to germinate. The first sign of growth will be a fat white root, followed by a shoot from the split in the top of the pit. It can then be brought into the light, but still must have warmth. Wait until there are plenty of roots before moving it into a peat-based compost, or a mixture of loam, peat and sand. When planting leave the top of the pit protruding a little above the surface of the compost. Alternatively the pit can be germinated in a peat-based rooting compost. Plant it blunt end down with the top just above the surface of the compost. Enclose the pot in a plastic bag and put it in a warm place in the dark, bringing it into the light when a shoot appears. When well-established, repot it into a peat-based potting compost, or into a mixture of peat, loam and sand. Whichever method is used it is essential when the stem has grown about 8in (20cm) long to cut it down to 5in (12.5cm). This involves the loss of all its leaves but new side shoots will soon appear. Thereafter from time to time pinch out the growing tips for bushy growth.

**Autumn and winter:** ▸ *P. gratissima* should be kept in the same range of temperatures as in spring and summer – 70–75 deg F (21–24 deg C). Keep it in a bright light and provide a humid atmosphere around it to counter the dryness of a centrally heated room. ◂ Water fairly frequently so that the compost is just moist. Do not feed.

# Phoenix canariensis

Canary Date Palm
Palm    Canary Islands

The stiff erect fronds of *P. canariensis* eventually form a plant up to 6ft (1.8m) high, with a spread of 3ft (90cm), but only after many years, as indoors it grows only about 6in (15cm) a year. The narrow pinnae of each frond, short at the base, gradually widening towards the centre and shortening again at the top, are arranged in pairs on each side of the main rib. *P. roebelenii* is not so coarse in appearance as *P. canariensis*. The fronds are similar in many ways, but they gently arch instead of growing erect – a graceful plant. This species will grow no more than 5ft (1.5m), but the spread will be between 3–4ft (90cm–1.2m).

## The year's care

**Spring and summer:** ▸The optimum temperature is between 65–70 deg F (18–21 deg C). When the weather is warm enough it is good to put the palm outdoors, if at all possible. *P. canariensis* needs bright light and direct sun, whereas *P. roebelenii* should be shaded from direct sun. If the light is not good enough the lower leaves will turn yellow. Water frequently so that the compost is moist throughout, but if waterlogged the roots are likely to die. If the palm is underwatered the tips of the leaves turn brown. ◂ Feed every two weeks.

**Potting-on:** Each year in spring in a well-draining loam compost until the maximum convenient pot size of 12in (30cm) has been reached. Thereafter remove the top 3in (7.5cm) of compost and replace with fresh.

**Propagation:** Sow seed in spring, but it takes months before the seed germinates and years before the plant grows to a decent size. *P. roebelenii* throws up suckers from the base of the plant and these can be removed and potted up.

**Autumn and winter:** ▸Both species should have a rest period at a temperature between 55–60 deg F

*Phoenix canariensis*

(13–16 deg C). *P. canariensis* needs bright light with direct sun, but *P. roebelenii* requires a shaded spot.◄ Water occasionally to keep the compost just moist. Do not feed.

# Platycerium bifurcatum

Staghorn Fern
Fern   Australia, East Indies

The grand unusual fronds of this epiphytic fern are always a talking point, but to stay worth being talked about the fern must have humidity. *P. bifurcatum* (syn. *P. alcicorne*) has sterile circular fronds which turn brown and die, to be replaced by new ones. The fertile fronds grow from the centre of the sterile fronds. They are forked, resembling the horns of a stag, and they grow to 2–3ft (60–90 cm), giving a spread in a mature fern of 3ft (90cm) or more. The dark green fertile fronds of *P. grande*, the regal elkhorn fern, are even longer, growing to 5ft (1.5m). Platyceriums look at their best when grown as hanging plants but this makes even more difficult the problem of providing them with a humid atmosphere.

## The year's care

**Spring and summer:** ►A temperature between 60–70 deg F (16–21 deg C) is essential. The fern requires bright light, but should be out of direct sunlight. If the plant is grown in a pot, stand it on wet

*Platycerium bifurcatum*

pebbles or surround it with moist peat. A plant grown in a hanging basket can be mist-sprayed every other day; excessive spraying removes the waxy covering of the fronds.◄ Water frequently so that the compost is moist all through, but allow it to dry out a little between waterings. Plants in pots are best watered by immersion in shallow water. Feed once a month.

**Potting-on:** Once every three years in spring in a mixture of peat and sphagnum moss. In other years merely repot to renew the compost.

**Propagation:** From spores on the undersides of fronds, but this is not always successful. The fern sometimes produces an offset at the base and this can be detached when repotting.

**Autumn and winter:** ►The plant will benefit from a rest period at a temperature between 60–65 deg F (16–18 deg C) in a bright spot out of direct sun. Maintain a humid atmosphere.◄ Water occasionally so that the compost is just moist. Do not feed.

# Pteris cretica
'Albolineata'

Ribbon Brake
Fern   Mediterranean, tropical
 regions

The brake ferns are comparatively easy to grow and reasonably tolerant of dry air. But if they are to stay in good condition over a period of years they need a certain amount of humidity and correct watering. *P.c.* 'Albolineata', which grows to some 18in (45cm), has up to four strap-shaped pinnae with a whitish green streak running the length of each one, and they are carried on a black stalk. *P. cretica*, the species, has plain mid-green fronds. Another variety, *P.c.* 'Wimsetii' is larger and the tips of each of the pinnae are crested. *P. ensiformis* 'Victoriae' is similar to *P. cretica*, but the fronds are a darker green and are streaked with silvery white along the rib.

## The year's care

**Spring and summer:** ►The ideal temperature range is between 60–65 deg F (16–18 deg C) and within that range humidity will not be important.

*Pteris cretica* 'Albolineata'

*Pteris ensiformis*

But it becomes so if temperatures go above 65 deg F (18 deg C) and the pot should then be put on a tray of wet pebbles or surrounded with moist peat.◄ The fern needs bright light, especially the variegated forms, but not direct sun. Water frequently so that the compost is always moist. If the compost dries out the leaves will shrivel and die, but the plant can still be saved. Cut off all the fronds at compost level and spray the stubble daily. Fresh growth will appear in a short time. Feed every two weeks. Cut away any dying fronds at compost level.

**Potting-on:** Every year in spring in a mixture of loam, peat and sand, or peat-based compost.

**Propagation:** New plants can be raised from spores more easily than with other ferns, but a temperature of about 75 deg F (24 deg C) is necessary for successful germination. A fern can also be divided in spring; each piece of rhizome should have several fronds and enough roots to support them.

**Autumn and winter:** ▶Give the fern a rest at a temperature between 55–60 deg F (13–16 deg C), in good light but out of direct sun. At these temperatures high humidity is not so important, but in warmer rooms a more humid atmosphere must be provided. Water fairly frequently so that the compost is always moist.◀ Do not feed.

## Schefflera actinophylla

Queensland Umbrella Tree
Foliage    Australia

*S. actinophylla* (syn. *Brassaia actinophylla*) is a particularly decorative plant with glossy arching foliage. The central stems send out stalks carrying three to seven bright green oval leaflets, up to 10in (25cm) long, in umbrella-like formation. If the plant is potted-on regularly it will grow to about 6ft (1.8m) in six years. The leaflets of *S. digitata* (syn. *S.*

*arboricola*) are much more delicate looking; there may be as many as ten narrow elongated glossy oval leaflets, about 6in (15cm) long. This schefflera also grows to about 6ft (1.8m).

### The year's care

**Spring and summer:** ▶In the period of active growth the temperature should be between 60–65 deg F (16–18 deg C). If it is any higher, additional humidity must be provided by standing the pot on wet pebbles or surrounding it with moist peat. Regular spraying with soft water or rain water will also help.◀ It needs good light but not hot direct sun. Water frequently so the compost is always moist. Feed every two weeks. Sponge the leaves regularly to maintain the natural gloss.

**Potting-on:** Every year in spring in a loam-based compost.

**Propagation:** New plants are raised from seed sown in summer.

*Schefflera actinophylla*

**Autumn and winter:** ▶The optimum temperature is around 60 deg F (16 deg C), and it should not fall below 55 deg F (13 deg C). Put the plant in a good light but away from direct sun. At this temperature high humidity is not necessary, but it does help to spray the leaves two or three times a week to keep them in good condition.◀ Water occasionally so that the compost is barely moist, but do not allow it to dry out. Do not feed.

## Sinningia speciosa hybrids

Gloxinia
Flowering    Brazil

After African violets the most popular gesneriad is probably the so-called florists' gloxinia, with its blousy flowers. These are hybrids of *Sinningia speciosa*. The oval leaves, in rosette formation, are mid-green with a velvety texture, and grow to 8in (20cm) long, carried on short hairy stems. It is a low growing plant, no more than 12in (30cm) high, with a similar spread of leaves. The trumpet-shaped velvety flowers, 3in (7.5cm) or more across, appear from spring until autumn. They have been bred in shades of violet, dark red, pink and white, and some hybrids have bi-coloured flowers.

### The year's care

**Spring and summer:** ▶During the growing season the temperatures should be between 60–70 deg F (16–21 deg C). The plant needs bright light for successful flowering, but not direct sun. Provide a humid atmosphere around it by standing the pot on wet pebbles or by surrounding it with moist peat. Do not spray the leaves and flowers because this will mark them.◀ Water frequently to keep the compost moist throughout. It is best to immerse the pot in shallow water to avoid marking the flowers and leaves. Feed every two weeks. Greenfly can be a problem.

**Propagation:** Raise new plants from seed sown in spring, or more easily from stem cuttings, about 4in (10cm) long taken in summer.

**Autumn and winter:** ▶When flowering has finished and the leaves

*Sinningia speciosa hybrids*

flowers. The plant grows to no more than 12in (30cm). The almost circular leaves, around 4in (10cm), are dark green and velvety, shaded with reddish brown about the veins. The long flower stalk carries clusters of tubular flowers from early summer until autumn. In the species the flowers are red with yellow throats, but among the many hybrids now available there are yellow, orange, pink or white flowers.

**The year's care**

**Spring and summer:** ▶The temperature should be between 60–70 deg F (16–21 deg C). The plant needs bright light to ensure a lengthy flowering season but must be protected from bright sun. Provide humidity by standing the plant on a tray of wet pebbles or by surrounding it with moist peat. Do not spray leaves or they will be permanently marked.◀ Water frequently by immersing the pot in shallow water; the compost should be moist always. Feed every two weeks.

**Autumn and winter:** When flowering has finished and the leaves begin to die down, gradually reduce the amount of water. Cut off the dead leaves and store the tuber in the compost, completely dry, at a temperature about 55 deg F (13 deg C). Alternatively, the tuber may be removed from the compost and repotted in late winter.

**Potting-on:** Tubers will need planting into larger pots once every three or four years in late winter, using a peat-based compost. In the years in between repot in the same size of pot. Gently break away the old compost and plant the tuber level with the surface of new, slightly moist compost. Start it into growth in a temperature between 65–70 deg F (18–21 deg C) and in a bright light. Water occasionally until new growth appears and gradually increase the frequency of watering. Do not feed.◀

# Smithiantha zebrina hybrids

Temple Bells
Flowering  Mexico

*S. zebrina* is another gesneriad from the same family as *Sinningia speciosa*, but this has small delicate tubular

*Smithiantha zebrina hybrids*

begin to die down, gradually reduce the amount of water. Cut off the dead foliage and let the compost dry out completely. The rhizome can stay in the pot of dry compost and be stored there in a temperature around 55 deg F (13 deg C). The rhizome may also be removed from the compost for storing and replanted in late winter.

**Potting-on:** In late winter replant the rhizome in fresh peat-based compost. Start it into growth at a temperature between 65–70 deg F (18–21 deg C) in a good light. Water occasionally until new growth appears and then increase the frequency of watering. Do not feed.

**Propagation:** Divide the rhizome into sections when replanting in late winter. (Leaf cuttings may also be taken in summer.)

# Spathiphyllum wallisii

Peace Lily, White Sails
Flowering    Colombia

The lance-shaped, glossy, bright green leaves of S. wallisii are about 6in (15cm) long, carried on 6in (15cm) stalks. Lily-like flowers appear in spring and given the right conditions they may flower off and on until late summer. The central yellow spadix is surrounded by an oval white spathe on a 10in (25cm) stalk. While S. wallisii grows to no more than 12in (30cm) the hybrid S. 'Mauna Loa' can reach twice that height, with leaves up to 12in (30cm) on stalks as long. The flowers are also much more dramatic, with spathes about 6in (15cm) long. The spathes of both

*Spathiphyllum* 'Mauna Loa'

*Spathiphyllum wallisii*

plants will last for many weeks, but they change colour to pale green after a few days.

**The year's care**

**Spring and summer:** ▶For healthy growth and good flowers the temperature should be between 65–70 deg F (18–21 deg C). The plant requires bright light, but shade from direct sun, which can damage the leaves. Provide high humidity by standing the pot on wet pebbles or by surrounding it with moist peat. Dry air will encourage red spider to which this plant is susceptible.◀ Water fairly frequently so that the compost is moist always. Do not let it dry out. Feed every two weeks.

**Potting-on:** Each year in spring in either a loam or peat-based compost.

**Propagation:** By dividing the plants in spring when replanting. Make sure that each piece of the rhizome has at least three leaves and enough roots to support them.

**Autumn and winter:** ▶Give the plant a rest at a temperature between 60–65 deg F (16–18 deg C), but no lower or flowering will be affected. Bright light is very important in the short winter days, but even then keep the plant out of sun. Maintain a humid atmosphere.◀ Water occasionally so that the compost is just moist. Do not feed the plant when it is resting.

# Vriesea splendens

Flaming Sword
Bromeliad    Central and South America

*V. splendens* is a spectacular epiphytic bromeliad grown both for its highly coloured foliage and its staggering bright red flower spike. The strap-shaped dark green leaves, up to 12in (30cm) long, are banded with brownish red markings. They grow in rosette formation, spreading to about 20in (50cm). The 15in (37.5cm)

*Vriesea splendens*

flower spike grows from the centre of the rosette and is topped with overlapping bright red bracts from which yellow flowers emerge in summer. When flowering is over the parent plant dies, but after throwing out offsets which can be removed to make new plants.

### The year's care

**Spring and summer:** ▶The ideal temperature range is between 65–75 deg F (18–24 deg C). In lower temperatures the bracts will soon fade. *V. splendens* needs bright light for flowering and for good leaf colour, but it should be out of direct sun. High humidity is vital. Stand the pot on a tray of wet pebbles or surround the pot with moist peat.◀ Water frequently so that the compost is always moist and keep the central rosette topped up with water. Feed once a month.

**Potting-on:** Once every two or three years in spring in equal parts of sphagnum moss, sand and peat. Repot to change the compost in other years.

**Propagation:** By removing offsets in spring, but let them get well-established first with leaves at least 6in (15cm) long.

**Autumn and winter:** ▶This plant requires similar temperatures to those in spring and summer – 65–75 deg F (18–24 deg C) – never falling below 65 deg F (18 deg C). Keep it in a well-lit spot, but out of direct sun. Maintain a humid atmosphere.◀ Water occasionally so that the compost is just moist and keep the central rosette dry. Do not feed.

# Hanging baskets indoors

The shape and growing habit of a plant decides where it looks its best; that depends to a large extent on the angle from which it is seen. In general the most effective position for a plant with a bushy spreading habit is where it can be seen from above; for an erect growing plant where seen in profile around eye level; for trailers and plants with long downward arching leaves where seen from below. That is why we grow them in hanging baskets, and our problems begin . . .

The first problem is where to place them. They are useful for brightening up corners and less interesting parts of a house such as hallways, corridors and stairwells, but the place where a plant in a hanging basket might look well is not necessarily where the plant will do well. The temperature must be right for your chosen plant. The other important consideration is how much shade that plant needs – or can stand. A plant in gloom will quickly languish and become sickly. On the other hand plants in a hanging basket placed near a window may suffer if they are exposed to direct sunlight. Draughty spots are also to be avoided; these are especially prevalent in passages or on stairs.

When you have found a place that satisfies you and the plant, there are the practical problems of fixing a hanging basket. It must be fixed securely, for the weight of a container, plant and compost, especially when the compost is wet, is considerable. If you can find a solid piece of wood into which to fit a hook you are fortunate. Plaster or plasterboard or lath and plaster ceilings are tricky; they may look solid but you could easily end up with a chunk coming down on your head. If the container is very light, spring toggles might be used, but it is far safer to find a beam or rafter above the plaster in which to put a hook. To do this probe in the area where you want to hang a basket with a thin steel knitting needle or bradawl until you hit a solid surface beyond the plaster or plasterboard. On a plasterboard ceiling it is often possible to detect by careful scrutiny the joins where the board was nailed to the beam; that is the spot to choose. As an alternative to fixing the basket to a ceiling it can be hung from a wall by wrought iron wall brackets. Make sure that brackets extend far enough out from the wall for the pot to hang freely, giving the plant plenty of room to spread and branch.

To hang the container use a sturdy material such as nylon cord, chains, strong wire, thickly plaited rope, flax or macramé work; thin string will not do.

The height of the container above floor level is important. It should be in a prominent position just above eye and head level. Too far above it will look totally lost, but too low it is likely to be a hazard. Moreover, the further out of reach the basket is the more likely you are to become careless in looking after the plants in it; hanging plants are by far the most neglected of all houseplants. A chain and pulley device to lower and raise the basket will vastly reduce the risk of this neglect. The regular removing of dead flowers and leaves, pruning, checking to see if they require watering and are in good health can then be done with little trouble.

The choice of basket is wide. Open weave wire baskets which need to be lined with sphagnum moss for water retention are more suitable for use outside. If you use them indoors each time you water the compost it will drip through the moss on to the floor. There are woven cane baskets into which a pot can be placed but it must have a saucer underneath it otherwise water will pour through the drainage hole on to the floor and the cane will also begin to rot. Pottery and plastic holders with built-in saucers are probably the most practical. Some hanging containers do not have drainage holes and the risk is that the compost becomes sodden.

Pot the plants in a peat-based compost, because it is not as heavy as loam and will hold moisture well. Place crocks at the bottom of the pot if there is a drainage hole.

Plants suitable for growing in hanging baskets are indicated in the panel opposite.

**Cool – easy**
*Asparagus densiflorus* 'Sprengeri'
*Browallia speciosa*
*Campanula isophylla*
*Chlorophytum comosum* 'Vittatum'
*Cissus antarctica, C. striata, C. rhombifolia*
*Cyanotis kewensis*
*Hedera helix*
*Impatiens wallerana*
*Passiflora caerulea*
*Pellionia pulchra*
*Philodendron scandens*
*Saxifraga stolonifera*
*Sedum morganianum*
*Senecio rowleyanus*
*Tolmiea menziesii*
*Tradescantia fluminensis*
*Zebrina pendula*

**Cool – difficult**
*Adiantum capillus-veneris*
*Ceropegia woodii*
*Duchesnea indica*
*Rhipsalidopsis gaertneri*

**Warm – easy**
*Achimenes longiflora*
*Begonia tuberhybrida, B. semperflorens*
*Callisia elegans*
*Ficus pumila*
*Nephrolepis exaltata*

**Warm – difficult**
*Columnea microphylla*
*Platycerium bifurcatum*

# Outdoors
## but almost indoors

So far the book has concentrated on plants indoors, but there is no reason why the house gardener should stay confined within walls. Rooms have windows and plants outside in window boxes are almost as much houseplants as those inside. Plants there also have a special impact because they are seen from within like a picture in the window frame. If a room on an upper floor has a balcony or verandah with plants growing on it the effect can be even greater – a horticultural tableau vivant. At ground level a window looking or opening on to a patio adds another opportunity to merge indoors and outdoors. Doorways and porches can do the same. Even flat dwellers without gardens may be able to extend their indoor gardening in one or more of these ways.

Adding these plants to houseplants also greatly increases the range of plants to grow; the selection of suitable plants described in the following pages shows how wide the choice is. Many of them would be too big for indoors, but would look magnificent in tubs on patios and balconies. For window boxes there are hardy annuals to give a cheap blaze of colour. Near-outdoors is also the best place for spring and autumn flowering bulbs, and such flowering plants as geraniums and fuchsias do better outdoors than in because the light is better. In their right place, indoors or outdoors, all can be plants at home.

# Hanging baskets outdoors

A hanging basket outdoors serves a different purpose from one indoors. It is partly a question of scale. One hanging basket in even a large room has far more impact than the same basket could ever have outdoors. It is no longer a focal point, but one of the ways of brightening up and softening the exterior of the house. Nor are you living with it, but seeing and admiring it when leaving and returning home or sitting out of doors, or, if you have found such a place for it, when you are looking out of the window.

Since you have no control over the climate outdoors it is important to choose plants that will thrive in a variety of weather conditions. The choice is wide because many brightly coloured flowering plants and variegated trailing plants fare better outside, with consistent good light and more sun.

Outdoor hanging baskets are a seasonal affair for the warmer months between late spring and early autumn. It is possible to have year round growth in a hanging basket, outside, for instance by planting ivies, but this is safe only in warm parts of the country. Even hardy plants are killed off by frost when they are grown in hanging baskets because the roots freeze in the shallow compost of the container.

It is even more vital to fix containers securely out of doors to stand up to the strongest winds; in the summer months they may not be frequent, but they do happen. Use a sturdy right angled bracket, firmly fixed to the wall. Do not fasten it into the mortar between the bricks since it will quickly crumble away and the screws will work loose. Screw the bracket against solid stone or brickwork, using a masonry drill to make holes to take plugs for screws. Semi-circular half-pots which fit flush against walls should be secured with sturdy hooks and not with wire nails which will rust quickly and snap.

The material used to hang the basket is again even more important out of doors. Chain is by far the best, followed by heavy gauge nylon cord. Never use string as this will rot rapidly in wet conditions, and even plaited rope will in time.

The type of container you choose will depend on what you want to spend. Ceramic or pottery containers can be used out of doors as well as inside, but they can be expensive. You may instead turn to the much cheaper open weave wire baskets which are just as good, but take more time to prepare for planting. They have the advantage that plants can be arranged to grow between the wires of the basket as well as to arch over the edges of the pot. Some are made of plastic coated wire, which give many more years of service than the plain wire baskets which soon rust. Collapsible baskets are available and they can be conveniently stored when not in use during the winter months.

To prepare the basket for planting you rest it on a bucket to keep it steady. If possible unclip the chains to make the job easier. Line the basket with a two-inch layer of sphagnum moss to help to retain water. Press it firmly between the wires to keep it in place. Cover the moss with a layer of plastic sheeting into which holes have been punched to allow excess water to drain away and through which plants can be slotted. Place crocks and a little charcoal in the bottom of the lined basket to ensure good drainage and to avoid a build up of acidity in the compost. Cover the crocks and charcoal with a layer of compost. Remove plants from their pots, keeping the compost ball intact and arrange trailers between the wires and around the edge of the container. Bed them in firmly with more compost. Upright growing plants can then be arranged in the centre, again bedded in firmly with compost. Give the compost a thorough watering until excess water begins to drip through the sphagnum moss lining.

A good rich compost should be used. This should contain enough nutrients to last a few weeks, but after that start feeding as indicated under each entry.

Finding the right place for the plants in a container is crucial. Many hanging basket plants will grow in full sun, but that does not mean full sun all day long. Four hours a day will be sufficient to keep plants in peak condition and ensure prolonged flowering. Continued exposure to the sun, especially scorching midday sun, will soon damage them. It is also vital to put the basket where it can be conveniently watered. During a hot summer plants will need to be watered every day and thoroughly until excess is seen dripping through the sphagnum moss. At least once a week take down the container and water it by immersing it in a bucket of water or washing-up bowl. Leave it for about half an hour, remove and allow to drain thoroughly. This will also give the opportunity to remove any dead flowers and leaves and to pinch out shoots of those plants, such as ivies, which need this treatment to ensure bushy growth. If plants are grown in containers without drainage holes, regularly stick your finger about an inch into the compost. If it feels dry at that level watering is necessary.

Any tender plants normally grown indoors and which are to be overwintered should be removed before the first frost strikes.

## Alyssum maritinum
## syn. Lobularia maritima

Sweet Alyssum    Hardy annual

Short lance-shaped hairy grey-green leaves. White, purple or red honey-scented flowers from early summer to autumn. Trails 4–6in (10–15cm) with 8–10in (20–25cm) spread. Sow seed in early spring. Full sun. Feed every two weeks when flowers appear. Cut back straggly growth.

## Aubretia deltoidea

Aubretia    Hardy perennial

Small spoon-shaped leaves and pink, red or purple flowers in spring. Trailing stems to 4in (10cm) and a spread of 18in (45cm). Buy small plants. Grow in full sun. Feed once a fortnight from appearance of flower buds until flowering is over.

## Begonia tuberhybrida

Begonia    Tuber

Heart-shaped leaves with serrated edges. Large single or double white, yellow, orange and crimson flowers from early summer to early autumn. Grows to 15in (37.5cm) with a similar spread. Start tuber into growth indoors in early spring at a temperature of 70 deg F (21 deg C). Transplant to basket in late spring. When flowering is over cut off dead foliage, lift tuber and store in dry place at 45 deg F (7 deg C) until following year. *B. semperflorens* has heart-shaped green, red or purple leaves and white, pink or red flowers from late spring to autumn. Grows to 12in (30cm) with a similar spread. Sow seed in late winter. Both require full sun or partial shade. Feed once a fortnight from appearance of flower buds until flowering is over. Remove dead flower heads.

*Browallia speciosa* 'Major'

## Browallia speciosa 'Major'

Sapphire Flower    Half-hardy annual

Bright green slender pointed leaves and violet tubular flowers with white centres from summer to autumn. Trailing stems up to 2ft (60cm) long with a 12in (30cm) spread. Sow seed in spring. Grow in sun or partly shaded, sheltered spot. Feed every two weeks from appearance of flower buds until they fade. Remove dead flower heads.

## Chlorophytum comosum 'Vittatum'

Spider Plant    Perennial

Clumps of long thin arching leaves with a creamy streak down the middle. In spring and summer arching strawlike stems carry several plantlets. Leaves up to 18in (45cm) long and similar spread. Buy small plants. Grow in slight shade. Feed once a fortnight in spring and summer. Bring indoors before first frosts.

## Convolvulus tricolor

Morning Glory    Hardy annual

Small oval leaves and funnel-shaped blue, pink, red and white flowers with yellow centres in summer months but each flower lasts for one day only. Grows to 12in (30cm) with a 2ft (60cm) spread. Buy plants or sow seed in late winter. Requires full sun. Feed every two weeks from appearance of flower buds until they fade.

## Fuchsia hybrida

Fuchsia    Flowering shrub

Many named hybrids are available suitable for a hanging basket. Oval leaves and clusters of bell-shaped flowers in combinations of white and red, purple and red, white and pink from late spring to autumn. Arching stems up to 18in (45cm) long with a similar spread. Buy plants. Grow in full sun or slight shade. Feed every two weeks in spring and summer. Remove dead flowers and seed pods. Bring indoors before first frosts if plants are to be overwintered. Cut back to 6in (15cm) when flowering is over.

## Hedera helix 'Glacier'

Ivy    Evergreen trailer

Small lobed mottled green leaves with white edges. Slow grower *H.h.* 'Green Ripple' again with small leaves and pointed lobes. Will trail to 6ft (1.8m) and more but regular cutting back will keep them in check. Buy plants. Grow in part or full shade. Feed once a month in spring and summer.

## Impatiens wallerana

Busy Lizzie    Half-hardy annual

Elliptic bright green rubbery leaves.
Single and double flowers in shades of
red, orange, pink and white from
early summer to autumn. Many
hybrids will grow no more than 10in
(25cm) with a similar spread. Sow
seed or take stem cuttings from
overwintered plants in early spring.
Full sun and shelter from strong
winds. Pinch out growing tips for
bushy growth. Feed every two weeks
once flower buds appear. Plants may
be taken indoors before first frosts and
they will continue to flower.

## Lobelia erinus

Lobelia    Half-hardy annual

Small narrow lance-shaped leaves.
Red, white or blue flowers from late
spring to early autumn. Grows to 6in
(15cm) with a similar spread. Sow
seed in late winter. Requires full sun
or partial shade. Feed every two
weeks from appearance of flower
buds. Remove dead flower heads for
continued flowering.

## Pelargonium peltatum

Ivy-leaved geranium    Perennial

Fleshy ivy-shaped leaves. Clusters of
single or double white, pink, and red
flowers, some bicoloured from late
spring to autumn and longer if not
caught by frost. Trailing stems to 2ft
(60cm) with a spread of 12in (30cm).

*Lobelia erinus*

*Pelargonium and Petunia hybrid*

Sow seed in late winter. Plants usually
available from late spring. To raise
new plants take cuttings in summer.
Grow in full sun. Feed every two
weeks when flower stalks and buds
appear. Remove dead flower stalks.
Bring indoors before first frosts if
plants are to be overwintered.

*Impatiens wallerana*

## Petunia × hybrida

Petunia    Half-hardy annual

Oval bright green leaves. Trumpet-
shaped double and single flowers in
shades of pink, red, purple, blue,
yellow and white from summer to
autumn. Grows to 12in (30cm) with a
similar spread. Sow seed in spring.
Requires full sun. Feed every two
weeks when flower buds appear. Good
seaside plant.

## Tradescantia fluminensis 'Quicksilver'

Wandering Jew    Perennial

Oval leaves striped green and white.
*T.f.* 'Variegata' has the same
colouring but broader stripes. Trailing
stems will grow to 2ft (60cm) or more,
but can be regularly cut back to keep
them a reasonable length. This will
also encourage bushiness. Buy plants
or take cuttings from indoor plants in
spring and summer. Plant out in late
spring when all danger of frost is over
in full sun or slight shade. Feed every
two weeks in spring and summer.
Bring indoors before first frosts if plant
is to be overwintered.

## Tropaeolum majus

Nasturtium    Half-hardy annual

Bright green circular leaves on long
stems. Double and single orange, red,
yellow and salmon flowers from early
summer to early autumn. Dwarf
cultivars grow to 18in (45cm) with
similar spread. Full sun or partly
shaded spot. Sow seed in spring when
frosts are over or they can be started
earlier indoors and moved outdoors
when weather is good. Feed every two
weeks from appearance of flower
buds.

## Vinca major

Lesser periwinkle    Evergreen shrub

Glossy oval leaves; some variegated
cultivars with creamy edges. Funnel-
shaped blue flowers from early spring
to summer. Trailing stems to 12in
(30cm) with a spread of 2ft (60cm).
Buy plants. Requires partly shaded
spot. Feed once a month from
appearance of flower buds until autumn.

*Zebrina pendula 'Quadricolor'*

# Zebrina pendula
## 'Quadricolor'

Wandering Jew    Perennial

Green oval leaves striped with cream,
pink and silver. Trailing stems to 15in
(37.5cm). Pinch out regularly for
bushy growth. Buy plants or take
cuttings from indoor plants in spring
and summer. Plant out in late spring
when all danger of frost is over, in full
sun or light shade. Feed every two
weeks in spring and summer. Bring
indoors before first frosts if plant is to
be overwintered.

# Window Boxes

Window boxes give passers by something to admire but more important is the pleasure they provide to people inside, for the window is a frame to a living picture of plants which can be changed from season to season.

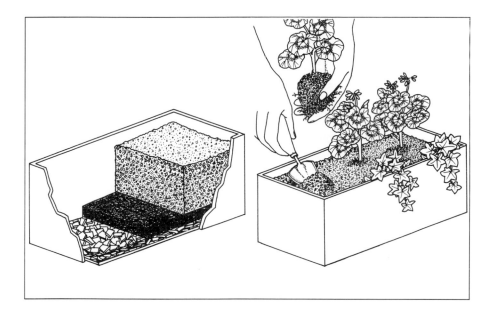

A window box greatly adds to your repertory of plants, for there are many hardy plants which will flourish better there than they would indoors, largely because they have better light and more air. Unfortunately many plants in window boxes will turn their backs on the room to reach for the sun. There are some obliging plants which look equally good when seen from inside or outside. Among them are geraniums, calceolaria, marigolds, dianthus, hyacinth, crocus, and muscari.

Looking on window boxes from the insider's point of view does not mean ignoring how effective they can look from outside. Trailing plants such as ivies can be planted along the front of the box to hang over the edge or the whole window can be framed with climbing plants, such as nasturtiums supported by plastic netting fixed to the wall.

Window boxes are made of many materials and the choice depends largely on how much you want to spend. The cheapest are moulded from plastic and are normally available in white, green, brown and beige. They are extremely light and if a lightweight peat-based compost is used in them they must be securely anchored to the window frame or surround so they do not blow over in high winds. The warm red of terracotta makes attractive, simple window boxes. The clay is porous and therefore the compost will dry out more quickly in a terracotta window box than in a plastic one. If you choose a wooden box – expensive to buy but much cheaper to construct yourself – it is vital to treat the wood with a preservative. Do not use creosote, which is poisonous to plants and gives off unpleasant smelling fumes in warm weather. All window boxes must have drainage holes in the bottom. If they have not, bore some before planting. In exposed positions it is wise to secure all window boxes to the window frame or surround, not only lightweight plastic but heavier terracotta and wood as well.

If you have sash windows the window box can rest on the sill, but casement windows which open outwards are a problem because a window box on the sill makes it impossible to open them. A more general drawback to placing window boxes on a sill is that they cut out a surprising amount of light, especially when they are full of bushy flowering plants. This can affect the growth of plants indoors, as well as making rooms gloomy to live in. The alternative is to lower the window boxes by supporting them on sturdy right angle brackets below the level of the sill; this dramatically increases the amount of light coming through a window. If the window overlooks a road a drip tray should be placed underneath the box to avoid dowsing passers-by.

To plant a window box first cover the bottom with a layer of crocks or pebbles about one inch (2.5cm) deep for good drainage. Follow this with a one inch (2.5cm) layer of peat for water retention. Fill the rest of the container with either peat or loam-based compost, leaving sufficient room for watering. The compost contains nutrients which will last for a few weeks only. Plants then need to be fed regularly as indicated under each entry. Compost should be changed every year for fresh.

During a warm summer a window box may need to be watered every day and it should be thoroughly soaked until water runs out of the drainage holes. To check whether the compost needs watering, stick your finger in about one inch (2.5cm). If it feels dry at that level it needs watering.

Following are short descriptions of plants and bulbs suitable for growing in a window box to provide spring, summer and autumn colour.

# Spring flowering plants

*Crocus chrysanthus*

## Chinodoxa luciliae

Glory of the Snow    Bulb

Bright green strap-shaped leaves. Pale blue starlike flowers with white centres about 1in (2.5cm) across from late winter to early spring. Some cultivars have pink flowers. Grows to 6in (15cm) with slightly smaller spread. Plant bulbs in autumn in either full sun or slight shade. Feed every month when foliage well-established until it dies down.

## Crocus chrysanthus

Crocus    Corm

Grasslike leaves with central white line running along their length. Oval cup-shaped flowers in shades of purple, blue, yellow and white, with six petals, which open in the sun from late winter to early spring. Grows to 4in (10cm) with a similar spread. Plant bulbs in autumn. Requires full sun when in growth. Feed every two weeks when foliage well-established until it dies down. Birds are fond of the yellow flowers.

## Galanthus nivalis

Snowdrop   Bulb

Narrow sword-shaped leaves and
pendant white flowers with central
petals tipped green from winter to
early spring. Grows to 6in (15cm)
with a 3in (7.5cm) spread. Plant
bulbs in autumn in full sun or slight
shade. Feed every two weeks when
buds appear until foliage dies down.

## Hyacinthus orientalis

Hyacinth   'Bulb

Strap-shaped leaves and tight clusters
of waxy red, pink, purple, blue,
yellow and white flowers on a tall
spike giving a bottle brush effect.
Grows to 10in (25cm) with a spread
of about 6in (15cm). Plant bulbs in
autumn in full sun. Feed every two
weeks from time flower spike appears
until foliage dies down.

## Iris reticulata

Iris   Bulb

Narrow grass-like leaves and violet
flowers marked yellow with distinctive
flaring petals from late winter to early
spring. Grows to 6in (15cm) with 3in
(7.5cm) spread. Plant bulbs in
autumn in full sun. Feed every two to
three weeks from time flower spike
appears until foliage dies down.

## Muscari armeniacum

Grape Hyacinth   Bulb

Narrow sword-shaped leaves and
spikes of bead-like blue flowers from
early to late spring. Grows to 6in
(15cm) with 3in (7.5cm) spread.
Plant bulbs in autumn in full sun.
Feed every month from appearance of
flower spike until foliage dies down.

*Muscari armeniacum*

## Narcissus bulbocodium

Narcissus   Bulb

Narrow rush-like leaves. Yellow
trumpet flowers with small petals
from late winter to early spring.
Grows to 6in (15cm) with a spread of
3in (7.5cm). Plant bulbs in autumn in
full sun or slightly shaded spot. Feed
every two weeks when flower buds
first appear until foliage begins to die
down.

## Scilla sibirica

Squill   Bulb

Strap-shaped leaves which first show
when bulbs are in flower. Blue

drooping bell-shaped flowers in early
spring. Grows to 6in (15cm) with
slightly smaller spread. Plant bulbs in
autumn in full sun. Feed every two
weeks from appearance of flower spike
until leaves die down.

## Tulipa forsteriana

Water Lily Tulip   Bulb

Dark green lance-shaped flowers up to
4in (10cm) long in spring. Grows to
10–15in (25–37.5cm) with a 5in
(12.5cm) spread. Plant bulbs in
autumn in full sun or slightly shaded
spot, sheltered from wind. Feed every
two weeks from the time when the
flower stalk appears until foliage dies
down.

# Summer flowering plants

## Ageratum houstonianum

Floss Flower    Half-hardy annual

Heart-shaped mid-green leaves. Tight clusters of feathery $\frac{1}{2}$in (1.25cm) flowers – blue, pink or white depending on the cultivar – from early summer to autumn or the first frost. Generally 6–8in (15–25cm), high with a similar spread. Sow seed in spring. Will grow in full sun or slight shade. Feed every two weeks after first flower buds appear. Remove faded flower heads.

## Alyssum maritinum syn. Lobularia maritima

Sweet alyssum    Hardy annual

Short lance-shaped hairy green leaves. Tiny white, purple or red honey-scented flowers from early summer to autumn; the tight clusters of flowers are so numerous that they give a carpeting effect. Between 4–6in (10–15cm) high, with a spread of 8–10in (20–25cm). Sow seed in early spring. Full sun. Feed every two weeks when flowers appear. Cut back straggly growth.

## Begonia semperflorens

Wax begonia    Half-hardy perennial

Heart-shaped green or bronzy red and purple leaves. Masses of small white, pink or red flowers from early summer to autumn. Up to 12in (30cm) high, but many cultivars are only 6–9in (15–22.5cm), with a similar spread. Raise from seed in late winter and early spring and plant out in the window boxes later. Grow in full sun or light shade. Feed every two weeks when flowers appear. Remove faded flowers.

## Calceolaria multiflora

Slipperwort    Half-hardy annual

Oval mid-green leaves, mostly hidden by the blousy multi-coloured flowers in shades of pink, orange, red and yellow, which appear from summer to autumn. Grows to 18in (45cm), but many hybrids stay a compact 9in (22.5cm), with a similar spread. Sow seed in early spring, and grow in full sun, but in a sheltered spot. However, very hot sun may scorch leaves and flowers. Feed every two weeks when flowers appear. Pinch out growing tips for bushy plants and remove faded leaves.

## Cineraria maritima: syn. Senecio cineraria

Dusty Miller    Half-hardy perennial

Long, deeply incised silvery grey leaves provide contrasting colour in mixed plantings. Heads of yellow flowers from late summer to autumn. Grows to 15in (37.5cm) but some stay a compact 8in (20cm), with a similar spread of leaves. Sow seed in early spring. Full sun or slightly shaded spot. Feed every two weeks when sturdy growth has been established. Usually treated as a hardy annual.

## Dianthus chinensis

Indian pinks    Half-hardy annual

Short grey green grasslike leaves. Flat double or single flowers in shades of pink, crimson, salmon and white, from summer to early autumn. Grows to 10in (25cm) with a spread of 8in (20cm). Sow seed in early spring. Grow in full sun or slight shade. Feed every two weeks when growing vigorously. Remove flower heads to encourage second crop of flowers.

## Fuchsia 'Tom Thumb'

Lady's eardrops    Flowering shrub

Dwarf form with oval mid green leaves and clusters of violet and carmine flowers from late spring to autumn. Grows to 2ft (60cm) with a similar spread. Rooted cuttings ready to flower usually available from late spring. For new plants take cuttings in summer. Grow in full sun or slight shade. Feed every two weeks from late spring to early autumn. Remove faded flower heads and seed pods. When flowering is over in autumn cut down to within 6in (15cm) of compost. Bring indoors before first frost if plants are to be kept for the following year.

## Impatiens wallerana

Buzy Lizzie    Half-hardy annual

Elliptic bright green rubbery leaves. Single and double flowers in shades of red, orange, pink and white, from early summer to autumn. Recently introduced hybrids grow to no more than 10–15in (25–37.5cm) with a similar spread. Sow seed in early spring or take stem cuttings from overwintered plants. Full sun, but must be sheltered from strong winds as the stems break off easily. Pinch out growing tips for a bushy appearance. Feed every two weeks once flower buds appear. Plants may be taken indoors before the first frost and they will continue to flower.

## Linaria maroccana

Toadflax    Hardy annual

Narrow long green leaves. Masses of small snapdragon flowers in shades of red, pink, purple, violet, yellow and white from early summer to autumn. No more than 15in (37.5cm) high and some hybrids are only 10in (25cm) with 8in (20cm) spread. Sow seed in early spring directly into window box. Grow in full sun or slight shade. Feed every two weeks when sturdy growth is established.

## Mesembryanthemum criniflorum

Livingstone Daisy
Half-hardy annual

Cylindrical fleshy leaves and pink, yellow, red and orange daisy-like flowers about 1in (2.5cm) across, from summer to early autumn. Forms a spreading carpet no more than 4in (10cm) high. Sow seed in spring. Needs full sun since flowers will open only in sun. Feed every two weeks when flower buds appear. Good seaside plant.

## Myosotis alpestris

Forget-me-not    Hardy biennial

Small lance-shaped leaves and clusters of blue, pink or white flowers from spring to summer. Grows to 12in (30cm) with a similar spread. Sow seed in summer and plant out in early autumn for following year's flowering. Some may be treated as annuals by sowing seed in spring. Grow in full sun or partial shade. Feed every two weeks from start of flowering. Remove faded flowers for continuous blooming.

## Nemesia strumosa

Nemesia    Half-hardy annual

Lance-shaped pale green serrated leaves. Trumpet-shaped pink, red, orange, white, yellow, blue and purple flowers, some marked with several colours from early to late summer. Grows to 10in (25cm) with a spread of 6in (15cm). Sow seed in early spring. Requires full sun. Feed every two weeks. Pinch out growing tips for bushy growth. Remove faded flowers.

## Pelargonium × hortorum F1 Hybrids

Geranium    Perennial

Circular mid-green leaves with brownish rings carried on 6in (15cm) stalks. Clusters of white, pink and red flowers on long stalks, from spring to late autumn and sometimes longer. Grows to a height of 12in (30cm) with a spread of about 10in (25cm). Sow seed in late winter. Rooted cuttings usually available from late spring. For

*Pelargonium hortorum and tagetes patula*

new plants take cuttings in summer. Grow in full sun. Feed every two weeks when flower stalks and buds appear. Remove dead flower stalks. Bring indoors before first frosts to save plants for the following year.

## Petunia × hybrida

Petunia    Half-hardy annual

Oval bright green leaves. Trumpet-shaped double and single flowers in shades of pink, red, purple, blue, yellow and white from summer to autumn. Grows to 12in (30cm) with a similar spread. Sow seed in spring. Requires full sun. Feed every two weeks when flower buds appear. Good seaside plant.

## Senecio cruentus

Cineraria    Half hardy annual

Bright green, heart-shaped leaves. Daisy-like flowers in shades of pink, red, blue and purple, often bi-coloured. Combinations of colours frequently planted together for a bright gaudy effect. Grows to 12in (30cm) with a similar spread. Sow seed in late winter. Grow in full sun or light shade. Feed every two weeks when good growth is established. Cut off dead flower heads.

## Tagetes patula

French Marigold    Half-hardy annual

Deeply incised feathery dark green leaves. Single and double pom-pom flowers in combinations of maroon and yellow or crimson and yellow from summer to autumn. Grows to 8in (20cm) with a similar spread. Sow seed in spring. Full sun or slight shade. Feed every two weeks when buds appear. Remove dead flower heads.

## Viola × wittrockiana

Pansy    Perennial

Oval bright green leaves. Flat large-petalled flowers in either single or mixed combinations of red, orange, purple, blue, yellow and white from late spring to autumn. Grows to 6in (15cm) with a similar spread. Sow seed in early spring. Full sun or slight shade. Feed every two weeks when flower buds appear. Remove dead flowers.

# Autumn flowering plants

## Colchicum autumnale

Naked Boys   Tuber

Wide, coarse leaves which appear
after flowering. Cup-shaped pink to
lilac flowers whose large petals open
until almost a flat saucer shape from
early to late autumn. Grows to 6in
(15cm) with a similar spread. Plant
tubers in late summer and early
autumn. Feed every two weeks from
appearance of flower stalks until
leaves die down.

## Cyclamen neopolitanum

Cyclamen   Tuber

Green leaves similar to ivy in their
shape with silvery markings. Pink or
white shuttlecock-shaped flowers, in
autumn. Grows to 4in (10cm) with a
similar spread. Plant tubers, dented
surface upwards, in summer in partly
shaded spot. Feed every two weeks
from first flower buds until leaves die
down.

## Crocus speciosus

Autumn Crocus   Corm

Grasslike leaves with central white
line running along their length. Oval
cup-shaped pale purple flowers with
darker coloured veins appear in
autumn. Grows to 4in (10cm) with a
similar spread. Plant bulbs in late
summer. Feed every two weeks from
the appearance of flower spike until
leaves die down.

## Leucojum autumnale

Snowflakes   Bulb

Narrow grasslike leaves which show
after the white bell flowers tinged
with pink have appeared in autumn.
Grows to 6in (15cm) with a 3in
(7.5cm) spread. Plant bulbs in
summer in a sunny warm spot. Feed
every two weeks from first flower buds
until foliage dies down.

# Balconies, porches, verandahs, patios

Plants grown in containers on balconies, verandahs, patios and in porches are a means of bringing the garden right up to the house. In a town these areas may indeed be all the garden there is and the plants there will be all the more greatly treasured. Since they are close to the house they can be admired both seen through windows and doors, as well as when you leave the house or come home.

Balconies present special problems even when they are two or three storeys up and even more so in high-rise blocks. The major headache is wind, but the exposed sides of a balcony can be sheltered by growing climbers, such as *Lonicera × americana* or *Clematis × jackmanii*. Shade may also somewhat limit the choice of plants which can be grown, especially flowering plants. Safety is important. Tubs and troughs when filled with wet compost are heavy; make sure that the balcony will take the weight.

Verandahs are more sheltered than balconies since they are usually at ground floor level, frequently with glassed-in roofs. Climbing plants provide attractive cover for the framework but do not choose too vigorous climbers, which will cover the roof, blocking out the light for plants below. Again make sure the floor is solid enough to hold the heavy weight of containers and wet compost. If the floor is wooden, containers should be raised a few inches by blocks of wood to enable water to escape freely and reduce the possibility of the wood rotting.

A paved area attached immediately to the house – terrace or patio, call it what you will – offers more scope not only because of its size but because it is open to the sky. Very often these areas are surrounded by two or more walls against which climbing plants can be grown. If the patio is in a basement area there are problems of light and shade-loving plants will have to be grown. There are many attractive green foliage plants such as *Buxus sempervirens*, *Fatsia japonica*, and *Ilex aquifolium* 'Argenteo-marginata', which will flourish in these conditions. Even a few flowering plants provide colour in these dark areas – *Impatiens wallerana* and *Viola × wittrockiana* among them.

Porches are often too small to hold many containers but an open porch can be livened up with two shapely bay trees standing sentry either side of the entrance. Protect them from severe frosts. Hanging baskets also add a splash of summer colour, but there should be sufficient clearance to walk underneath without banging your head. Porches which have been enclosed with doors can be used to overwinter plants, such as geraniums and fuchsias.

The type and size of container used will depend on the space available and the kind of plants you intend to grow. There are deep tubs and pots suitable for shrubs; shallow containers do not have enough room for roots to spread. Shallow containers can be used for colourful shows of annuals, but they dry out quickly and will need to be watered daily in periods of warm weather.

Before planting a container make sure there are drainage holes in the bottom so excess water can escape. Cover the bottom with a one inch (2.5cm) layer of crocks or pebbles followed by an inch (2.5cm) layer of peat to help retain water. Fill the rest of the container with either a loam or peat-based compost, not garden soil. Loam-based composts are more suitable for shrubs and provide weight to keep the container steady and upright in winds. Leave about two inches (5cm) of space between the compost and container rim for easy watering.

It is impractical to change all the compost every year but the top three or four inches (7.5 or 10cm) can be removed in spring and replaced with fresh. Take care not to disturb or damage the roots. Provide the plant with the food it needs for sturdy growth by regular liquid feeding as directed in the lists of plants which follow.

# Plants for tubs

### Aucuba japonica 'Variegata'

Spotted Laurel    Evergreen shrub

Shiny dark green serrated leaves flecked with yellow, insignificant maroon flowers are followed by red berries in spring, but only on female plants pollinated by male flowers. For berries a male and female shrub must be planted together. Grows to 6ft (1.8m) with a similar spread but can be pruned to keep in good shape and check growth. Grow in full sun or partly shaded spot. Feed every two weeks in spring and summer.

### Berberis candidula 'Amstelveen'

Barberry    Evergreen shrub

Glossy bright green leaves with bluish white undersides carried on arching branches forming a dome-shape. In spring small yellow flowers appear followed by blue-black berries. Grows to 30in (75cm) with a similar spread. Grow in full sun or slight shade. Feed every month in spring and summer. Prune back every two to three years if becoming straggly.

### Buxus sempervirens

Box    Evergreen shrub

Small shiny oval dark green leaves; variegated cultivars also available with yellow or white markings. Grows to 3ft (90cm) and is usually clipped to whatever shape is desired. Grow in full sun or slightly shaded spot. Very wind resistant. Feed once a month in spring and summer.

### Camellia japonica

Camellia    Evergreen shrub

Glossy oval green leaves. Many cultivars available with single, semi-double and double flowers in shades of red, pink and white, sometimes bicoloured, from late winter to late spring. Remove faded browning flowers. Grows to 6ft (1.8m) with 3ft (90cm) spread. Put the plant in a sheltered, slightly shaded spot. Feed once every two weeks in spring and summer. To keep the plant compact prune back stems by a third after flowering.

### Ceanothus thyrsiflorus repens

California Lilac    Evergreen shrub

Glossy green leaves and clusters of pale blue flowers in late spring and early summer. Grows to 3ft (90cm) with a 5ft (1.5m) spread. Needs full sun and a warm spot and is not recommended for cold areas. Cut off dead flower spikes. Feed every month in spring and summer. Prune to shape after flowering if getting out of control.

### Chamaecyparis lawsoniana 'Ellwood's Gold'

False Cypress    Conifer

Small scaly leaves on branches growing in a conical or pyramid shape. The feathery foliage is tinged with golden yellow. Grows to 3ft (90cm) with a 1ft (30cm) spread. Will grow in full sun or slight shade. Feed once a month in spring and summer.

### Choisya ternata

Mexican Orange Blossom
Evergreen shrub

Shiny green aromatic leaves and clusters of starlike hawthorn-scented flowers which appear in spring and early summer. Grows to 5ft (1.5m) with a similar spread. Requires full sun, but sheltered position. Good seaside plant if protected from winds. Feed once a month in spring and summer.

*Camellia japonica*

## Daphne odora
### 'Aureo-marginata'

Daphne   Evergreen shrub

Narrow oval green leaves edged with yellow. Clusters of starlike white and reddish purple flowers with a spicy smell appear from mid winter to early spring. Grows to 3ft (90cm) with a similar spread. Grows in full sun or partial shade but needs to be sheltered. Feed once a month in spring and summer. *D. mezereum* is a deciduous shrub with purplish flowers which show in late winter and early spring. Similar height and spread to *D.o.* 'Aureo-marginata' and requires similar growing conditions.

*Daphne odora*

## Elaeagnus pungens
### 'Maculata'

Wood Olive   Evergreen shrub

Oval green leaves splashed with golden yellow in centre. Good winter colour. Grows to 5ft (1.5m) with a spread of 6ft (1.8m). Tolerant of a windy position. Grow in full sun or partly shaded area. Feed once a month in spring and summer.

## Erica carnea

Winter Heath   Evergreen shrub

Short needle leaves and clusters of pink to red bell-shaped flowers from mid-winter to early spring. Grows to 1ft (30cm) with a similar spread. Full sun or partial shade. Tolerates lime soil. *E. cinerea* has pink, purple or white flowers from early summer to autumn and those of *E. vagans* appear from summer to late autumn. Both are similar in size to *E. carnea*. Require full sun and lime-free soil. Feed once a month in spring and summer. Prune after flowering.

## Euonymus fortunei
### 'Emerald Gold'

Spindle Tree   Evergreen shrub

Shiny oval leaves with gold variegations in summer, turning bronze tinged with pink in winter. Grows to 18in (45cm) with similar spread. Full sun or partly shaded spot. Feed once a month in spring and summer.

## Fatsia japonica

Evergreen shrub

Shiny, deeply lobed leaves up to 12in (30cm) across. Clusters of creamy white flowers in late autumn. Grows to 5ft (1.5m) with a similar spread. Full sun or slight shade. Requires protection from frost. Feed once a month in spring and summer.

*Fatsia japonica*

*Fuchsia magellanica, Petunia and Lobelia*

# Fuchsia magellanica

Fuchsia   Deciduous shrub

Oval mid-green leaves and clusters of bell-shaped red and purple flowers from late spring to autumn. Grows to 3ft (90cm) with a similar spread. Place in full sun or slight shade. Feed every two weeks in spring and summer. Remove dead flowers and seed pods. Cut back to 6in (15cm) in autumn when flowering is over. Protect from frost.

# Garrya elliptica

Evergreen shrub

Glossy dark green oval leaves with grey undersides. Long grey catkins appear in late winter and early spring. Grows to 6ft (1.8m) with a 5ft (1.5m) spread. Full sun or partial shade. Grow near a wall for protection in cold areas. Feed once a month in spring and summer.

# Hebe brachysiphon

Veronica   Evergreen shrub

Bright green oval leaves with long spikes or tails of lilac mauve flowers in summer. Grows to 5ft (1.5m) with a 4ft (1.2m) spread. *H.b.* 'White Gem' with white flowers is more compact, growing to 3ft (90cm). Grow in full sun, but in sheltered spot. Needs protection in cold areas. Good seaside plant. Feed once a month in spring and summer.

# Hedera helix

Ivy   Evergreen climber or trailer

Three to five lobed leaves. *H.h.* 'Goldheart' has green leaves with golden centres on reddish stems. *H.h. erecta* has plain green leaves on erect stems. *H. canariensis* 'Variegata' (syn. 'Gloire de Marengo') has large leathery leaves, dark green in the centre and creamy white at the edge. All will grow to 15ft (4.5m) with a 10ft (3m) spread, but can be kept in check by regular pruning. Grow in part or full shade. Variegated ivies will do better in slight shade. Feed once a month in spring and summer.

# Hydrangea macrophylla

Hydrangea   Deciduous shrub

Broad oval toothed leaves and large mopheads of pink or blue flowers in summer. Grows to 4ft (1.2m) with a similar spread. Requires partial shade and a sheltered spot. Feed every two weeks in spring and summer. To keep flowers blue they must be grown in acid soil, with blueing agent added during the growing period. Non-acid or alkaline soils will produce pink flowers only.

# Hypericum patulum

St John's Wort
Semi-evergreen or deciduous shrub

Broad oval leaves and large five-petalled saucer-shaped yellow flowers from summer to early autumn. Grows to 3ft (90cm) with a similar spread. Requires full sun or slight shade. Feed once a month in spring and summer. Prune each spring for bushy growth and prolific flowering.

# Ilex aquifolium
## 'Argenteo-marginata'

Holly   Evergreen shrub

Bushy pyramid of broad leaves with silver edges and bright red berries from late autumn to winter. Male and female shrubs have to be planted together to produce berries. Grows to 6ft (1.8m) with a 3ft (90cm) spread. Place in full sun or partial shade. Feed once a month in spring and summer.

*Phormium tenax*

## Juniperus communis
'Compressa'

Juniper   Evergreen conifer

Compact conical plant with short
needle-like green-grey almost blue
leaves. Grows slowly to 18in (45cm)
with a 6in (15cm) spread. Requires
full sun. Feed once a month in spring
and summer.

## Laurus nobilis

Bay laurel   Evergreen shrub

Lance-shaped leathery leaves and
greenish-yellow flowers in spring.
Plants are either standard with a
round head or pyramid shaped. Trim
to shape in spring. Grows to 5ft
(1.5cm) with 2–3ft (60–90cm) spread.
Grow in full sun or slight shade. Feed
once a month in spring and summer.
Protect from sharp winter frosts.

## Mahonia japonica

Evergreen shrub

Oval leaves with toothed edges and
long racemes of yellow flowers with a
Lily of the Valley smell from late
winter to early spring. Grows to 6ft
(1.8m) with a 4ft (1.2m) spread. Will
tolerate quite deep shade. Feed once a
month in spring and summer.

## Phormium tenax

New Zealand Flax   Evergreen shrub

Sword-shaped leaves growing in
clumps from the base of the plant.
Large flower spike of red flowers
appears from summer to early
autumn. *P.t.* 'Veitchii' has creamy
stripe along middle of the leaf and *P.t.*
*purpureum* has bronzy purple leaves.
Grows to 4ft (1.2m) with a 3ft (90cm)
spread. Requires full sun. Feed once a
month in spring and summer. Protect
from sharp winter frost.

## Punica granatum
'Nana'

Pomegranate   Deciduous shrub

Narrow shiny leaves and orange to
scarlet funnel-shaped flowers from
summer through to autumn. Will not
produce fruit. Grows to 2ft (60cm)

*Punica granatum* 'Nana'

with a similar spread. Requires full
sun in sheltered spot. Feed once a
month in spring and summer. Keep
under cover in winter; it will not
survive frost.

## Rhododendron kaempferi

Azalea   Evergreen shrub

Oval slightly hairy leaves, which may
fall in winter in cold areas. Clusters of
funnel-shaped flowers in shades of red
and pink appear from late spring
through summer. Grows to 6ft (1.8m)
but can be kept to a compact 4ft
(1.2m) by regular pruning. Grow in
full sun or slightly shaded spot with
shelter from wind. Use a lime-free
compost. Feed once a month in spring
and summer. Remove dead flower
heads. *R. yakusimanum* has narrow
glossy leaves and beautiful bell-shaped
white flowers in late spring.

## Rosmarinus officinalis
'Severn Sea'

Rosemary   Evergreen shrub

Small aromatic grey-green leaves on

arching stems. Lilac blue flowers
appear in spring. Grows to 3ft (90cm)
with a 2ft (60cm) spread. Requires
full sun and sheltered spot. Feed once
a month in spring and summer.
Protect from severe frost.

## Viburnum carlesii

Viburnum   Deciduous shrub

Broad oval toothed leaves with downy
undersides. Pink buds open to reveal
white flowers, smelling of almond, in
spring. Grows to 4ft (1.2m) with a 3ft
(90cm) spread. Requires full sun or
partial shade. Feed once a month in
spring and summer.

*Rhododendron hybrid*

## Yucca filamentosa

Yucca   Evergreen shrub

Architectural plant with rosette of stiff blue-green sword-shaped leaves. Large panicles of creamy white flowers appear in mid summer. Grows to 3ft (90cm) with a similar spread. Requires full sun. Feed once a month in spring and summer.

*Yucca filamentosa*

# Climbers for tubs

## Clematis × jackmanii

Clematis   Deciduous

Groups of three oval leaves and large purple blue flowers in summer. Grows to 10ft (3m) with a 4ft (1.2m) spread. Grow in full sun or partial shade but the container itself should be shaded since the roots prefer cool conditions. Feed once a month in spring and summer. Prune in late winter, cutting back stems to a height of 3ft (90cm).

## Forsythia suspensa

Forsythia   Deciduous shrub

Narrow lance-shaped leaves and clusters of bright yellow flowers in spring. Grows to 6ft (1.8m) with a 5ft (1.5m) spread. Place in full sun or partial shade. Feed once a month in spring and summer. When flowers have faded cut back the stems to within two buds of old wood.

## Jasminum officinale

Jasmine   Deciduous

Mid-green pinnate leaves with several oval leaflets and clusters of white scented flowers from early summer to early autumn. Grows to 15ft (4.5m) with a 5ft (1.5m) spread. Grow in full sun or partial shade in a sheltered spot. Feed once a month in spring and summer. When flowering is over thin out shoots.

## Lonicera × americana

Honeysuckle   Deciduous

Broad oval leaves and tubular yellow-pink flowers in summer. Grows to 10ft (3m) with a 5ft (1.5m) spread. Full sun or partial shade. Feed once a month in spring and summer. Prune that year's flowering shoots after flowers have faded.

*Clematis × jackmanii*

*Lonicera × americana*

*Passiflora caerulea*

*Vitis coignetiae*

## Passiflora caerulea

Passion Flower    Evergreen

Shiny five to seven lobed leaves and unusual bluish flowers with intricate arrangements of petals, sepals and stamens in summer. Grows to 8ft (2.4m) with a similar spread. Requires full sun and a sheltered spot. Feed once a month in spring and summer. Protect from severe frost. Thin out shoots in spring.

## Solanum crispum

Chilean Potato Tree
Semi-evergreen

Oval downy leaves and dark purple flowers with yellow centres from summer to late autumn. Grows to 10ft (3m) with a similar spread. Grow in full sun or partial shade. Feed once a month in spring and summer. Prune back in spring.

## Vitis coignetiae

Vine    Deciduous

Large oval to round leaves, dark green on upper surface and brown underneath, covered in down during summer. Leaves turn brilliant crimson in autumn. Vigorous growth to 15ft (4.5m) and may need to be pruned back to keep in check. Feed once a month in spring and summer.

# The right place

# Country style in the city

A small manor house, once surrounded by fields and orchards miles from the centre of London is now, a hundred years after it was built, a large family home in the suburbs of the city. The problem is how best to balance the space when there are plenty of rooms within but only a small garden. The answer has been to demolish a tiny conservatory and build a large one that links the traditional spaces of kitchen, dining room and sitting room to the garden and to each other. The integral design provides an interesting view from the inside of the glasshouse looking out and introduces more light to the whole house. The concept of a glass extension creates more house room for plants.

By the step to the sitting room door are grouped a composition of thin perpendicular shapes balanced by a clump of flowers and greenery.

An antique globe and pink conch shell look well with the abundance of cyclamen and azalea, the cascade of *Ceropegia woodii* (String of Hearts) and tall succulents. The wicker cakestand forms a tiered container and an aglaonema sits in the wicker basket.

# Country style in the city 2

Marine blue and white Italian tiles, the graceful lines of a modern conservatory and the winter landscape beyond form a pleasing framework for a profusion of indoor trees, plants and flowers. Peering through the leaves on the staging shelf is a Victorian marble figure and the ochre pot containing the agave and almost covered by the *Cissus antarctica* is art nouveau. Ivy and jasmine thread through the iron casement on the wall – *Philodendron scandens*, *Schlumbergera truncata* or asparagus would fulfil this role as well. Most of these trailers are easy to care for, as long as they have good light, but the schlumbergera needs warmer temperatures and particular attention during its resting period when light should be restricted. Codiaeum, howea, maranta, cyclamen and azalea are also on display.

# Country style in the city 3

A freezer is more than just a freezer when crowned with a headdress of interestingly shaped plants. Same with the kitchen units. Still room to manoeuvre but it all looks good. Ceropegia and vine decorate the freezer, while trailers of variegated ivies decorate the shelf room above and potted plants, including philodendron, cyclamen and azalea, go on show, but stay out of the way, below. Pot plants act as a space divider by helping to screen the work-top area from the traffic of the passage-way on the other side. The colours of kitchen utensils, pots and potted plants all blend attractively with the pillar-box red Aga cooker.

# Studio apartment

The main room has a large bay window but the kitchen, bathroom and bedroom are devoid of light. The natural place for the plants to congregate is over in the corner, making a comfortable focal point for chairs, table and lamp. The adaptable shelving of the bookcase makes a good niche for plants as well as objects. Their frequent rearrangement introduces variety and change of mood in a small place. Tall jasmine plants are used to define the two columns halfway down the room, and the decor also includes a visually rich mix of calatheas, dracaenas, codiaeum, dieffenbachia, *Saxifraga stolonifera* (mother-of-thousands), and in the pink and blue art nouveau pot, a sheltering ficus; the total combination forming an interesting balance of shapes.

# Looks good on the wall

Details from the last two homes show how trailing green clouds of glory can be made immensely effective. These three make pretty, rather romantic ideas for party decoration, too.

This page: The planting is up on the wall with a Victorian cast-iron gallery which can also hold fairy-lights and candles for evening; here entwined with jasmine and variegated ivies, which need sunlight to maintain their variegation, but thrive best in fairly cool conditions. Jasmine can be trained round an inverted wire to keep its shape under control, giving the appearance of the handle to a basket garlanded with greenery. More arms of ivy wrap themselves round the stone head on the wall leading from the Aga kitchen to cellar steps.

Opposite: An awkward corner in the studio is effectively put to use with a set of simple shelves, and a collection of china jugs and bowls house the primulas and greenery-yallery of tolmiea, ivy and tradescantia. The lass in the big hat was cast as an ornament for a pub.

# Formal flat

In contrast to the informal gatherings within the country style house with the conservatory and the one room studio apartment, these are ideas for decoration with plants in a compact bachelor apartment. Here the brilliant interior design by Stanley Falconer gives the feeling of much more space than there is in reality.

This page: Views of the sitting room with a study leading off through mirror glass doors. A container for mixed ferns including *Asplenium nidus*, adiantum (Maidenhair fern) and pteris, and plant holders covered with book endpaper for the cyclamen on the chimney-piece and on the side table. Plants include dizygotheca, dracaena and dieffenbachia. Through the mirror doorway to the study, and in here the sparmannia takes up position for full light on the window sill, and down the sides of the oak bureau are tendrils of ivy, and a column of trailing-stemmed ceropegia or rosary vine.

Opposite: Maidenhair ferns and spring flowers fill spare space in the bathroom. Because of their love of humidity they respond well to frequent mist-sprays in very warm rooms, but they should be brought out regularly into brighter light for a few days.

# Plants and pattern

The combination of plants with prints and colour in pattern creates an effect that is even more richly visual. The family town house here has every wall surface stippled, marbled or bordered with interesting patterns, and flower prints abound in the materials. First glimpse is at the immensely feminine bedroom and bathroom adjoining. The master bedroom combines a howea and *Ficus benjamina* (in the corner) with flower chintz curtains. Adding colour emphasis: a line up of pink and red poinsettias and azalea. In the bathroom next door a howea palm in the corner looks perfectly at home in the art nouveau jardinière and the arrangement of lilies, *Codiaeum variegatum pictum* (croton), azalea and cyclamen offset the gladioli panels in the Roman blind. Design here and overleaf by Osborne and Little.

# Plants and pattern 2

Downstairs, the colour, pattern and plants combine to make a bold design statement.

Right: Seen from the stairs, a view of the entrance hall leading to drawing room and the garden room. The shiny green of the banana tree and *Ficus lyrata* are cool relief against the rich tones ranging from vermilion to amber. *Ficus elastica* would provide a similar contrast. In the drawing room the cascade of scindapsus with its variegated leaves finds a suitable perch on the marble chimney-piece, its line harmonising with that of the carving and the looking-glass. Trailing *Ficus pumila* creates a similar effect. The *Codiaeum variegatum pictum* looks effective in the fireplace for an evening, but should not be left in such a shaded position long.

Opposite: Green plants for the green room, a family of palms, dracaena and ivy manage to survive in a rather dark space. The palms are put in the window to benefit from maximum light for a few hours whenever possible.

# Trailers and climbers

Then and now

Still in the same house, an Arts and Crafts high back chair on the half-landing. The colourings are again subtle, and the greens and yellows in the china container echo the ivy. Just as the Victorians decorated their dining tables with swags of smilax, so they strived for decorative effect with ivy to the extent of draping the creeper around sofas and chairs. Here, the idea of ivy round the banisters is right in the mood for celebration. A lovely way to decorate the house at Christmas. And, in summer, lengths of jasmine or honeysuckle used in the same way would look original and pretty.

Opposite: A glance back over the shoulder to steps leading to somewhere a hundred years ago. This photograph of a Victorian house shows the way we were with indoor decoration: ivy round the stairs, arches of morning glory over the top, to make a secret, enchanting roofscape. Unlike the plain modern carpet in today's photograph, the stair carpet in the conservatory has a stylised leaf pattern border to reflect the real thing on the woodwork.

# Trailers and climbers 2

Ceilings, corners

Opposite: Blissfully on the climb, tendrils of swift-growing greenery that rampage up the walls and decorate the ceiling. The effect is inviting, cool and suggests a mood of relaxation similar to the feeling of sitting under a pergola of vines. A network of thin wire is used to lace the creepers across the top of these different rooms. In the modern English country house orangerie the trailing garlands are passiflora and ipomoea (morning glory), with dracaenas and palms below, and the room is designed with an iron table and deep modern sofas. Altogether, an atmosphere of comfort.

Below: A *Philodendron scandens* (heartleaf philodendron) cheerfully legs it up the walls and across the white ceiling of a simple room. This idea would be easy to carry out for fast-growing plants such as passiflora that would cheer up a small bed-sitting room.

Right: A waterfall of passiflora creates an interesting alternative to an upright plant such as a potted palm in the corner of a study. Design by Nina Campbell.

# Jungle story

From climbers into complete jungles

Creating an indoor forest is a fine idea if you would love a garden but live in a flat, and it is a noble undertaking if you already possess a garden and are prepared to look after a host of indoor plant life as well. Soft dappled light, such as you would find in a thick woodland, is one effect from suspending a battery of plants, such as ficus or tradescantia. However, in direct sunlight, the effect of a coloured canopy could be achieved with a combination of cascading beauties such as abutilons and the red and white flowered twining clerodendron. Another reason for jungling is when you have little furniture but plenty of space to fill up with interesting foliage instead, or when you want to use the plants like ground cover and apply them to hide an eyesore. The jungle look succeeds in creating the illusion of privacy and peace.

Opposite: In the kitchen of a 'factory house' outside Milan, baskets of philodendron and tradescantia are set on a wide plank hung by chains from the ceiling and tall bamboos and more potted plants act as a room divider.

Above left: Under the skylight on the minstrels' gallery of a London studio flat is a gathering of nephrolepis, chlorophytum, dracaena and scindapsus grouped for reflection in the wall-to-wall mirror at the end of the passage. None of these plants is difficult to grow, but, like all variegated plants, they need good light and most prefer warm temperatures, although chlorophytum (spider plant) is very adaptable.

Above right: To add interest to the area around the hatch linking kitchen to dining area and to work like a leafy collar, a handsome group of plants, including the curious *Platycerium bifurcatum* (staghorn fern) and zebrina hang on or sit around the shelf.

# Jungle juxtaposition

Continuing the jungle theme, but tailoring it by placing the real and the fake side by side and grooming the shapes of all parties.

The result produces a green glade for a highly picturesque kitchen with a ficus and *Cissus antarctica* (kangaroo vine) well out of the way of the work space but still an integral part of the decoration. The sturdy corkscrew-like topiary makes delightful contrast with its mirrored reflection. Note the interesting mix of objects: period piece wireless, copper and brass tree container, attractive candle holders. The leafy wallpaper design works well with the sympathetic mix of wood surfaces.

# Plants in windows

## Window gardens

The idea of the window garden was introduced in the nineteenth century as part of the Victorian fascination with houseplants and indoor gardening. The aristocracy had reared exotic plants brought from their expeditions faraway down the centuries but it was the new middle classes that aspired to cultivate what the upper classes had already long become accustomed to. Hence, the growth of the conservatory. The indoor garden was often constructed on a half-landing in a terrace house and sometimes included a small aquarium. The elaborate themes are shown in the pictures below and fit in the whole clutter of the times, from pelmets to pools and birdcage to brackets. Here the then fashionable cyperus, hyacinths, fern and cissus jostle for position. From these beginnings to the present-day interpretation – still the antique lace and coloured glass in the lantern, but with log cabin woodwork and gloss painted furniture. A lush, warm mood is inspired by the purple and scarlet composition including hippeastrum, fuchsia, begonias, saxifraga, aspidistra and maranta.

Opposite: Less of the set piece, more of everyday life, a window makes the frame for a kitchen garden. A birdcage makes the centrepiece to a collection of potted herbs. An example of how decoration can take rudimentary basics and produce a result that is realistic, visually pleasing and costing little to put together.

# Plants
# in windows 2

Ornamental variations

Decorative windows offer great scope
for houseplants. In the basement
room shown opposite the leaded glass
creates the atmosphere of a secret
glade opening into a magic courtyard.
There is no garden here and so the
light-well was white-washed, then
trellis affixed to the wall and a group
of ivies trained to the woodwork. The
contrast of windows and plant is
visually satisfying. So, too, is the
completely different idea of the
plump-fingered *Fatsia japonica* framed
against the port-hole shaped window
below. Fatsias like plenty of air and
can safely be kept by a window.

# Plants in windows 3

Ornamental, and on to shelving surfaces

Above right: Shrine-like arrangement of plants worships the light in a basement window, the glass made the most of in terms of filtering shafts of colour by two painted glass panels. Among plants shown are clivia, aspidistra, nephrolepis (Boston fern), microcoelum, chlorophytum and hyacinths, all of which can happily sit in the basement window where the sun is not too strong.

Above left: In the family room of a south London house there is more stained glass with the comfortable combination of wicker chairs and baskets for the philodendron, tradescantia, nephrolepis and chlorophytum.

Inset: In a tiny bathroom plants are interspersed with bottles and other bits and pieces – the glass shelf supports against a mirror background create the effect of a window as well as adding the illusion of space with reflected surfaces.

Opposite: The use of a table in the window for plants is an alternative to window seat, ledges or shelves. The coarse lace blind is in keeping with the no-nonsense basic trestle and all easy enough to assemble. Choose plants flourishing in lots of light, such as *Ficus benjamina* and *F. lyrata*, nephrolepis and *Fatsia japonica*, all shown here. Hydrangea, also in the picture, is not easy to keep indoors, particularly in a centrally heated room, and it should spend some time in a shaded spot outside if possible.

# Solving the slope

Here are some sloping solutions to the interesting and tricky gradient of dormer and attic windows.

Above: Scarlet hippeastrum looms large and a green puffball of tradescantia hangs over the immaculate still life of dracaenas and objects in a countrified loft room. Such an arrangement could be adapted below a window in any spare area such as a landing or not too draughty passage.

Right: A jolly group of seven different plants and cut flowers all gathered on the landing: mauve geraniums fit comfortably on to the window ledge. Easter lilies mix happily with the informality of a robust marguerite, and calatheas and aspidistra flourish in the limited light.

Bottom picture: Way up in the rooftops, a nephrolepis fills an awkward corner. It should be moved to the brighter light of the windowsill from time to time.

Opposite: Where there is no window ledge or where the light falls in one area of the room only (such as in the basement room shown earlier), then a table grouped with plants maximises the surface for display. An unusual white gateleg table is the support for white, pink and green plant group with the stephanotis trained on a wire arch. Chosen to match the colour scheme of paint and wallpaper, the plants transform an otherwise awkwardly shaped alcove.

# Traditional drawing rooms

In the pale creamy Knightsbridge drawing room, the window area is dominated by a robust banana tree. The cool tones are in striking contrast to the bold butcher's apron stripes chosen for the bathroom of the same flat, which complement the boldly shaped yuccas doubling up at their reflection in a wall-to-wall mirror.

# Traditional drawing rooms 2

More about the traditional drawing room space, but to demonstrate how you can take one kind of plant and achieve much the same effect in a totally different setting. The example here is the fuchsia.

In the corner of a red drawing room the tall plant looks well with the very English flowery chintz and cut flowers arrangement of red roses and lilies. Interior design by Colefax and Fowler.

In the little picture the fuchsia again makes a fine focal point near a window but here it is in a more rustic setting, suitable for a country kitchen or the corner of an entrance hall. In the drawing room the container is blue and white porcelain and for the country look the pots are in similar rounded shape but more utilitarian. One holds *Plumbago capensis*, ideal for this brightly lit position.

# Traditional drawing rooms 3

Traditional drawing room still, but this time informal and showing a pair of sparmannias; the larger of the two capturing as much light as possible by the croquet mallets in the window corner of The Abbey Hotel, Penzance.

# Purely decorative

This page: More very English elements combine for ideas that are purely decorative and like the different themes shown earlier on page 16 suggest attractive possibilities for party decoration. Here in a country kitchen with buttercup yellow Laura Ashley provençal style curtain fabric, a white iron rise-and-fall lamp is wreathed in ivy. The plant pot can be fixed to the chain at the top. An Edwardian birdcage can be filled with any one of a number of trailing plants, pellionias for instance, or small-leaved philodendrons, and the cage is convenient to reach when watering is needed. On a small corner table, a crisp white lace-edged cloth and orange tree turn an unused or awkward corner into something special.

# Bold statements

A taste for the exotic

Turn an ordinary bathroom into an
oasis, strongly stated with the choice
and shape of plants and the colour of
their surroundings. The bathroom is a
perfect setting for epiphytes which are
content to grow on a piece of bark or
will flourish in perforated baskets.
These plants survive better if you
lower the temperature at night and
half open the window or turn on a fan
during the hot weather – but don't
direct the fan towards the plants
themselves. Over the bath hang a
group of three dendrobium orchids
and the other plants hung from bar or
ceiling are epiphytic bromeliads.

# Bold statements 2

Say it with stripes

Stripes on a buff and black canvas upholstered easy chair, stripes from the perpendicular pull-back blinds, stripes reflected in bars of light on the floor, wooden slats. All make the same observation: when you want to make a very definite comment in terms of design you do well to stick to straight, no-frills, hard shapes. The yucca plant carries through this notion with its spiky, sharp leaves and rather aggressive shape.

Above left: Tidy ordered interior with wood slat base for holding avocado and philodendron.

Above right: A corner with yucca trio, an efficient enough setting for any office reception. Note the good choice of container and under-planting that softens the severity of the main threesome.

Opposite: A kitchen with bold primary colours, clean lines, no clutter – and a *Monstera deliciosa* (Swiss cheese plant) whose shape has leaves made like stripes and tendrils that harmonise well with all the thin rods and grids of silvery metal. A similarly bold effect could be achieved with *Ficus elastica*, or a softer effect with *Ficus benjamina*.

# The Wardian Case

The forerunner to the bottle garden was the Wardian case in the nineteenth century invented by the English botanist, Nathaniel B. Ward. From his concept of growing plants in a sealed glass container the ideas of the terrarium, bottle garden and other sealed containers in which to grow plants have all been derived. The Wardian case was the solution to growing indoor plants successfully in spite of the gas fumes. It resembles a doll's house size conservatory. Later, the famous plant writer Shirley Hibberd made popular the glass window garden which he rather pompously called a 'hortus fenestralis'. The drawing is of a particularly pretty Wardian case constructed in a shape like a miniature conservatory and in the Crystal Palace style. The three coloured Wardian cases show the charming shapes that the glass chambers were made into. The central casket has a marvellously dotty fern, tiered like a wedding cake with cacti flourishing in the top storey and a fernery down below.

Below: A present day hortus fenestralis filled with geraniums – a practical way of maximising the available light for plant life and a pleasing miniature extension to the house from the outside view.

# To Let

This painting of oil on canvas is by James Collinson and entitled 'To Let'. The subject is a Victorian landlady and the notice for rooms to let hangs in her window. The potted plants are placed in a wire jardinière of identical style to the antique one painted white on page 61. A hundred years ago garden room and outdoor furniture was often painted dark green as in the picture here and not glossy white according to the fashion now.

# Plants and their containers

What the well dressed plant is wearing is based on the same philosophy as what being well dressed amounts to for a person. In other words, to be well dressed is to be suitably dressed. Here are some ideas to adapt for your own plants, your own setting and the planters you have available.

Opposite: A *Ficus lyrata* at the bottom of the stairs and a monstera halfway up them are firmly rooted in huge Ali Baba jars like the empty one seen down the cloistered corridor. These plants will tolerate occasional draught and are appropriate in this spartan villa interior in Malta.

This page: Three totally different disciplines. For the entrance to a London house, the pitch painted Versailles tubs for the bay trees match the black railings. Baroque white wall bracket on a rough white wall holds *Campanula isophylla* with an *Aglaonema crispum* 'Silver Queen' below. Protect the campanula from frost and from too much sun; the aglaonema will thrive in warm temperatures, but again should be sheltered from direct sunlight. And in a sitting room with ikat fabric on the wing chair and curtain borders, the turquoise of the generous Minton tub is totally in keeping and the cyclamen look right in rush planters. This arrangement would be successful only in the warmer months – the cyclamen would not last long when the radiator was hot.

# Plants well-contained

Good ideas for planters

Right: A cordyline in an art nouveau tub, with geraniums stacked around a verandah chair, create the mood of yesteryear nostalgia but with a present day application.

Below right: Maidenhair fern looks even more fragile in a delicately painted Chinese box. The pattern shows a similar fern design and a feathery bird of paradise. Both these interiors by Designers Guild.

Bottom: Good use of empty space. A fireplace painted glossy white makes a good backdrop and resting place for a strong shaped collection of asparagus and fern. The sansevieria appears even more sharp-tongued in the green and yellow bowl decorated with similar leaves.

# The touch of white

Here a mixture of dried flowers and plants in white china containers or placed against white.

Above left: A jolly rose-patterned chamber pot makes a handy receptacle for a family of ivies.

Above right: A pink and white porcelain mug picks up the colour tones of the heather; the same plant is seen again in the glass paper weight.

Left: Graceful camouflage for a fireplace out of use in summer or altogether in disuse. Spider grass flops from its niche on the open brickwork and cut dried flowers are right for all seasons in the china jug.

# Plants and their containers 2

Natural resources

Wicker, rush, rattan – all are the raw materials for planters which so long as the shape is kept simple, you will rarely grow tired of. They are classics. Here are five ways of applying the same principle.

Opposite: A group including a *Ficus benjamina*, pteris, monstera and cyperus make a beautifully proportioned arrangement in a pair of deep wicker baskets and four circular smaller ones. The wooden slatted staging shelf and the rush blind make sympathetic natural textures, and as with this simple white painted background are all easy to achieve.

Right: Formal plant shape, formal setting. Standard azalea in a lacquered brown and black wicker basket for the corner of a dressing room. Design by Pandora Astor.

Below: The bold shaped yucca, *Ficus benjamina* and palm all play jack-in-the-box out of a wicker hamper painted grass green to match the little armchair and seagull pattern cottons.

Inset: Myrtle is said to survive well if looked after by a person of great virtue. Here it flourishes in a wicker container in a cool, airy dressing room. Note how the natural texture of the wicker blends with the tan in the colour scheme of the paper and materials. Design by Colefax and Fowler.

Below right: House-plants including scented geraniums are grouped in natural rush containers (and beyond, the African violets are placed in a green glazed pot to match the lamp base).

# Colour it bright

Groups of all green plants suggest cool and restfulness, and the gathering of different tones of plants is a visual feast. Sometimes there is simply a need for bright colours.

Opposite: A kaleidoscope of colour in a Côte d'Azur fabric and room all designed by Collier Campbell. The sturdy aechmea carries on the bold theme.

Right: An eternally happy triangle in the open window creates an attractive silhouette whether on the outside looking in or the other way around: *Kalanchoe blossfeldiana*, cascades of *Campanula isophylla* and the pretty-leaved peperomia create a well balanced threesome in shape and tone. They need the bright light they receive in this position, but should not be allowed to get hot. The campanula's flowers do not last long in normal summer temperatures, and strong midday sun will be too much for all these plants.

Below right: Gloxinia, browallia and begonias are placed in front of a blind painted with a dream landscape and painted tulips. The Russian lacquer box emphasises the rich jewel colours.

Below: Full bloom hippeastrum with dizygotheca, asplenium and nephrolepis ferns on a living room side table make an interesting, bold group for a small apartment.

# Springtime

Imaginative ways to decorate with spring bulbs

Left: Pine corner cupboard houses hyacinth bulbs and cut hyacinths, and the top ledge supports a *Cissus antarctica* (kangaroo vine).

Below left: Narcissus are planted in a setting that creates a restrained mood: white china glazed cache-pot in a simple bathroom.

Below right: A cast-iron conservatory stove opens its doors for spring and is filled with a vase of cut daffodils. In the Victorian wash bowl are pots of daffodil bulbs and against the background are cut hyacinths in a blue tin kitchen jar and a scented geranium. The Laura Ashley materials of blue and yellow pick up the bright theme.

Opposite: The bathroom shows ways of dressing the simple alcove wash basin, and in the bedroom the white Victorian jardinière is full of hyacinths, primulas, cyclamen and cineraria. Altogether a very pretty way to decorate a teenage girl's bedroom.

Overleaf: More narcissus, this time in a wide shallow bowl, creating a marvellous clash of colour on colour, and flower on flower print.

# Palms predominate

Palms are striking and elegant additions to the furnishing of a room. They tend to be hardy and comparatively undemanding provided they are kept moist, though some – *Cycas revoluta*, *Phoenix canariensis*, *Chamaerops humilis* for example – require bright light even in winter.

Below: Almost any drab bathroom can be improved with paint and plants, and the rose red walls and handsome foliage here demonstrate the point. The graceful palm, calathea and pteris disguise the ordinariness of the bath and add a feeling of warmth and theatrical style.

Below right: In the corner but certainly not in disgrace, the howea palm illuminated from below adds flamboyance to a dining table by the window.

Right: Period piece – Laura Ashley's leafy trellis design cushions and a trellis pattern garden chair shelter in a glass room corner filled with the fronds of palms, and in the background the leaves of a ficus.

# Living with glass

Once more into the conservatory. All manner of houseplants are looked after here and reach to ceiling height. Plumbagos clamber to the sky and below are imaginative plantings of lilies and a multitude of ferns. The water colour painting is by Gerald Mynott.

Right: The white wicker table and chair are as good in a garden room as they would be in a bathroom where plenty of plants are used. *Spathiphyllum wallisii* and white cyclamen are next to the chair, while caladium and primulas are sandwiched in the table vent. Design by Nina Campbell.

The two glimpses of an octagonal conservatory and roof top garden plantings are at a house in Chelsea. Here the plants make a magical environment with the domes from Brighton Pavilion and the tall skylights of the purpose-built artists' studios.

# Just geraniums

Instead of conventional window dressing, a jigsaw of petals and leaves act as a safety curtain to hide the view from outside the window of a disused room. The house is on the main street of a Northamptonshire village. Geraniums are particularly long suffering if their owners take them for granted. But give them good light, water and proper pruning and they will soldier on out and upwards, as seen here.

Opposite: Complementing the gentle lines of the ogee arch, ivy-leaved geraniums at the narrow windows of a village house on the borders of Switzerland and France.

# Beautiful balconies

Opposite: Blue wooden balcony in Switzerland.

Right: Concrete house in the same village, each step punctuated with a potted plant and a ruff of geraniums round the ironwork.

Below: On the white balcony the French windows lead out to a space-saving pyramid arrangement of geranium planters with hanging baskets.

BIRRA BIER FORST

# Window boxes

Attractive ways to look out on the world

Above left: A frame for the window in the summer foliage of wisteria which appears after the graceful purple or white flowers. The green framework is a good foil for the beautifully understated planting of white geraniums edged with plain and variegated ivies.

Above right: For a brief midsummer moment it is curtain up on the window box as these morning glories come into full bloom and screen the view either side of the glass. A bamboo garden cane pinned across the stems halfway up keeps the plants in place. Underneath, struggling for recognition are bright pink tobacco plants, busy lizzie and more wisps of ivy.

Opposite: The window of a mews house down a narrow cobbled passage gives endless pleasure to the passer-by. White paint, white and green plants (cheerful same size conifers, busy lizzie and variegated ivy) and a perfectly arranged white cotton blind combine to give an impression of care, respect and love.

# Goodbye

The dark green front door, steps of black and white marble, polished brass and shiny immaculate white paint all present an extremely smart exterior, which can only be complemented by the addition of bay trees in plain black tubs. A picture that speaks volumes about the happy relationship between plants, their home and their owner.

# Acknowledgements

Special thanks are due to the Flower Council of Holland for permission to use many of the photographs in this book. The photographs of Dutch plants are those appearing on pages 65 (bottom), 67 (right), 68, 69 (bottom), 70 (bottom left and top), 73 (top), 74, 75 (top), 77 (right), 78 (left), 79 (right), 80 (bottom right), 84 (left), 85 (top), 89, 90 (bottom), 91 (top), 92 (bottom), 95 (bottom), 96 (top), 102 (both), 107 (bottom), 108 (bottom), 109 (left), 112 (right), 113 (bottom), 117 (bottom), 121 (bottom), 125 (both), 126 (bottom), 127 (top), 128 (top), 129 (bottom), 131 (both), 133 (bottom), 127 (top), 128 (top), 129 (bottom), 131 (both), 133 (both), 134 (three pictures), 135, 136 (both), 145 (left), 146, 147, (both), 148 (top), 149 (bottom), 152 (right), 154 (both), 155 (both), 157, 158 (left), 159, 160 (bottom and bottom right), 161, 162 (top), 163 (bottom), 164

Nearly 400 million pot plants are cultivated each year in Holland and their exports represent 45% of the world's total. In Holland floriculture is a major industry, providing over 60,000 jobs. Sales from growers to wholesalers are conducted at one of the twelve major auction centres, run as co-operatives and established as a means of preventing fierce competition from working against the growers. In the 'Dutch auction' a certain price is asked at first and gradually reduced by the clock system until a willing buyer is found. Most plants auctioned in the morning reach shops all over the world within 24 hours.

Research is of major importance in Dutch horticulture, aiming to broaden the assortment and to improve quality constantly so that plants are healthier and flourish longer.

Further information about the Dutch floriculture industry may be obtained from the Flower Council of Holland at the following addresses:

Alt Pempelfort 6
4000 Düsseldorf 1, Germany
Telephone: 91-325 0597

79 Avenue Denfert Rochereau
75014 Paris, France
Telephone: 01-325 0597

50 Upper Brook Street
London W1Y 1PG, England
Telephone: 01-726 4291

250 West 57th Street
New York NY 10019, USA
Telephone: 212-307 1818

Verbeekstraat 11-13
2332 CA Leiden, Holland
Telephone: 071 312 031

Other photographs for *The Right Plant A-Z* are supplied by:

Harry Smith Horticultural Photographic Collection: 66, 67 (left), 70 (bottom right), 71, 73 (bottom), 77 (left), 82 (top), 84 (bottom right), 85 (bottom), 86 (bottom), 94 (top), 96 (bottom), 97 (top), 99 (bottom right), 101 (bottom), 103 (left and centre), 110 (top), 112 (left), 114 (both), 118 (both), 119 (top), 122 (top), 124, 126 (top), 128 (bottom), 129 (top), 130 (both), 132, 138 (bottom), 140 (both), 141 (top), 148 (bottom), 149 (top), 153 (top), 170, 171 (top and bottom), 174, 175, 181 (right), 183 (top), 185 (top left and bottom left)

Michael Warren: 69 (top), 72 (bottom), 75 (bottom), 79 (left), 81 (top), 82 (bottom), 83 (bottom), 86, 87 (top), 88 (top), 93 (both), 94, 99 (bottom left), 104 (bottom), 105 (top), 107 (top), 108 (top), 110 (bottom), 111, 119 (bottom), 120 (top), 138 (top), 139 (bottom), 142, 150 (right), 151 (bottom), 156 (left), 160 (top), 172, 180, 182 (bottom), 184 (right), 185 (left)

A–Z Botanical Collection: 65 (top), 76 (top), 80 (top), 84 (top right), 87 (bottom), 104 (top), 105 (bottom), 109 (right), 113 (top), 115 (right), 137 (both), 139 (top), 156 (right), 162 (bottom), 163 (bottom), 177

Tania Midgley: 76 (bottom), 141 (bottom), 151 (top), 171 (centre), 181 (left), 182 (top), 183 (bottom), 184 (left)

William Keen: 78 (right), 91 (bottom); Holly Gate Nurseries Ltd (Clive Innes): 83 (top); The Iris Hardwick Library of Photographs: 72 (top); Bernard Alfieri Photo Library: 116 (left); Eric Crichton: 81 (bottom left), 95 (top), 103 (right), 127 (bottom), 145 (right), 150 (left), 152 (left); Heather Angel/Biofotos: 115 (left); B. M. Lamb: 117 (top); Pat Brindley: 90 (top); David Bradfield: 158 (right)

Thanks also to Garry and Carol Todd for help in obtaining photographs.

Photographs and drawings in *The Right Place* section are provided by:

Camera Press London: p. 210 (top), 211 (La Maison de Marie Claire), 215, 216 (top), 217, 224, 226 (both pictures), 234 (bottom left), 235; The Mansell Collection: p. 203; Michael Boys Syndication: p. 205: Susan Griggs Agency/Michael Boys: p. 212 (bottom), 221

Inset: Tania Midgley: p. 214 (bottom): Paul Redman (design by Nina Cambell Ltd): p. 204 (top), 214 (inset), 243 (top); Steve Lovi: p. 188, 202 (all pictures), 209 (Kitchen by Hannerle Dehn) 230 (left and bottom), 231, 239, 249; Richard Nicholson/EWA: p. 206 (top right); Eric Crichton: p. 230 (top), 234 (top right), 235 (right and bottom right); Richard Eiinzig: p. 207, 227 (design by Richard Rogers); BBC Hulton Picture Library: p. 210 (bottom pictures), 232 (top); Bill McLoughlin: p. 214 (top right), 216 (bottom pictures), 218, 219, 228 (bottom pictures), 233 (top left and left), 238 (bottom left), 244, 245, 246, 247, 248, 250; David Montgomery: p. 221 (top), 234 (inset) design by Colefax and Fowler; Lucinda Lambton: p. 234 (bottom right); Tessa Traeger: p. 223; David Bradfield: p. 222, 236 (bottom), 238 (left and bottom right), 239; James Mortimer/Designers Guild: p. 232 (right); Christine Hanscombe: p. 237; Harry Smith Horticultural Photographic Collection: p. 232 (bottom); Arabella McNair Wilson: p. 241 (bottom right); Martin Summers: p. 244 (bottom pictures); Mark Lebon: p. 235 (top right) – designs by Pandora Astor.

Detail of 'To Let' by James Collinson (1825–1881) reproduced by courtesy of Forbes Magazine Collection, New York (p. 229); Detail of painting by Gerald Mynott © 1983 by permission of Francis Kyle Gallery, London (p. 242): Plate from *Rustic Adornments for Homes of Good Taste* by Shirley Hibberd 1857 (p. 228)

Thanks also to Caroline Brakspear, Ros Dale-Harris, Tim Dale-Harris, Osborne and Little Ltd, The General Trading Company Ltd, Casa Fina Ltd, David Mellor Ltd, Laura Ashley Ltd, Clive Wainwright of the Victoria and Albert Museum, Stanley Falconer, Tom Parr, the Abbey Hotel, Penzance, and for the loan of plants, The House of Rochford, the New Ruaton Garden Company Ltd and Molly Blooms Flowers.

The photograph on the title page is by Bill Richmond, and the illustration on the contents page courtesy of the BBC Hulton Picture Library.

# Index